CIVIL SOCIETY AND CORRUPTION

Mobilizing for Reform

Edited by
Michael Johnston

With a Foreword by
John Brademas

Proceedings of the
Center for Ethics and World Societies
Colgate University
Hamilton, New York 13346

Center for Ethics and

COLGATE

World Societies

University Press of America,® Inc.
Lanham · Boulder · New York · Toronto · Oxford

Copyright © 2005 by
University Press of America,® Inc.
4501 Forbes Boulevard
Suite 200
Lanham, Maryland 20706
UPA Acquisitions Department (301) 459-3366

PO Box 317
Oxford
OX2 9RU, UK

Library of Congress Control Number: 2004117931
ISBN 0-7618-3124-X (clothbound : alk. ppr.)
ISBN 0-7618-3125-8 (paperback : alk. ppr.)

1

Civil Society Mobilized against Corruption:
Russia and Ukraine

Louise Shelley

A strong and independent civil society is essential to grassroots reform, providing a framework, sustaining resources and leadership, and a measure of security to citizens working to improve social conditions. Often, however, civil society is weakest where it is needed most, or at the very least faces major obstacles created by history, the policies of old regimes, and the problems of the new. Louise Shelley compares two of the most important such cases in this chapter—Russia and Ukraine—showing both the obstacles and problems on the one hand, and the surprising tenacity of some aspects of civil society, on the other. International efforts to build a strong civil society frequently are not attuned to such historical and social factors; as a consequence organizations and initiatives spring up reflecting outsiders' agendas, but lacking "resonance" in society. Those efforts will likely be short-lived and perhaps even counterproductive as scarce opportunities and citizen support are wasted. The authoritarian tendencies in Russia and Ukraine are undermining much of the progress made in this area in the first decade of post-Soviet independence.

I. Introduction

By the late 1920s the rich religiously based civil society of the pre-Revolutionary Russian Empire had been exterminated by the Soviet leadership. Any groups outside of Party control ceased to exist because the central objective of the Communist Party was the consolidation of economic and political power.

Former leaders of sports, religious and even philatelic organizations were sent to the gulag (the Soviet system of labor camps) to suppress any potential manifestations of civil society whose members might attempt to mobilize against the central state.

The elimination of civil society had inadvertent consequences that the Party leadership did not anticipate. Lord Acton once commented, "Absolute power corrupts absolutely." Without civil society there were no checks on Soviet power. The corruption that accompanied the absolute power of these elites proved to be a major contributing force to their ultimate collapse.

The post-Soviet states are heirs to the deeply entrenched political corruption that dominated the Soviet Union in its final decades. The countries that have emerged from the USSR are ranked, according to Transparency International (TI) and World Bank indexes, as among the most corrupt countries in the world.[1] The capacity to address corruption in the region's countries is significantly affected by the extent by which they can develop a civil society capable of monitoring the state and serving as a check on its authority.

The Soviet successor states have very different levels of civil society – a consequence of historical traditions, the legacy of Soviet era corruption and the current economic state of the citizens of the respective countries. Therefore, the presence of a rich civil society in the pre-Soviet Baltics has made it easier for these groups to resurface than in Central Asia where there are now highly authoritarian governments and little tradition of civic society. Ukraine, which was severely repressed during the Soviet era, has a more limited civil society than Russia, which was allowed more artistic and other forms of expression during the Soviet era.

This chapter contrasts the experiences of Russia and Ukraine in developing civil societies capable of addressing pervasive and institutionalized corruption. In the decade following the collapse of the USSR, civil society has diverged significantly in the two countries. But there are similarities too: women have emerged as leaders in civil society in both countries and also in activities directed against corruption. In both countries the independent media initially emerged as powerful forces against corruption. This is no longer the case in either country. The killing of Giorgiy Gongadze, a Ukrainian journalist investigating high level corruption, whose murder was allegedly ordered by President Kuchma, and the subsequent intimidation of journalists have eliminated the media as a force against corruption. In Russia today, only a few small circulation newspapers like "Novaya Gazeta" and a few brave journalists scattered around the country work against corruption. These individuals are now more the exception than the rule.[2]

In both Russia and Ukraine there are severe obstacles to the development of a vibrant and effective civil society. In Ukraine, the more limited financial resources and the greater economic precariousness of daily life limit citizen participation in civic organizations. The higher standard of living in Russia provide more opportunities for participation in civil society, but corruption and the abuse of charities and civic organizations by organized crime and corrupt *nomenklatura* (members of the former Party elite) have made it more difficult to establish a credible civil society. The initial growth of civil society in the Yeltsin era has been curtailed sharply under Putin through crackdowns on the media and the use of the legal system to curb independent citizen action.[3]

The funding for anti-corruption activism has been problematic. Domestic funding for civil society has been limited. Mikhail Khodorkovsky, the arrested head of the oil giant, Yukos, has funded human rights, anti-corruption, and other groups. His Open Russia Foundation, whose projects exceeded $100 million annually, was under investigation by the Tax Ministry. The Soros funding for much anti-corruption activity in the former USSR has diminished as philanthropic activities in the U.S. are being favored.[4] Efforts by foreign aid organizations, in particular those from the United States, to foster anti-corruption activity in civil society has promoted much activity in Ukraine and Russia. But that activity is not a genuine reflection of citizen interest; rather, it is a market response to the availability of funding. With the decline of foreign assistance to Russia and Ukraine from the United States and with limited support for such activities from Europe, many aspects of civil society have withered. Some of this is a natural consequence of the lack of available funds but additionally it is a consequence of the absence of political support for civil activists.

Groups face other fundamental problems of survival in Russia. Soldiers' Mothers' Committee, Moscow Helsinki Group, and environmental groups—all of whose work will be discussed below—have recently experienced difficulties in re-registering, face frequent visits from the federal security service and have trouble with local authorities. Under these conditions it is hardly surprising that Russia has fallen from 71st to 86th place in the Transparency index in the past year. Ukraine is not doing any better, having fallen to 106th place.[5]

II. Historical Background

By the end of the first decade of Soviet rule, Russian, Ukrainian and Caucasian civil society had been obliterated in the USSR. Much pre-Revolutionary civil society had been sponsored by the Orthodox Church, an institution swiftly repressed by the Bolsheviks. No officially sanctioned independent religious, sports, ethnic, youth, or cultural organizations existed in the Stalinist or even the more liberal Khrushchev period. The Komsomol and Pioneer organizations were Party-based structures, controlling recreational activities including the summer camps, sports, and cultural programs of Soviet children and youth. All adult activities were under the control of the Party and every aspect of personal expression and collective activity was subject to Party regulation.

By the mid-1960s, however, there were the first signs of an independent society outside of state control. Human rights activists emerged, often grouped around independent writing and journals (*samizdat*), and some underground religious activity began to surface in a covert manner.[6] The trial of the independent writers Andrei Sinyavsky and Yuli Daniel galvanized the small civil societies of the 1960s;[7] sympathizers met during and after the trial. Many of these circles would subsequently blossom into a human rights movement.[8]

During the détente era of the mid-1970s there was some thawing in Soviet society and groups began to coalesce.[9] These groups were still very limited, and could be categorized into dissidents and human rights activists, nationalist groups, independent artists, and religious groups outside the state controlled Orthodox Church. Although the USSR was still a highly controlled society, unsanctioned public demonstrations grew steadily in the decades after Stalin. In the first decade after his death there were thirty-two known demonstrations in the entire country. From 1965-74 the figure rose to 174, and during the following decade the number increased to 203.[10] Both the number of demonstrations and their size increased after the mid-1960s. Sometimes these demonstrations were spontaneous responses to police brutality or outbursts after a sports event, such as those occurring in Uzbekistan in the mid-1960s. But by the final years of the Brezhnev period, the early 1980s, the number of planned protests had increased, reflecting the capacity of an emerging Soviet society to mobilize and express its point of view. Despite this development skillful militia work combined with intelligence by the security police managed to control the numbers who demonstrated in public.[11]

Emergent civil society existed in many non-political areas. In the mid-1970s, a growing artistic movement developed outside the dictates of socialist realism. The movement built to a crescendo in 1974, when artists mobilized to exhibit their works publicly. An initial display of artistic works in the South of Moscow was bulldozed; several foreign journalists covering the event as well as Russian artists were injured. A large-scale public exhibition followed in Izmailovo a couple weeks later.[12] The highly visible art movement had parallels in the theater and music worlds, but these spheres did not assume such a public stance or suffer from public suppression. The *samizdat* of both literary and political materials was widespread during this time and involved the dissemination of such famous authors as Aleksandr Solzhenitsyn.[13] Although the reading of these works was a private activity, the networks that supported their dissemination and printing were another important manifestation of civil society.

There were significant limits to the growth of these organizations during the 1970s. A highly punitive criminal law was readily applied against members of these visible groups. Enormous efforts were made to deprive activists and their families of their livelihoods. This was possible because all employment was controlled by the state and there were no private businesses. Reprisals were particularly severe in Ukraine. Ukrainian activists were sent to labor camps for lengthy sentences; members of their immediate families were fired from their jobs and even denied the opportunity to sell their handicrafts through state handicraft stores. Therefore, family members were forced into the illegal second economy to survive. Secret financial support groups were established by private citizens, often dissatisfied Russian intellectuals, whose significant salaries permitted them to support the diverse elements of the dissident, nationalist and human rights movements.[14] Financial support also came from other sources. Independent artists sold their work to foreigners. Nationalists and religious groups received s ome su pport f rom Russian, U krainian a nd o ther d iaspora c ommunities, in covert ways. On occasion, this support was detected and the recipients prosecuted. The participants in the growing second economy did not support civil society because their survival was dependent on their ties to Party structures.

In the late 1970s and early 1980s, the Soviet state cracked down severely on independent political movements. Nationalists and dissidents received long prison sentences or were sent into exile. The groups, however, did not disappear. They m erely went u nderground and reemerged rapidly w ith the political f reedom of the Gorbachev era.

Gorbachev's assumption of power in the mid 1980s ushered in *perestroika*. A rich civil society emerged in many parts of the former Soviet Union. In many regions of Russia a strong press emerged independent of the fossilized state-controlled Society of Journalists. Workers' movements began to take hold, particularly in the mining regions of the country, and independent unions existed for the first time.[15] Nationalist movements emerged with great force in the three Baltic countries and in Ukraine. Even in Belarus, a nationalist revival movement served to mobilize thousands. By the end of the 1980s, women's movements began to emerge as a potent force in Russian society, a consequence of the difficult economic situation of women in the economic transition and the possibility of articulating longstanding grievances.[16] Environmental, ecological movements also assumed great importance in the overall fabric of civic society.

By the end of the Soviet period there was a diversified civil society in many regions of the former Soviet Union. Unfortunately, there was only a limited tradition of domestic support; no foundations existed, and a newly rich emergent class was not interested in philanthropy. Moreover, most newly-rich were part of a crony capitalism that had no interest in supporting civil society.

III. Civil Society and Anti-Corruption Work in the Post-Soviet Era
Both Russia and Ukraine emerged from the Soviet era with very severe problems o f c orruption. I n b oth n ewly i ndependent s tates, o rganized c rime g roups penetrated state structures at the local, regional and national levels. A criminal-political nexus prevailed that undermined the transition to rule of law and the state based mechanisms to control corruption.[17] Crony capitalism emerged as a predominant factor in the economy and the political structure of society.[18] Petty corruption existed in every element of society including education, law enforcement and the distribution of social benefits.

There w ere no powerful forces to counter the pervasive culture of corruption[19]—no core religious or ideological beliefs that laid out expected standards for citizen conduct. Furthermore, civil society was too weak and poorly financed to provide much of a counterweight to the increasingly systemic corruption. Many citizens, overwhelmed by the difficulties of day-to-day survival, could not donate their limited time to civic organizations. A mere three to nine percent of Russian citizens took part in any form of civic activity.[20] Moreover, business people did not initiate anti-corruption campaigns because they believe this is a function of the state and do not see themselves as agents of anti-corruption activity.[21]

In the early post-Soviet years, almost no foreign and international resources were devoted to fighting corruption. Most of the international community failed to recognize the corrosive impact corruption would have on all aspects of post-Soviet development. Rather, the focus of foreign financial assistance in the early 1990s was on privatization and economic reform. Scant attention was paid to the safeguards needed to prevent the looting of state resources by Soviet era elites and o rganized c rime.[22] After t he mistakes o f t he e arly 1 990s b ecame e vident, much foreign assistance in the later 1990s was devoted to anti-corruption programs. But these foreign sponsored programs often had little resonance or support within the societies.

Russian-Ukrainian Differences

According to World Bank and TI surveys, Russia and Ukraine are among the most corrupt countries in the world.[23] Although both emerged simultaneously from the collapse of the Soviet Union, they have very different capacities to mobilize against corruption (see Table 1.1). Russia retained m ost of the f inancial and bureaucratic resources of the Soviet state. Rich in natural resources and with a less precipitous economic collapse than other successor states, it could focus some attention on the construction of civil society. Ukraine, by contrast, had to focus on building a bureaucracy, establishing a foreign policy, a diplomatic corps and an independent military. Its immediate priority was on state building rather than on the construction of civil society.

Prior to the collapse of the USSR, three primary forms of civil society predominated in Ukraine: nationalist, workers' rights and environmental. Rukh, the People's Movement for Perestroika, became a dominant force in preindependence Ukraine. Its objective was to achieve "economic prosperity through the development of the ideals and values of civil society."[24] A large scale workers' movement existed primarily in the eastern mining regions pressing for greater workers' rights and expression. A large ecology movement emerged in reaction to the Chernobyl crisis that was broad based. Women were represented in Rukh and the environmental movement rather than being a strong separate movement of their own.[25] Ukraine had distinct and powerful galvanizing movements.

TABLE 1.1:
Civil Society in Russia and Ukraine: The Soviet Period

	Russia	**Ukraine Ukraine**

Forms	Diverse forms:
	   Human rights
	   Religious
	   Artistic
	   Women's
	   Ecological
	   Media
	   Independent unions
		Nationalist-based
		   civil society
		Environmental groups
		Unions

Attitudes to- ward civil society	Increasing tolerance of civil society	Intense repression of civil society because of its political basis

Funding	Domestic, limited foreign
	   Support
		Domestic, limited foreign
		   Support

Russia, in contrast, had more diverse forms of civil society. No group reached the level of mobilization that was found with Rukh in Ukraine. Women Russia, by contrast, had more diverse forms of civil society. No group reached the level of mobilization that was found with Rukh in Ukraine. Women formed more distinct groups than their Ukrainian counterparts. The *glasnost'* (openness of expression) of the Gorbachev era had a strong central base in Moscow and became a potent force in Soviet, and subsequently Russian, society. The environmental movement was strong, but without the tragedy of Chernobyl it was not such a unifying force across all segments of society. The freedoms of the Gorbachev era diminished the human rights movement as many of their decades-long concerns such as psychiatric abuse, jailing of dissidents, and suppression of free expression were no longer the major problems facing Soviet society.

With the collapse of the USSR, civil society in Russia and Ukraine diverged rapidly. With independence, many of the objectives of Rukh became institutionalized within the incipient Ukrainian state. The tolerance and multi-ethnic focus of the newly independent Ukraine, once platforms of Rukh, eliminated the need for this important independent movement. In fact, some would contend that Rukh not only ceased to be a manifestation of civil society but rather, in spite of itself, became the presidential party.[26] The incorporation of civil society into the state eliminated a possibly powerful check on executive authority and had important long-term consequences for anti-corruption efforts.

The effectiveness of anti-corruption efforts in Russia and Ukraine cannot be evaluated solely by examining the anti-corruption activists. In both countries, groups dedicated to other causes such as freedom of the press, protection of the environment and prevention of trafficking in women. These focused groups proved to be more potent forces in controlling corruption than the explicit anti-corruption activists because they reflect deep-seated indigenous concerns of the citizenry and have not developed as a response to foreign stimuli to create anti-corruption movements (see Table 1.2).

TABLE 1.2:
Civil Society and Focus of Anti-Corruption Efforts: The Post-Soviet Period

Groups	**Focus and Main Issues**
Journalists	All levels of political corruption
Women's trafficking group • in Russia, Soldier Mothers	Law enforcement and border guards • military corruption (Russia)
Human rights groups (Russia)	Monitoring local and law enforcement Corruption
Environmental groups • stronger in Russia	Official corruption undermining the Environment
Academic community research centers	Research and analysis • monitoring of judiciary and the courts
Anti-corruption groups • stronger in Ukraine	Low level corruption • municipal corruption

The Russian experience

Civil society in Russia diversified rapidly after 1991. Corruption became a key concern of many sectors of civil society. Human rights groups reconstituted themselves as a strong force in the mid-1990s addressing such critical issues as abuses of civilians in Chechnya, labor rights, electoral violations and abuses by law enforcement personnel.[27] Academicians and scholars—sources of integrity in the Soviet era—developed strategies to address corruption in state institutions and in institutions of higher learning. Women are active participants in many areas of civil society and have established their own organizations to assist women who suffered particularly in the transitional period.[28] Journalists were at the front line of anti-corruption investigations in the *glasnost'* era under Gorbachev and continued this after the establishment of the Russian state.

Russian journalists have suffered significantly for battling corruption. The

Committee to Protect Journalists, located in the west, has identified numerous killings and assaults on journalists investigating corruption.[29] Among the most notable a re t he Ju ne 1 998 k illing o f L arisa Yudina, e ditor o f *S ovietskaia Kalmykia Sevodniia*, who w as shot in Kalmykia.[30] She had been engaged in long term i nvestigations o f high-level c orruption b y the l eader of K almykia whose leadership of an international chess federation provided ample opportunities for abuse on both the local and international level. In mid-2000, Igor Domnikov, an investigative journalist with the prominent newspaper *Novaia Gazeta* was bludgeoned and died as a result of the attack.[31] Journalistic activism continues to carry severe costs (see Table 1.2, above).[32] In October, 2003, the editor of a Togliatti n ewspaper, Alexei S idorov, w as murdered j ust e ighteen months a fter his predecessor was assassinated. Togliatti is the site of the large *AvtoVaz* autombile plant that has been heavily infiltrated by organized crime.[33] Yuri Shechochikhin, editor of the muckraking *Novaia Gazeta* and a Duma member, died under mysterious circumstances in July 2003.[34]

In the first years of the new millennium, there has been little television independent of the government or the oligarchs, neither of which have had an interest in exposing corruption. Journalists, a potent force in the final y ears of the Soviet period, have been muzzled in the anti-corruption arena. Although some vigorous anti-corruption reporting is available through smaller newspaper outlets and internet sites, the purchase of many national newspapers by the oligarchs restricts the reporting of anti-corruption news.

Women's activism has been strongly focused on anti-corruption through their participation in the environmental movement, the media and such organizations as the Committee of Soldiers' Mothers, one of the largest and most geographically diverse NGOs. Started primarily by poor women whose sons were sent as young recruits to Chechnya, by the mid-1990s the Committee was challenging the corruption of military officers. Interviews conducted by the author with members of the Committee in the mid 1990s in Ekaterinburg revealed that they h ad j oined forces with human r ights l awyers i n t hat c ity to p ress c laims against corrupted military officials who had deprived them and their families of their legally entitled benefits. According to human rights activists, the Ekaterinburg situation was not unique.

The Soldiers' Mothers committee, unlike many other women's organizations, depends on Russian resources for its continued existence. It is not a creature of the f oreign aid community and has developed on the h uman and f inancial resources of Russian women. It stands in sharp contrast to many of the women's organizations that have developed mostly as a response to the availability of foreign assistance funds.[35]

Organizations to combat human trafficking, like the Soldiers' Mothers, have strong indigenous roots. Yet as anti-trafficking has become a western concern, some of these organizations h ave shifted their priorities to satisfy the funding objectives of their donors.[36] These organizations are confronting the nexus of organized crime and law enforcement corruption that facilitates trafficking. Their particular focus has been on the corruption of lower-level law enforcement personnel and border guards implicated in human trafficking. Groups such as the Angel Coalition, Miramed and others work in many parts of Russia to raise awareness not only of the problem of trafficking but also of the complicity of law enforcers in the process. The anti-trafficking movement exists on a national level a nd e ngages i n o utreach t hrough su ch v enues a s l ectures a nd u se o f t he Internet to reach large audiences.[37]

Human rights groups once viewed corruption as an issue extraneous to their concerns. But in the late 1990s this changed: corruption-related abuses by law enforcement bodies became a concern to human rights activists. Leading groups such as Citizens Watch in St. Petersburg and the Moscow Helsinki Group began to address these issues, with regional chapters of the Moscow Helsinki Group evaluating local law enforcement corruption.[38] More recently the Moscow Helsinki Group has devoted considerable resources to addressing the municipal corruption that impedes service delivery to citizens.[39]

Trade unions once mobilized millions of citizens in the Soviet period. Post-Soviet independent trade unions, initially strong supporters of Yeltsin, were co-opted, however. Also contributing to their eclipse as a potent societal force after 1991 was the fact that President Boris Yeltsin favored official unions at the expense of the independent ones. President Yeltsin, dependent on regional leaders for support, did not support the unofficial unions that pressed regional leaders on the non-payment of w ages.[40] Workers w ere often not paid because corrupt regional leaders siphoned off their wages. High-level corruption thus helped stifle one of the most potent anti-corruption forces in Russian society.

Legal institutions and scholars have assumed an important role in addressing corruption, as the scholarly community w as a less corrupted sector during the Soviet era and academicians saw themselves as voices of integrity. Scholars and academicians have participated in coalition building, addressing corruption in higher education, and in judicial reform. Faculty at Moscow State University and elsewhere have sponsored research on corruption within law schools including assessments of the level of corruption in admissions and in the exam process. The Law Faculty of St. P etersburg University, u nder t he leadership of its Dean, has instituted strict procedures and greater transparency to prevent the proffering of bribes at entrance exams or during the examination process.

The St. Petersburg law school has also embraced the "law in action perspective", initiating reforms not only within its institutions but also assuming a lead role in the reform of the judicial process in the larger community. Dean Nikolai Kropachev believes that greater oversight of legal decisions and greater transparency would reduce corruption in the judicial process. To address this issue, the law faculty has been a focal point for review and analysis of court decisions of the St. Petersburg region. The law faculty raised the money to equip the St. Petersburg judiciary with computers. The judges are required to p rovide their decisions to the law faculty where a group of faculty reviews the decisions, and selected decisions are analyzed in the publication *Iuridicheskaia Praktika* (Juridical Practice) issued quarterly by the law school. Judges, aware that their decisions are scrutinized by knowledgeable lawyers, are much more hesitant to accept bribes. The availability of published legal cases serves as a form of precedent in a civil law society, enhancing transparency and consistency in decision-making.[41] Despite this major effort, there are serious limitations on the ability to control corruption in the courts because judges do not cooperate to the extent desired. The failure to place decisions on the internet further reduces the transparency of the process.

Since 1995, organized crime and corruption research centers have sprung up throughout Russia. These Centers, funded through grants administered by the Transnational Crime and Corruption Center (TraCCC) at American University in Washington, D.C., represent a partnership between American and Russian scholars. Located in cities from Moscow and St. Petersburg to the Urals, Siberia and the Far East, they were founded at the impetus of Russian colleagues concerned that the rise of organized crime and the concomitant corruption would undermine the post-Soviet transition. With support from the MacArthur Foundation and subsequently the U.S. Government, they have proved to be a consistent source of research and policy advocacy in the anti-corruption field. Building on a team of leading scholars and practitioners, and based primarily in leading legal institutions throughout the country, the Centers identify and address issues of organized crime and corruption affecting their own regions and contribute to the larger national debate on how to address corruption. Members of the Center contribute to legislation and policy formation at the national and regional levels. They undertake multi-disciplinary research and analysis including press and public opinion surveys, and engage the public, policy makers and law enforcement practitioners in public fora through executive seminars and the media.

These Centers have conducted diverse research on corruption in the natural resources and banking sectors, surveys of law enforcement officials incarcerated for corruption and other offenses, corruption of the elite, trends in state sanctioning of official corruption and the role of corruption in the trafficking of women. The diverse publications of the research centers as well as the Centers' *Organizovannaia Prestupnost' i Korruptsiia* (Organized Crime and Corruption) journal have allowed the centers to reach a larger audience. Their research is increasingly recognized and cited in foreign reports and analyses of Russian corruption. Websites and regional conferences have also been key vehicles to communicate their insights and analysis.[42] Through small grants and summer school programs, the Centers engage in outreach beyond the cities where they are based. They have developed significant domestic capacity to address organized crime and corruption issues. Integrated into a Russian framework, they are viewed as a Russian-American partnership, albeit one funded by foreign funds. The presence of significant contributions in facilities and human resources from the Russian side makes this an indigenous Russian network.

Scholarly centers addressing corruption also include the Indem Foundation, headed by Georgi Satarov and other former staffers of the Yeltsin era, and the Carnegie Moscow Center.[43] Satarov has given much visibility to the anti-corruption surveys conducted by the INDEM foundation. These surveys have shown not only the pervasiveness of corruption but the high cost to Russian society.[44] The Carnegie Moscow Center of the Carnegie Endowment for International Peace has focused primarily on the corruption of administrative structures and prospects for democratization.[45] As they are primarily Moscow-based, these initiatives do not function on a national scale like that of the organized crime study centers located across Russia. They produce high-level research that remains within a small circle of intellectuals and Moscow-based policy makers. Indem's survey research results on corruption, however, have been disseminated broadly across the country.

Transparency International's chapter in Moscow, like other former-Soviet region chapters, was launched with funding from George Soros. Still in its early stages of development, it has not yet been able to galvanize a national constituency for anti-corruption activity. It has organized public meetings in Moscow and elsewhere where it has invited experts from different research centers and the government. TI personnel have spoken at conferences of the organized crime and corruption Centers in order to reach individuals in Russian regions not aware of the Moscow-based Transparency program. It has conducted survey research, along with INDEM, on corruption in the Russian regions.[46] It also maintains a reference library for researchers. and activists in the anti-corruption arena.

Supporting civil society in Russia is difficult, since there is little tradition of giving to charity or civil groups and few incentives to do so. The imprisonment and investigation of Mikhail Khodorkovsky will probably further limit pro-transparency philanthropy in the near future. The absence of tax deductibility for charitable contributions and the prohibition against giving to non-state organizations during the Soviet period have made Russian members of civil society heavily dependent on foreign assistance. When the plans of activists with roots within civil society dovetail with those of foreign donors, the programs are most successful. When westerners conceive of anti-corruption programs without Russian input, the programs often have little impact.

The Ukraine case

Ukraine had large NGOs at the close of the Soviet period. Once independence was achieved, however, many of the objectives of existing civil society had been realized. State building rather than the construction of civil society was of paramount importance. Ukraine therefore had less of a civil society capable of fighting corruption. Ukrainian activists mobilized around many of the same corruption issues as their Russian counterparts—the environment, trafficking of women, and local municipal corruption. Yet critical events gave each society a different focus. The long-term consequences of the Chernobyl catastrophe were a defining issue for Ukraine, in the same way that the Chechen war mobilized many poor Russian women whose sons and husbands served in the conflict.

Privatization of state property occurred more slowly in Ukraine than in Russia. Whereas Russia's economic reformers vowed to transfer state property into private hands as rapidly as possible, the Ukrainian elite favored the maintenance of s tate o wned i nstitutions. I n R ussia's r apid p rivatization, l ittle a ttention was paid to who acquired property and the methods they used to get it. In contrast, spontaneous privatization occurred in Ukraine with top officials grabbing pieces of the state without a legislative mandate. Ukrainian activists in the anti-corruption a rea b egan t o monitor t he a ppropriation o f s tate r esources b y government officials.[47] Those activists paid special attention to the insider privatizations in former centers of Party power such as Donetsk and Dniprpetrovsk. Former Party officials from Dniprpetrovsk, key officials in independent Ukraine, benefited s ignificantly f rom the spontaneous privatizations of m ineral, oil and gas resources and state-owned factories.[48]

Russia inherited the core of the *glasnost'*-era press from the final Soviet years, and tremendous opportunities were given to the Moscow-based press to conduct wide ranging investigative reports. Ukrainian central authorities, by contrast, tried to keep a lid on nationalism and did not allow the media to develop freely. Therefore, journalists in the early years of Ukraine's existence were not as potent an anti-corruption force as in Russia. Moreover, many Ukrainian journalists were hesitant to criticize the government, fearing that to do so would weaken Ukrainian independence. However, by the end of the first decade of Ukraine's existence, independent journalists were a potent force within society.

Epitomizing the potency of the anti-corruption investigations of muckraking journalists is the killing of Giorgiy Gongadze, a journalist with an on-line news service, in September, 2000. Gongadze went missing; later, a beheaded corpse was found whose identity was only established after a tortured tale of DNA analysis. Hidden recording equipment placed by a member of the President Kuchma's security apparatus within the presidential offices allegedly recorded the President ordering the killing of Gongadze. While President Leonid Kuchma has survived these allegations through consistent denials, the Gongadze case greatly discredited the President's standing both among his population and in the international community.[49] Although there were not as many journalists in Ukraine conducting such investigative work as in Russia, the potency of the investigations is no less strong. The fear by the presidential administration of Gongadze's revelations indicates that the media were seen as key in monitoring high level corruption. No anti-corruption figure as visible as Gongadze has emerged since his murder.[50]

As in Russia, Ukrainian women are pillars of anti-corruption activities. They are active participants in programs at the municipal level, the foreign funded anti-corruption coalitions and the significant anti-trafficking organizations. The large number of Ukrainian women trafficked around the world has led to broad-based activism at the community level, including prevention campaigns and mobilization to combat the local corruption that allows the traffickers to operate. Much of this has strong indigenous roots but as foreign and multilateral funds for anti-trafficking have become available, w omen with experience in g ender-based civil society issues have moved into foreign-sponsored anti-corruption initiatives.

Other anti-corruption programs in Ukraine are also the result of the availability of foreign assistance. Some of these efforts correspond to, and help support, broad based initiatives in society. Others are essentially western efforts to promote engagement on this issue. In contrast with Russia, significant sums have been directed by the U.S. Agency for International Development (USAID), the World Bank and the European Community to explicitly address Ukrainian corruption.[51] As a result, Ukraine has foreign-sponsored newsletters on corruption and has hosted numerous national and regional conferences sponsored by multilateral organizations and the United States on corruption. NGOs have sprung up in response to the availability of funds, some—such as the Ukraine National Coalition for Integrity—combining strong local groups with opportunistic NGOs.[52]

Foreign-sponsored initiatives have focused almost exclusively on low-level corruption a ffecting t he d evelopment o f p rivate b usiness a nd e ntrepreneurship and impeding the delivery of municipal services. Among the most successful of these is the Partnership for Transparency that works in many regions of Ukraine and with key policy makers.[53] The Freedom of Choice Coalition has focused on electoral campaign financing, a national anti-corruption survey and meetings on anti-corruption between 2000 and 2002. The need for transparency in customs procedures, licensing, as well as municipal budgets have also been prime concerns. These efforts have not addressed the crippling political-criminal nexus that has allowed oligarchs to consolidate economic and political power and to erode press freedom through intimidation of journalists.[54] Instead, the concern has been to mobilize the citizenry of major cities such as Donetsk, Kharkiv, and Lviv to address issues over which they may possibly assert some leverage.[55]

TI's Ukrainian Chapter, funded by George Soros, is housed within the Ukrainian Legal Foundation. The Foundation, headed by Serhiy Holovaty, former Minister of Justice of Ukraine, has conducted high-level public opinion surveys on corruption in Kyiv and other parts of the country. This organization has also implemented programs on public awareness, youth education and governmental oversight.[56] As in Russia, however, "transparency" remains primarily a creature of the west that lacks broad-based indigenous support within Ukraine. By merging its own activities with those of an opposition politician—Holovaty—TI has violated its policy of political neutrality and undermined its own potency. It has failed to maintain an active presence in Ukraine,[57] although in 2001 it partnered with TI-Russia and the Freedom of Choice Coalition in

Ukraine to host a regional anti-corruption event.[58]

Academicians and scholars are a less potent anti-corruption force in Ukraine than in Russia, a legacy in part of the repression of independent thought in Ukraine during the Soviet period. The organized crime study center, based in the Kharkyiv National Legal Academy, is less focused on corruption than its counterparts in Russia. The same can be said for the newly established center in Odessa. Kharkyiv's focus was on developing the needed legal framework for an independent Ukraine, whereas Odessa is primarily concerned with understanding the manifestations of organized crime within Ukrainian society and in the Black Sea region. Academicians in Kyiv have worked with the World Bank to develop excellent surveys and analyses of corruption. Their work has been more analytical than a manifestation of civil-society activity.

In conclusion, the most effective forces in Ukraine to mobilize against corruption were the journalists and women activists both within and outside the women's movement. Exposés of high-level corruption have made citizens aware of the costs of these issues for national development but little tangible success has been recorded in diminishing either small or grand corruption.

IV. Conclusion

The emergence of any civil society at all in the post-Soviet era is remarkable in light of seventy years of repression in the USSR. Belonging to civil society was a risky undertaking in the Soviet period; citizen leaders faced intimidation and possible incarceration. Although many more individuals can freely take part in civil society in both countries, participation remains risky for journalists and others who probe deeply into corruption and the other ills of contemporary society. Journalists have been killed in both Russia and Ukraine, yet in neither country have the murders been solved or responsible individuals brought to trial. Still, human rights, nationalist, and religious movements acquired strength as Soviet power receded, providing the basis for the civil society of contemporary Russia and Ukraine.

The corrupted power structures still enjoy extensive impunity. With weak rule of law, corrupted law enforcement and no independent judiciary, neither country can offer protection to the individuals who challenge the grand corruption of the oligarchs or the petty corruption that depletes municipal budgets and contributes to the trafficking of women. The absence of domestic financial support for civil society in Russia and Ukraine has made many groups highly dependent on foreign assistance to sustain their activities. The desire of western countries to fight corruption has produced significant funding for anti-corruption programs. Many such initiatives have sprung up in response to market conditions, but too many lack domestic support. Such civil society groups sometimes need to mold their objectives to the desires of the foreign community rather than to their own perceived methodology for addressing corruption. Groups that are more western in orientation often receive more aid than those having greater resonance with Russians and Ukrainians.[59] Not only are these programs unsustainable without western aid; they are unlikely to develop extensive support within the society. They create the veneer of an anti-corruption program without actual substance or tangible results.

The culture of corruption in Russia and Ukraine remains predominant over the culture of civil society. The nascent civil society is not yet a counterweight to the deeply entrenched corruption in political, economic and daily life. Until this balance shifts, there are limited prospects that Russia and Ukraine will develop into democratic societies with functioning market economies. Without this shift, there can only be the external trappings of democracy. The increasing authoritarian tendencies of Putin's Russia have severely crippled civil society and the independent media. President Kuchma's efforts to hold on to power despite very important revelations of his corruption make efforts to sustain anti-corruption civil society difficult except at the most local level.

The first decade of post-Soviet rule in Russia and Ukraine gave some hope that a vibrant civil society might emerge. This hope was much stronger in Russia than in Ukraine, but some held out hopes for Ukraine too. However, intimidation, apathy and the failure of the business community to engage as a form of civil society against corruption have severely limited the possibility of these two societies to effectively move against corruption. Over a decade since the break up of the Soviet Union, the problems of corruption seem as intractable as they were in the early 1990s. Few citizens have the courage, the incentive or the desire to engage in anti-corruption activism in Russia and Ukraine. Efforts in this direction are much more limited in the two major states to emerge from the USSR than in the neighboring countries of Eastern Europe.

ENDNOTES

1. Oleinik, Anton N. 2003. *Organized Crime, Prison and Post-Soviet Societies*. Aldershot, Hampshire, U.K.: Ashgate Publishing; Transparency International Corruption Perception Index. (2003).
http://www.transparency.org/pressreleases_archive/2003/2003.10.07.cpi.en.html (retrieved, March 30, 2004); Kaufmann, Daniel, Kraay, Aart and Zoido-Lobaton, Pablo, "Approaches to Measuring Governance." *Global Corruption Report.* Berlin: Transparency International. (2001), pp. 244-48. Retrieved on November 13, 2001 from
http://www.worldbank.org/wbi/governance.
2. Orttung, Robert. 2004. "Russia," in Freedom House, *Nations in Transit 2004*. Lanham, MD: Rowman and Littlefield. Online at
http://www.freedomhouse.org/research/nattransit.htm (viewed July 30, 2004).

3. *Ibid.*

4. *Ibid.*

5. Transparency International Corruption Perception Index. (2003). http://www.transparency.org/pressreleases_archive/2003/2003.10.07.cpi.en.html (retrieved, March 30, 2004)

6. Bukovsky, V. 1978. *To Build a Castle.* London: Andre Deutsch.

7. Tökes, Rudolph (ed.). 1975. *Dissent in the USSR: Politics, Ideology and People.* Baltimore: John Hopkins University Press.

8. Alexeyeva, L. and Goldberg, P. 1990. *The Thaw Generation: Coming of Age in the Post-Stalin Era.* Boston: Little Brown and Co.

9. Alexeeva L. 1985. *Soviet Dissent: Contemporary Movements for National, Religious and Human Rights.* Middletown: Wesleyan University Press.

10. Alexeeva, L. and Chalidze V. 1985. *Mass Unrest in the USSR.* Vol.1. Washington, D.C.: Office of Net Assessments, pp. 222-224.

11. Shelley, L. 1996. *Policing Soviet Society: The Evolution of State Control.* London: Routledge, pp. 182-183.

12. *Ibid.*, pp. 185-6; Curatorial Assistance. 1998. *Forbidden Art: The Post-War Russian Avant-Garde.* New York: Distributed Art Publishers, p.80. The author was present there and lived in the USSR from 1974-76.

13. Hopkins, M. 1983. *Russia's Underground Press: The Chronicle of Current Events.* New York: Praeger.

14. Alexeyeva and Goldberg, *op. cit.*

15. Schapiro, L., and Godson, J. 1981. *The Soviet Worker: Illusions and Realities.* New York: St. Martin's Press.

16. Waters, E. 1993. "Finding a Voice: The Emergence of a Women's Movement." In N. Funk and M. Mueller (eds.), *Gender Politics and Post Communism.* New York: Routledge, pp. 287-302; Mamonova, T. 1994. *Women's Glasnost' vs. Naglost: Stopping Russian Backlash.* Westport, Conn.: Bergin and Garvey.

17. Shelley, Louise I. 1999. "The Political-Criminal Nexus: Russian-Ukrainian Case Studies." *Trends in Organized Crime* 4:3, pp. 81-107.

18. Coulloudon, V. 1997. "The Criminalization of Russia's Political Elite." *East European Constitution Review* 6:4, pp. 73-79; Center for Strategic and International Studies 2000. *Russian Organized Crime and Corruption: Putin's Challenge.* Washington, DC: CSIS Press.

19. Miller, W., Grødeland, A., and Kosechkina, T. 2001. *A Culture of Corruption? Coping with Government in Post-Communist Europe.* Budapest: Central European University Press.

20. "*Sud'ba demokratii v Rossii v rukakh bezrazlichnogo bol'shinstva.*" http://www.democracy.ru/article.php?id=538, 28 October 2003, accessed 30 March 2004.

21. Olimpieva, I. , Panchenkov, O and Nikiforova, E. 2004. "Fighting Corruption in State-Business Relations: Small and Medium Business in St. Petersburg" (forthcoming).

22. Menges, Constantine C. 1996. "An Initial Assessment of U.S. Aid to Russia, 1992-1995, and A Strategy for More Effective Assistance." *Demokratizatsiya* IV:4, pp. 538-560; Wedel, Janine R. 1996. "Clique-Run Organizations and U.S. Economic Aid: An Institutional Analysis." *Demokratizatsiya* IV:4, pp. 571-602.

23. Transparency International Corruption Perception Index. (2003). http://www.transparency.org/pressreleases_archive/2003/2003.10.07.cpi.en.html (re-

trieved, March 30, 2004); Kaufmann, Daniel, Kraay, Aart and Zoido-Lobaton, Pablo. 2001. "Approaches to Measuring Governance." *Global Corruption Report*. Berlin: Transparency International, pp. 244-248. Retrieved on November 13, 2001 from http://www.worldbank.org/wbi/governance.

24. Zviglyanich, V. 1995. "The State and Economic Reform in Ukraine." *Demokratizatsiya* III:2, p. 134.

25. Juviler, P. 1998. *Freedom's Ordeal the Struggle for Human Rights and Democracy in Post-Soviet States*. Philadelphia: University of Pennsylvania Press, pp. 70-73.

26. Harasymiw, B. 1993. "Democracy in Ukraine." *Demokratizatsiya* I:3, p. 8.

27. International Federation for Human Rights. 2001. *Human Rights in Russian Regions*. Moscow: Moscow Helsinki Group.

28. Azghikhina, N. 1995. "Will Russia Become the Capital of Western Feminism?" *Demokratizatsiya* 3:3, pp. 243-51.

29. Committee for the Protection of Journalists. 2003. "Attacks on the Press: Russia 2003" http://www.cpj.org/attacks03/europe03/russia.html (accessed March 20, 2004).

30. Global Organized Crime Project. 2000. *Russian Organized Crime and Corruption Putin's Challenge*. Washington, D.C.: Center for Strategic and International Studies, p. 67.

31. Committee for the Protection of Journalists. 2000. "Europe and Central Asia." Retrieved on November 13, 2001 from http://www.cpj.org/attacksoo/europe00/Russia.html.

32. Commission on Security and Cooperation in Europe. 2000. "The Putin Path: Are Human Rights in Retreat?" (CSCE 106-2-9) Hearing before the Commission on Security and Cooperation in Europe, Washington, D.C.: May 23.

33. Committee for the Protection of Journalists. 2003. "Attacks on the Press: Russia 2003" http://www.cpj.org/attacks03/europe03/russia.html (accessed March 20, 2004).

34. See http://www.eng.yabloko.ru/People/Shekoch/Schekoch.html (accessed March 30, 2004).

35. Henderson, S. 2000. "Importing Civil Society: Foreign Aid and the Women's Movement in Russia." *Demokratizatsiya,* 8:1, pp. 65-82.

36. In Russia, as in Ukraine, when these groups have shifted to job training programs in response to donor assistance, they have moved away from the corruption problems that facilitate trafficking.

37. United States. Department of State. 2001. "Trafficking in Persons Report." Victims of Trafficking and Violence Protection Act 2000 (H.R. 3244): U.S. Department of State Annual Report. (July).

38. International Federation for Human Rights. 2001. *Status Report on Human Rights in the Russian Federation*, 8.

39. Alexeeva, Luidmilla. 2001. Speech delivered to Radio Liberty/Radio Free Europe. Washington, DC., September 20.

40. Alexeeva, Ludmila. 1995. "Free Trade Unions in Russia." *Demokratizatsiya* III:1, pp. 38-43.

41. Kropachev, N. and Shakhtikihina, N. 2001. "Scientific Institutions: Law Schools as the Bridge between Law in the Books and Law in Action in Countries Reforming their System." *Law and Society Conference*. Budapest, Hungary, July 5.

42. See research conducted and links to the Russian research and work. Retrieved on November 11, 2001 from http://www.american.edu/traccc.

43. Indem Foundation. 1998. "Russia vs. Corruption: Who Will Win?" Analytic Report.

44. See for example http://www.rand.org/nsrd/cre/events/corruption.html (accessed March 30, 2004).
45. See website of Carnegie Moscow Center, http://www.carnegie.ru/en/search/advsearch.asp?search=Corruption&searchCatalogue=0 &cP=3 (accessed March 30, 2004).
46. Marina Grigorian, Marina. 2003. "A Portrait of Corruption in Russia." July 11. http://www.cdi.org/russia/johnson/7246-19.cfm (accessed March 29, 2004).
47. See the work of the publication "Corruption Watch" of the Ukrainian Center for Independent Political Research.
48. Ukrainian Center for Independent Political Research 1996. "The Dnipropetrovsk Family." Kyiv: Democracy Fund.
49. Pascual, C. and Pifer, S. 2002. "Ukraine's Bid for a Decisive Place in History." *The Washington Quarterly* 25:1, pp. 175-192.
50. Committee for the Protection of Journalists. 2003. "Attacks on the Press 2003: Ukraine." http://www.cpj.org/attacks03/europe03/ukraine.html (accessed March 30, 2004)
51. For an example, see Ukraine National Integrity Survey. 1997. "Citizens' Experiences of Public Service Quality, Integrity and Corruption." Washington, D.C.: World Bank.
52. "Corruption Watch." Electronic Journal. Sponsored by the Ukrainian Independent Center of Political Research and the Ukraine National Coalition for Integrity. Retrieved November 11, 2001, from: http://www.nobribers.org/unci.
53. More information can be obtained from its website www.prozorist.org.ua (accessed March 31, 2004).
54. Shelley, Louise. 1999. "The Political-Criminal Nexus: Russian-Ukrainian Case Studies." *Trends in Organized Crime* 4:3, pp. 81-107.
55. For example see the *Newsletter* of the Ukraine National Council for Integrity, Issue No.2, May 2000; Issue No. 4, July 2000; and Issue No.6-7, September-October 2000.
56. *Newsletter* of the Ukraine National Council for Integrity. Issue No.2, May 2000.
57. Transparency International Ukraine website, http://www.transparency.org.ua/ (accessed March 30, 2004.)
58. For more information see http://www.transparency.org.ru/conf_ukr.asp (accessed Feb. 27, 2002).
59. Henderson, *op. cit.*

2

Contributions, Covenants, and Corruption:
Politicians and Society in Japan

Susan Pharr

Corruption does not always defy the values and wishes of society. Sometimes, a culture of corruption can grow up that sustains misconduct and that can frustrate reforms designed without regard to the ways people understand the links among wealth, status, and power. But those social value systems also contain limits and constraints; moreover, while rooted in tradition they are not unchangeable. Susan Pharr, in this discussion adapted from a lecture presented under the auspices of Colgate University's Center for Ethics and World Societies, examines the fascinating case of Japan, where traditions of gift-gifting and status relations both sustain and, in important ways, have long restrained corruption. Understanding those connections can help us see why Japan had both high levels of corruption and rapid economic growth for several decades after World War II. Both economic problems and the excesses of politicians who disregarded traditional values, however, have begun to change that culture of corruption.

I. Introduction: Growth and Corruption

I am talking tonight about Asia and East Asia, with a focus on Japan, but I am also talking about a part of the world that is very different from where we are now. I hope to convey a sense of some of those differences, specifically as regards the ways Japan and the West perceive each other.

As the centerpiece of my talk I would like to set out a puzzle. We are talking about a part of the world that has experienced some of the most dramatic economic growth of the post war period, or really in world history. We can speak of double-digit growth of the 1960s and 1970s in much of Japan's neighboring region. More recently, the trend has expanded to include China, and even after the crisis of the late 1990s growth is continuing today in other parts of East Asia. But we are also talking about corruption, and by many measures some of the most corrupt countries in the world are those same Asian miracle economies. Most people and most scholars would argue that corruption is very bad for economic development—so, how can we explain this anomaly? That is the puzzle I put out before you—one I will address later on.

First, how corrupt is Japan, relative to other parts of the world? Given Japan's problems with corruption, what are the reasons behind it? I'll be talking about Japan, but asking you to think about the kinds of explanation I am offering, and how they might apply to other countries. Next I want to focus on the puzzle itself that I have just put before you, explaining the growth-with-corruption anomaly. And then I want to say a word about what has changed in Japan. I will make the case that the country has undergone a seismic shift in terms of its attitudes towards corruption, and towards the environment in which corruption operates—a change, I think, for the better. This is happening in the context of what many people would say has been a "lost decade" economically. There are positive developments in Japan in terms of controlling corruption; how can we explain *that* shift? Why the turnaround?

So let me now begin by asking, "how black is the sheep?" When we compare Japan to other countries in Asia in terms of the usual corruption indices, Japan actually starts looking pretty good. Singapore and Hong Kong receive favorable ratings, but Japan is up there too, not far from the least corrupt countries in Asia. If we take a broader perspective, however, and take a look at the countries that are the most corrupt countries in the world on the indices, we see that Asian countries are widely scattered, some ranking among the most corrupt in the world: Indonesia, Vietnam, the Philippines, and India, for example. Overall, Japan comes out around number twenty-three out of about a hundred countries on the scale. On the other hand, when you look at the countries that are at the top of that scale—the ones regarded as the cleanest countries in the world, such as Finland—you can see the most advanced industrialized countries come out ahead of Japan. So in that sense Japan is a laggard in dealing with its level of corruption. It is more towards the corrupt side than almost any of the industrialized countries, with only a few like Belgium and Italy ranking below Japan. Japan doesn't look as good as it does against the Asian comparison.

Japan's level of corruption is actually very surprising. What I mean by that is that theories of change and theories of modernization, industrialization, and economic transformation would lead us to expect that as countries become more and more developed, they develop more law; and that as they develop law, corruption gradually gets contained. Historically England had problems with the wholesale buying of offices, but as it became more developed the level of corruption diminished. That is roughly the trajectory that most industrial countries have followed. When you think about Japan however, it is an anomaly: here is a country that is one of the most developed in the world in terms of the percentage of people working in the tertiary sector—that is, in the information and service areas as opposed to industry—and one of the most literate countries in the world with the highest newspaper readership of any country. Japan had achieved almost universal literacy by 1912. So by all of those measures we would expect it to be much cleaner than it actually is. How can we explain Japan's post war period of high economic growth and achievement while it was a laggard when it came to dealing with corruption?

II. Japanese Corruption: Four Major Influences

Let me now offer you an anatomy of Japanese corruption that brings out some of the factors that help explain that pattern.

A dominant party and its constituencies

The first has to do with a political system that has had one party in power for a very long time. That is the Liberal Democratic Party, or LDP as it is generally called; it was in power from 1955, with almost unbroken rule, up until 1993, and has been back in power since 1995. So basically one party has ruled Japan during the era that interests us. One-party systems, as opposed to turnover systems where parties alternate in power, are a complex way of describing a simple thing: that is, when parties alternate in power they tend to check each other's excesses, whereas if one party holds power unchallenged, over time it tends to become more corrupt. If you are interested in China, for example, or in other countries that have one party in power, that is an important fact: generally speaking, a one party system tends to be conducive to, or permissive of, a culture that supports corruption, compared to systems in which power changes hands more frequently.

The exact dynamic, though, needs some thought. Why is it, exactly, that one party system would promote corruption? Think about each political party as having a certain constellation of interests that are closely associated with it over time. An obvious example is the United States: the Republican Party is closely associated with big business interests, labor unions tend to support the Democratic Party, and so on. A party with a particular base or constituency tends to pursue policies that favor the interests that they can count on to get elected. Now in a turnover system that means that one set of interests get favored for a certain period of time, but then there is an election and a new set of interests come in. Of course, that doesn't mean that a political party serves *only* its constituents; it can't do that and stay in power over long periods of time. Still, the scales do get tipped towards one set of interests.

Over time we see that particular set of interests dominating—as happened in Japan. The LDP's constituent interests were agriculture and big business, and they developed cozy inside relations with the party in power. Over time more and more policies got pushed their way, and they had privileged access. In that situation large amounts of money moved, both over *and* under the table, from big business to the party in power. The dynamic in Japan works like this: if you run a business, and you want a certain contract with the government, you need the bureaucrat in charge of administering the policies to give you the contract. So what businesses in Japan have typically done, for a long time, is to cultivate the politicians through giving money. Then the politicians put pressure on the bureaucrats to favor the interests of those businesses. Notice that I'm not saying businesses give bribes to bureaucrats, but rather that they do give campaign contributions above and below the table to encourage the politicians to lean on the bureaucrats to help them out.

So is this corruption? The laws in Japan are rather lax; it is not always the case that what as I have portrayed here is corrupt. But over time these relationships are conducive to corruption. Such close relationships can be abused, and in post-war Japan they have been abused.

The bureaucrats

The second point in all this has to do with the nature of regulations. What do bureaucrats do? Bureaucrats make policies, but they also carry out policies—and in doing that they have varying degrees of discretion. For example, in the mid-1980s there was a big issue in U.S-Japanese relations called the large retail store law. Imagine that you wanted to start a retail store in Tokyo. In the United States you don't have to go to national bureaucrats to get permission to start a retail store. But in Japan, if you wanted to open a store with more than 1500 square feet of floor space you had to go to bureaucrats in the national government to get permission. Therefore, you will also go to a politician who can encourage those bureaucrats to give you permission. Japan's bureaucrats have a great deal of discretion, a great deal of power, and a whole range of decisions they can make, and they have not had strict rules to follow in deciding who gets what. That creates incentives for people to try to influence those bureaucrats, and that is one of the features of Japan that, one could argue, supports a culture of corruption. Japan by many measures doesn't have a large bureaucracy; in fact, it has fewer bureaucrats than the United States per capita. But those officials have more discretionary authority as to how they make decisions.

Informal norms and the law

The third feature of the Japanese arrangements that tends to support a culture of corruption has to do with the laws. Corruption is a particular kind of crime—unlike any other—in which law enforcement almost totally depends upon arresting the little fish and getting them to talk. Those of you who watched the Monica Lewinsky scandal unfold several years ago know that several features of the United States political and legal system were very important in the way that particular scandal came to light. One of them is plea-bargaining. If you remember, Monica Lewinsky did a deal: she would not be prosecuted, and in return investigators were able to get her cooperation in talking about President Clinton and bringing charges against him. Plea-bargaining becomes a very valuable tool: prosecutors can promise one person a deal in order to get at higher-level individuals in corruption. Another feature of the legal system, important in corruption investigations in particular, is wire-tapping and similar ways of recording evidence. Linda Tripp wore a body "wire" during conversations with Monica Lewinsky in a hotel in Virginia, and the information recorded was later used against Clinton.

But in Japan, plea-bargaining and wire-tapping have not been a part of the legal system. Why would that be? Japan had a long legacy, in the pre-war period, of fascism, and had a very active secret police force. In the post war period the police were interested in cleaning up their image, and it came to be regarded as unacceptable to use methods associated with the pre-war secret police. So wire-tapping and making deals through plea-bargaining are uncommon in modern Japan. But when it comes to corruption, wiretapping and plea-bargaining are essential for nailing the person that you are trying to accuse or convict of corruption. Without these tools it is very difficult to pursue corruption cases.

One party, lots of weddings, and many funerals

A fourth important factor is the nature of the electoral system in Japan. Electoral systems have all kinds of different consequences depending on exactly how the rules work. In the United States we send one person from each Congressional district to the House of Representatives in Washington. It is a winner-take-all system. In Japan, for much of the post war period up until 1994, the three to six top vote-getters were sent to Tokyo from each constituency, with each party putting up a list of candidates for those seats. That meant that the LDP, as the largest party, often had its own politicians competing with each other. That involves some difficulties, because after all, on the issues most would agree on things—same party, same constituencies, same ideology, same positions on practically everything. So the kind of campaigning that developed was highly personalistic: you wined and dined your constituents. You gave them all kinds of benefits in order to cultivate their personal loyalty and to keep them under your tent.

What is the problem with this? It takes a lot of money in an electoral district to keep your constituents happy. The kind of campaigning created by the electoral system also raises important points about Japanese culture. For example, in the late 1980s an ordinary Japanese politician laid out all his expenses—what he did with millions of dollars of political money. We might expect that much of it must have been for television, because in the United States about 60 percent of all campaign money is spent for television—but not so for Japan, because there are strict rules on using television. So what were these huge amounts of money used for? One thing might strike many Americans as odd: much of it goes for weddings and funerals. On a given day this politician (or his representatives) might go to five weddings.

Certainly that is time consuming; but why is it expensive? Japan has a custom: when Japanese go to weddings and funerals they are expected to put money in an envelope and give it as gifts. In the case of a funeral, elaborately decorated envelopes containing money are given to the family of the deceased; at a wedding, money goes to the young couple. The amount to give is based on status. A politician is a high status person, and the current expectation is that a politician attending a wedding will give a gift of about $500. Five weddings a day comes to $2500; it all adds up. For weddings alone in just one year, this politician spent about $912,500. For funerals it is the same thing: between $400 and $500 is routinely expected. Put the money in an envelope; go to the funeral, and give the envelope: this is a normal Japanese custom and a part of politics.

Japanese politicians develop a personal relationship with their constituents by circulating in their constituency and going to a lot of weddings and funerals. Now consider that in Japan, a member of the Diet is only given funding for two staff people. Everything else, the Member pays for. And it is typical for a well-established Member of the legislature to have about twenty staff members to go to weddings and funerals, personally cultivating members of their district. Those staffers easily cost *another* $900,000 or million dollars a year at late-1980s prices. That, like other costs, creates a constant demand for contributions. So this gives you a sense of how the costs of politics add up for things that, while they have nothing to do with the way American politicians spend their money, reflect important values and traditions in Japan. In an electoral system in which politicians mostly compete with others from the same party, personalistic campaigning and gifts are the only way they can cultivate their constituents.

III. The Political Culture: Gift-Giving and Conceptions of Corruption

The final point I would like to discuss is the political culture itself. As I have suggested, Japan, and East Asia more generally, have gift-giving cultures. This deeply affects the climate of corruption. All of you have gone to airports and have seen Duty-Free shops. People who run those shops have two kinds of passengers that they talk about. "JPAX", or Japanese passengers, account for 75 percent of duty free shops' business all over the world. "OPAX" are everybody else in the world. In duty-free shops, staff talk about Japanese passengers, and then about everyone else in the world. This is changing because today Thailand, Korea, and Taiwan are also entering the zone of the big, big gift purchases. But the point is that the Japanese have always been major gift givers.

Japanese routinely give many, many gifts to many kinds of contacts. Each year, for example, there are two gift giving seasons in which people give not simply to personal friends but to their range of associates; and if you are in business you have quite an extensive circle of people you deal with. This kind of gift giving affects how people feel about corruption, because it is an exchange of gifts or favors, and gifts in Japan in normal life are given, and expected, in certain ways. For example, in a school it is quite usual for professors or teachers to get gifts from parents of their students. The expectation that comes with getting the gift is that the teacher will also look after the student. There is an implicit notion that "I'm good to you and you will be good to me," and it seen as a very reasonable thing. My colleague Robert Putnam at Harvard, who studies "social capital," argues that it is all about exchanges and the trust that we all have in each other—that I care about you, I trust you, and you will trust me. This is the reciprocity of normal life in many healthy societies. But gift-giving colors the way people think about corruption and it makes it harder for people to draw the line. When is something corrupt?

I have explored this issue by doing focus groups in Japan in rural areas, cities, and suburbs. I have asked people to think about a series of scenarios describing conduct—people doing things of various kinds—and then asked the people in the focus groups what they thought of them. Here is one of my scenarios: a politician is given a set of golf clubs by some businessmen in his district. Japanese people love to talk about things like this; they talk about how much the golf clubs must have cost, and in some groups people didn't really know but most in Japan did. It is a big golfing country, so people always have opinions about golf and some would have an opinion about how much a set of clubs would cost. People routinely thought the cost would be somewhere between $1,000 and $10,000 for top-of-the-line golf clubs—the kind that high status business people would give to a politician. (You can't give cheap golf clubs to a politician because he is a high-status person.) What was interesting was that only 34 percent of people in the focus groups thought it was wrong for business people to give such a pricey gift to a politician in their district. I conclude that because gift giving is so usual in their own lives, and they are constantly thinking about gifts in terms of the status of the person, it seems reasonable to them that gifts would be exchanged at another level among well-to-do, high-status people.

Social customs therefore make it difficult to judge what is corrupt, and with respect to the political culture gift-giving practices create problems in terms of what is expected of politicians. People expect gifts of their friends; they tend to expect gifts from politicians they consider close associates; and they expect them to behave like friends and therefore to come to their weddings and give them their $500. Not only does this drive up the cost of politics; it also creates a tolerance of practices that in many western countries would be considered very questionable, because politicians have to obtain those funds from business contributors or from other party leaders.

These considerations also make corruption very difficult to prove, partly because many of the gifts are in the form of cash. That makes the Japanese courtroom a very strange place. In a corruption case we hear the prosecutor asking strange questions about the actual money that was being given. For example, they might ask, "Was it wet?" "Was it clean?" They ask this because, if a family is giving cash gifts, Japanese housewives will iron the bills and make them all spiffy and clean. So if the bills are all nice and crisp and look ironed, the defense will say, "It is just a gift." When cash changes hands between citizens and politicians in a Western society, by contrast, there is a reasonable assumption people make that it is probably a bribe—an assumption you can't make in Japan given its gift-giving customs.

Tradition: not just exchanges, but limits too

All of these factors that I have described are parts of, and support, a culture of corruption. But let me return to the puzzle that I posed in the beginning. If we say that Japan has a culture supporting corruption, then we are faced with the anomaly of the high growth that Japan long experienced despite the corruption. How can we explain it? I would argue that in Japan, and in other high-growth countries in East Asia, corruption has operated within limits that amount to a series of covenants among the Japanese public, politicians, and bureaucrats. This covenant defined how much corruption people were prepared to tolerate. I think of this in terms of three "shall-nots"—that is, that corruption has been acceptable so long as it stays within a domain defined by three sets of informal limits. The first of those "shall-nots" confined corrupt payments primarily to politicians; they were not generally accepted among bureaucrats, as I suggested above. Why does this matter? If you look at the countries that have the most serious corruption problems, typically the money flows directly to the bureaucrat. Cash usually changes hands and the bureaucrat takes money in exchange for a contract, for example. This is the Italian style of corruption, to name one case. Many local-level bureaucrats engage in corruption, which is one of the reasons why Italy is so far up the list of corrupt countries. But in Japan I described to you a triangle in which, while people gave to politicians, the politicians are not giving money to the bureaucrats, nor are people giving it directly. Bureaucrats do sometimes favor the interests of the business people who pay the politicians, but not through an automatic *quid pro quo*. This meant that Japan could maintain a rather efficient bureaucracy that worked very effectively for economic growth and development, as did several other countries in Asia that have had periods of high growth.

The second "shall-not" really has to do with politicians themselves. Although the Japanese public was prepared to tolerate fairly high levels of corruption in their politicians, that was acceptable only as long as it was for their own political purposes—that is, to maintain their constituency and get themselves elected. It was "practical money", necessary to stay in politics, and people accepted that. The "shall-not," however, meant *not for personal gain*: politicians could not have lavish homes, and could not live like Imelda Marcos with her three thousand pairs of black high-heeled shoes. They could not have mansions as you find in the suburbs of Amman, Jordan today among many elites. A politician had to keep a modest personal profile, even though it could be raised for political purposes. That part of the covenant set some limits on corruption, and on the amounts that changed hands.

The final "shall-not" had to do with the legal system. Generally speaking, the legal system itself was not corrupt. Again, if we consider the most corrupt countries in the world, typically corruption there goes right down to the legal system. If you run a red light in Moscow, for example, the policeman comes over, puts out his hand, and says, "You ran a red light." You reach for your currency, and you pay him, and everything is done. These sorts of bribery and extortion are very widespread in many parts of the world. But Japan's legal system did not exhibit that kind of behavior at all. It remained outside the corruption loop, and that helps explain how Japan successfully maintained the rule of law, which is basic and essential for high levels of economic development.

Those are the three "shall nots." You can see that, in a larger sense, in Japan during this high growth era there was a kind of passive understanding between the public and the leaders: "We will tolerate a certain amount of corruption in exchange for high economic growth." Citizens said, in effect, that if leaders keep treating us well in terms of high economic growth, we will look the other way on the corruption. That helps explain the anomaly of Japan, and of other countries in East Asia, where high levels of corruption coexisted with high levels of growth for several decades.

IV. Conclusion: Changes in the Culture of Corruption?

One question remains: what has really changed? How much of the above no longer holds true in Japan? Some people in Japan refer to the last ten years as the lost decade, and in economic terms it has been a very difficult time of recession and economic hardship. I would argue that during that decade there have been very important changes in Japan in which the culture of corruption has itself been changing. The country is indeed in economic trouble, but there are some profound developments underway that in the long term will be good for Japan. How have they affected the culture of corruption? They tested the three "shall-nots." First, politicians stopped working within the limits I have described. In the late 1980s, partly because Japan had entered a "bubble economy," businessmen and people with enormous affluence—some of the latter, politicians—raced after a wealthy lifestyle and lived far more lavishly than they ever had before. This violated the limits of how much corruption could go for personal gain, and made the Japanese public very angry. Moreover, bureaucrats were no longer staying out of the loop on corruption. During the 1990s there was a whole series of scandals involving, almost for the first time, powerful bureaucrats personally implicated in corruption cases. And finally, accelerating the process of change in the 1990s, there has been corruption involving police corruption. Many of these cases do not involve large amounts of money by third world standards today. In the case of Indonesia's former President Suharto, for example, we would be talking about over a billion dollars taken by the leader in Indonesia for personal gain. In the case of police corruption in Japan, we are talking about several hundred thousand dollars—not huge amounts of corruption.

But all of these cases cumulatively have made the public reexamine corruption and, by focusing attention on it, are shining a bright light over a whole series of cases that in the past would have been kept under wraps. The media would not have reported them in the 1990s, but now the lid is off. Of course the major thing that opened itself in the 1990s up has been the recession itself. The basic social-political bargain between the public and the political leaders—give us growth and we will look the other way on corruption—broke down when growth itself came to a halt. That is a change with major political implications; and, over the longer term, it is likely to alter Japan's culture of corruption as well.

3

States, Networks, and Rents: Contrasting Corruption in Africa and Asia

Alice Sindzingre

Reform does not begin with a blank slate. Informal networks and other social institutions of long standing shape individual behavior and development in important ways. Social networks are often regarded as a source of corruption—and thus, as a problem to be "reformed"—or have been ignored altogether by international aid and lending agencies, on the assumption that rolling back the scope of the state will be sufficient to revitalize civil society and the economy. In this chapter, however, Alice Sindzingre shows that development processes and social networks differ from one region to another. In Asia, social networks have had positive development effects and, in important respects, are distinct from corruption. In many African societies, by contrast, the colonial heritage, post-independence problems, and the policies of international agencies discourage the rise of a local private sector and undermined the economic efficiency of social networks. Both development and anti-corruption efforts must place greater emphasis upon the actual networks in place, rather than upon idealized scenarios for creating a private sector and building civil society. That, in turn, requires an understanding of the longer-term forces shaping social networks.

I. Introduction

Since the 1990s "bad governance," usually meaning corruption, has often been one of the main explanations offered for the economic stagnation of Sub-Saharan Africa, especially in the literature of development assistance agencies.

At the same time, it was not seen as a relevant phenomenon in East Asia during its decades of dramatic growth, but suddenly became a prominent factor in accounts of the Asian financial crisis of 1997-98. Corruption, therefore, refers to broadly defined phenomena, and it enters into loose and *ex post* causalities with economic growth, being either neutral or harmful according to the part of the world under consideration.

This chapter develops comparisons between Asia and Sub-Saharan Africa (SSA), with a focus on Southeast Asia and West Africa. It will not devote a thorough analysis to definitions of corruption, which have been the subject of numerous studies. It is well known that corruption is a polysemic phenomenon, encompassing large-scale and international corruption as well as local petty corruption. Some studies point to an economic and institutional continuum between both forms. Other studies consider that large-scale corruption, often involving states and firms from developed countries, cross-border financial flows, organized transnational networks and frequent dealings in other illegal goods—arms or drugs—is heterogeneous, influenced by the local routine demands for bribes characterizing the civil service in developing countries.[1] Likewise, corruption is often confused with related phenomena, such as rent-seeking, which includes both legal and illegal rents, bribery, and so on. It may also be confused with clientelism and patronage relationships, which are the possible channels for these legal or illegal rents.[2] Developing countries often exhibit "traditional" or "neo-traditional" social relationships, such as patronage or neo-patrimonial systems. In these relationships, power and high status are given to "big men" with extensive capacities for redistributing goods, money and social protection in exchange for allegiances and flows of labor, services, and so on. An example is the traditional Mediterranean patronage systems.

It is obviously risky to compare entire continents over a long period of time, especially when discussing concepts that are still not clearly defined. Thus, this chapter does not aim at a precise and detailed comparison between all the forms of corruption existing in Asia and Africa. It develops certain aspects described in a previous analysis,[3] raising a series of relevant questions and pinpointing the possible levels of differences or analogies between both contexts. An understanding of these levels should make it easier to go beyond clichés about African stagnation on the one hand and Asian successes on the other. It also shows that corruption is not in itself the relevant explanation of economic and social phenomena. Corruption is a derived—secondary and not primary—fact because it reflects underlying historical, economic, political, social relationships, representations, beliefs and norms. While it is now admitted that corruption is always welfare-reducing, compared to a state of affairs without corruption, it may nonetheless be used in a productive as well as in a destructive way.[4]

Corruption is pervasive in both regions, but a series of levels highlights contrasting economic, political, and social processes and outcomes. This chapter first examines the role of economic factors in the emergence of corruption. The developmental or anti-developmental nature of political regimes appears to be a more relevant explanation of the existence of corruption, and most of all, its detrimental nature for development, than are the relationships of governments with their private sectors, i.e. alliance, collusion or antagonism. The exploitation of rents towards productive aims is what makes the difference between both regions in terms of economic performance and the extent of the negative effects of corruption. Social norms, in particular those related to the structure of networks, constitute a crucial difference in terms of the economic impact of corrupt activities in the two regions.

II. Economic Causalities: Complex Relationships between Bad Governance and Economic Performance

The inconclusive results of econometric regressions

"Bad governance" is a phrase that the World Bank popularized in the late 1980s to explain the economic problems of sub-Saharan Africa (SSA) and the failure of its adjustment programs in that region to yield desired results. Public sector management did not have an adequate capacity, or it was inefficient, to cope with a situation in which there was no accountability or legal framework for development and which lacked transparency in decision-making. Since then the Bretton Woods institutions' (BWI) view of good governance has slightly evolved. It is no longer being equated with administrative reforms or the application of private sector management strategies to public institutions, but now refers to a greater degree of "ownership," the participation of people in the development process, decentralization and concerns for achieving social equality.

This stance has been supported by academic research, especially econometric studies aimed at determining a correlation between bad governance—deficits in accountability, transparency and the rule of law—and types of political regimes, especially those relating to democracy and economic performance. However, uncertainty persists over the relationship between lack of corruption, or democracy, and growth, this relationship being weak if cross-country regressions are used.[5] The relationship is less uncertain at the analytical level, when using case studies or qualitative analysis.[6] At cross-national levels many studies show a negative relationship between corruption and economic performance.[7] Other economic indicators, such as a more volatile composition of international capital inflows, are also associated with corruption and crony capitalism.[8] However, there remain severe problems of measurement and methodology. Likewise, as is often the case in cross-country regressions, the direction of causality is difficult to assess, as it can move from the existence of corruption to poor economic performance and inefficient public administrations, or the contrary.[9]

Some studies have found associations between corruption and certain types of economies—for instance, a dependence on exports of natural resources, especially oil.[10] Others reveal a negative link between the absence of the rule of law, domestic regulation, fair judicial institutions and property rights, i.e. corruption on the one hand, and foreign direct investment (FDI) on the other. However, countries like Nigeria and Angola are among the big recipients of FDI, even though they are known for the massive international corruption of their oil economies as well as for their instability. In any event, SSA receives very little

FDI, and the few recipient countries are mineral exporting countries with oil resources or mines, such as Angola, Congo, and Nigeria.[11] It is widely acknowledged that such sectors are open to international corruption. Governments with budgets relying heavily on oil or mineral extraction are particularly exposed to international and domestic corruption through public procurement, under-invoicing, financial fraudulent practices, dishonest banking, and so on. Those problems, however, did not prevent some countries from becoming the preferred recipients of FDI or exhibiting positive growth rates, as in Gabon and Angola. Southeast Asian countries, such as Thailand, Malaysia, Indonesia and China, are affected by corruption. In the case of China it has even been accompanied by exceptional growth. Some countries have been helped by improved accountability in the public sector. Others have displayed good economic performances with non-existent property rights and authoritarian regimes, again as in the case of China.[12] In terms of welfare costs, countries are nevertheless different. In the Philippines and Indonesia, flagrant autocratic and predatory regimes, under President Suharto for example, and corruption have been deleterious.[13] In Korea, Thailand and Malaysia, on the other hand, corruption has not been so devastating, even though cronyism and the protection of firms through political connections constitute significant costs for the economies.[14]

Cross-country regressions cannot explain such complexities. The existence of populist leaders like Silvio Berlusconi, elected Prime Minister of Italy again in 2001, demonstrates that even in developed countries, governments can create laws designed by and for the leader. This practice does not apply exclusively to developing countries ruled by arbitrary autocrats or weak SSA democracies, Côte d'Ivoire with its constitution being a case in point. Such a choice has not been detrimental to Italy's economic performance. The persona of a populist leader—suspected of bribery, opaque sources of personal wealth, collusive business practices, and patronage politics—nonetheless elected and supported by the citizens (who only retain the positive image of successful entrepreneurship and are indifferent to his offences), is found in developed as well as developing countries. The Italian Prime Minister has thus been compared to the one of Thailand, Thaksin Shinawatra, who exhibited similar features of a businessman owning wealth from questionable sources, elected by plebiscite.[15] The point is that these populist characters are perceived by voters as being close to the private sector, having a deep knowledge of its specific problems, and therefore as more capable of fostering economic growth than, for example, an honest government and a well-enforced rule of law.

Qualitative causalities, thresholds and corruption traps

A series of reasons prevent econometric regressions from being a useful method, one reason being threshold effects. Above a certain threshold of development, corruption is harmful but not destructive for economies, the resilience of institutions, and political legitimacy, but this does not apply to fragile and small economies. Corruption has not been deleterious for growth in Southeast Asia, or in France, Italy and Japan, because these economies are big and diversified enough to bear the economic leakages caused by corruption scandals, or the costs and loss of welfare for the final consumer created by bribes in specific sectors. African economies are much smaller and more vulnerable. For instance, in sub-Saharan Africa, in the WAEMU[16] part of the Franc zone, countries have between three and sixteen banks respectively, a handful of export commodities, and so on.[17] The state is the main economic actor, with the average rate of state expenditures oscillating around 20 percent of the GDP.[18] This means that if private interests siphon off public resources, the economic impact can be serious. It is widely acknowledged that corruption breeds corruption. One of the major risks for SSA countries is the vicious circle—the "corruption trap" or negative equilibrium caused as corruption provides incentives for further corrupt practices. In such cases, the best-designed policies frequently remain powerless. Very strong political signals are needed.[19] It is difficult to avoid stabilized microeconomic calculations and trade-offs when honest behavior brings no rewards and is socially more costly than a dishonest approach.

Two factors contribute to maintaining this state of routine corruption. First of all, at the extreme end, this corruption equilibrium can be a comparative advantage. It is an advantage for the government because it enables it to pay civil servants salaries that are below the subsistence level and to keep the wage bill low—the so-called "capitulation wages".[20] It also allows politicians to carry out their own corrupt activities, such as collecting funds for political purposes, using the opacity of legal texts to control clienteles and distribute favors while enriching themselves. For public choice theorists, many legal rules are in fact deliberately designed to be opaque and burdensome in order to facilitate corruption. It is also an advantage for individuals. The latter can take advantage of the fact that states do not have strong public institutions and their civil servants can be easily corrupted, whether they are in the customs service, the police force, the judiciary, at border controls, or other key sectors. They can use the state as a hub for international illegal trafficking, for example, drugs, arms, or terrorism. SSA seems to have some worrying capacities for attracting international criminal groups that previously used to operate in Latin America or Asia, and for exporting its own criminals to the US or Russia. This is a harmful way of harnessing the "comparative advantage" of the dereliction of SSA states and public institutions.

Secondly, the political illegitimacy of many SSA governments, associated with weakly institutionalized bureaucracies and poor physical infrastructures, sometimes makes it difficult for them to be well informed, and to impose their decisions among civil servants working in the field, including customs or police officers. In some countries, like Côte d'Ivoire in 1999, despite the government's decision to curb their permanent rackets, road transportation officials simply continued as before. Such cases illustrate the classic difficulty of imposing effective supervision, for that requires a supervisor who does not subscribe to the norms of the supervised.[21] It also showed a dimension of many SSA political regimes: poverty and illegitimacy. Such regimes can be simultaneously authoritarian and powerless.

Another series of reasons for the irrelevance of econometric methods stems from the relationships among political elites, institutions and citizens. First of all, these relationships imply qualitative, individual, and changing perceptions impossible to summarize in quantitative measures. Secondly, these regressions use variables that are formal and, above all, apolitical, like the "rule of law", and they therefore miss the crucial political dimensions of legitimacy and adhesion to shared values, which are the conditions for accepting particular political regimes and institutions. For instance, corruption can be economically ruinous when it creates stronger inequality, with predatory and comfortably off elites in contrast to the poor. It undermines the trust between a state and its citizens, discouraging productive activities, and becomes an incentive to cheat and to imitate corrupt elites. There is no trust in microeconomic transactions and public decisions. Individual strategies aimed at making assets secure lead to capital flight and are obstacles to growth. Modes of redistribution are equally important: corruption may be accepted if its products are redistributed in a spillover way, without having excessive inegalitarian effects. An important point is that in Asia, enrichment has been less used for consumption, as in SSA, than for productive purposes – although it may have led to speculative bubbles, for example in the real estate sector. The family members who receive assistance engage in work, and the money tends to be invested within the region. In SSA, individuals secure their wealth abroad, resulting in a huge capital flight. [22] This highlights the importance of political perceptions and the lack of trust in leaders.

III. The Effects of Corruption: Political Regimes and Institutions

Developmental states and anti-developmental political regimes

Colonial histories have obviously been very different, and within Asia, Northeast Asia should be distinguished from Southeast Asia. Although accompanied by atrocities, Japanese colonization in Korea and Taiwan implemented a more "productive" coercion, left significant physical infrastructure and improved the level of human capital.[23] In Taiwan, unlike many countries in SSA where the end of colonization still left expatriates in key administrative positions, governments pursued strategies to diminish their reliance on expatriate competencies.[24] The "developmental" states in Northeast Asia relied on active public policies of the "big push" type, and on state intervention in the economy. In contrast to orthodox theories and the free-market paradigm, Asian governments relied on selective market "distortions": industrial policies deliberately created rents, and distributed them to private firms (for instance through export credit programs in Korea), but in ways linked to export performance and international competitiveness.[25] Growth has been based on proactive outward-oriented state plans and on selective industrial strategies, supported by trade and investment policies.[26] From a political point of view, the rulers calculated that the enrichment of their countries and citizens could be profitable to themselves. The time frame is as long as for any autocrat, but the object of the calculation, as well as the trade off, is different. These regimes are less fragile and illegitimate, and they therefore do not feel threatened by the development process.

On the contrary, according to the "pessimist" view[27] Sub-Saharan Africa was marginalized at an early stage and locked into the model of a small, open, colonial economy, while Asia integrated into the global system. Colonization left little capital and few developmental institutions, especially in Central Africa where its extractive nature was linked to the massive displacement of populations, the destruction of local societies and the lack of education and human capital building.[28] Before colonization there were dynamic traders: British indirect rule did not interfere with the local structures while French direct administration, on the contrary, competed with them.[29] As for international trade, the colonizers not only locked their firms and market shares[30] but also neglected to create a class of local entrepreneurs. British rule, however, left more room for the emergence of local entrepreneurs, as in the case of Nigeria where there are now a number of third-generation businessmen.[31]

In SSA, even after decades of adjustment programs aimed at reducing state intervention, the public sector remains dominant, coexisting with narrow private and formal sectors, mainly with a foreign ownership or management, and significant "informal sectors" arising out of diverse phenomena (illicit trade, petty traders and small artisans). State intervention has created rents, but not the appropriate conditions for using them for greater competitiveness and productivity. The external integration of states is unbalanced, SSA being the most open region of the world in terms of trading outside the region, with a notable unregistered regional trade. There is a permanent racket on the roads run by customs or police officers, which does not impede trade but imposes additional costs finally borne by individuals and firms. While being poorer, Africans pay more for international goods—20 percent higher than the international prices, a broad figure that includes corruption on both the selling and the buying sides.[32] Even if the requested fees do not account for a large portion of the total costs, these extortionate practices result in congestion, queuing, and inefficiencies, which *in fine* enrich a small group of civil servants and their entourage.

SSA political regimes are often not "developmental," and sometimes are clearly anti-developmental, due to their colonial history, deficit of legitimacy, military coups, political instability, competition for state power and available resources at the time of independence. The time frame of the rulers and politicians of developmental states has been long in Asia, especially in Northeast Asian states. In Korea, as in Taiwan, political leaders realized the interest of building capable bureaucracies.[33] SSA autocrats may also have long time frames, for they are determined to remain in power for as long as possible (in Togo and the Côte d'Ivoire, for example, where autocrats ruled for more than three decades). But their calculations were focused exclusively on their own individual welfare and enrichment, in an apparently irrational way, leading to the collapse of their countries. In these cases, petty corruption is less relevant and costly in terms of economic growth than the predatory character of certain SSA leaders. Their calculations are rational if analyzed in the context of fragile political regimes, in which anti-developmental policies and the destruction of institutions may be optimal strategies if staying in power is their only goal.[34]

The existence of effective institutions

Even with their collusive practices and opaque government-business relations, East Asian states—more in the Northeast than in the Southeast—have a rule of law that is in contrast to many SSA states. The rule of law—formal and "informal"—allows for the stability of trust and of individual calculations. Even if it is necessary to bribe, there is a stability and predictability in the fact of bribing and the act of payment. Even if there are military coups, the stability of the expectations of private entrepreneurs is not destabilized, and investment decisions continue to be made. In Thailand, despite the domination of the military, a tradition of "functional government" may explain its economic performance, unlike the socially divided Philippines.[35] The rules may be informal, linked to communities and not written as state rules, but they are nevertheless stable, which is a definition of institutions: even if there is corruption, it is institutionalized. In SSA, personal rule and arbitrariness have prevented the formation of stable expectations relying on long-term rules, which are the prerequisites of entrepreneurship.

This stability of norms and expectations may be a dimension not only of the formal norms, laws and obligations provided by states, but also their combination with "informal" social rules, which they cannot contradict, such as family links and intra-firm relations. In SSA, the legacy of colonial rule and post-colonial regimes produced two devastating elements. One is the illegitimacy of state institutions due to the illegitimacy of the individuals who are supposed to represent it. The second is a discrepancy between the state's norms and the daily norms provided by various social memberships: kinship, village, territory, religion, and so on. This gap between multiple sets of norms resulted in two public spheres, one legitimate and the other illegitimate, thus creating opportunities for legitimate siphoning and theft.[36] This has been detrimental for economic expectations and the sustainability of institutions: no "transplant effect" occurred.[37]

One crucial point is the arbitrary nature of political power and decisions, and their dependence on the state of mind of an individual, the leader, which is in fact synonymous with the absence of institutions. For efficient economic performance or the emergence of a developmental state, the presence or absence of corruption or property rights is less relevant than the possibility of having stable expectations and calculations, and projecting decisions and their consequences into the future. This is one of the dimensions of institutionalization. This kind of construction is fragile; both institutions and states may see their developmental dimension eroded by diverse events, external shocks, domestic policies and so on. This has been an effect of global financial liberalization.[38]

When power is totally decentralized, i.e. each individual holding some capacity of coercion on others can freely exercise it, the absence of rights-cum-corruption has been demonstrated as leading to the collapse of national production, and in extreme cases, the collapse of the states themselves (for instance, ex-Zaire, post-communist countries).[39] In SSA, corruption and levies on powerless citizens can also be centralized, stabilized and organized, with public agents in certain posts levying bribes and sharing them with others at higher levels. In such circumstances, the expectations of individuals in their economic transactions are not necessarily disturbed, they are not rendered impossible in the medium term, and production can continue. The final cost is borne by the consumers who pay a higher price than that of a non-corrupt market and include such costs *ex ante* in their economic calculations, particularly regarding investment. The difficulty in maintaining stable expectations is not only the product of a type of political regime, but also of instability in the value of goods or currencies since the pre-colonial period. In SSA, in the long run, "no condition was permanent".[40]

For the poorest groups, there is no time horizon at all. Rights and property are subjected to the hazards of decisions taken by individuals, rulers and politicians, and in this sense, there is no institutionalization in the sphere of the state. Institutions do exist; they are, however, provided by other types of community and the rules that govern them, the easiest candidates being ethnic and religious groups. SSA states reveal poor internal integration, and they are unable to provide stable norms or institutions to support the stability of expectations because their institutions are weak. This is why there is no "third party" in individual contracting and no provider of security or coercion. Individuals must find the necessary norms to frame their transactions within other systems, and these norms must be accepted by every transacting party. Ethnic memberships, as well as religious ties or any acquired membership, whether residential, occupational or of another type, often provide these common norms. Thus, in many SSA countries, private firms rely on "ethnic" links. It is difficult to assign causality: ties are "ethnic" because ethnicity easily provides common beliefs and norms. The common norms and beliefs are *ex post* "proofs" of common membership, as shown by the great capacity of African societies to assimilate foreigners. However, the use of such links as the main channels of trust creates constraints and hinders the economic performance of private firms. These are the constraints of interlocked contracts, which operate simultaneously on several markets including credit, insurance and goods markets. In Kenya, for example, it has been shown that the use by entrepreneurs of members of the same ethnic group for supplier credit limits the scope of their markets.[41] The economic effectiveness of such links is therefore limited; they extend only with difficulty beyond the limits of the commonly recognized memberships of certain shared features (religion or ethnicity).

IV. The Relationships of Political Regimes with the Private Sector
The coalescing of political regimes and private sectors

Historically, during the pre-colonial period, Southeast Asia was characterized by close links between alien communities, especially the tax collectors, and rulers in the important trading locations (mainly ports) of the region. The system resembled revenue farms found in Europe, for example, the French *fermiers généraux*. More than the other alien trading groups, the Chinese settled in the region and did not restrict themselves to trading networks. Rulers and sultans on the one side, and Chinese foreign merchants, moneylenders and tax collectors on the other, shared strong mutual interests. The former could reduce their dependence on local bureaucracies and exchange their political protection for collected taxes, while keeping the Chinese community under control. As foreigners, Chinese were vulnerable and could always be threatened and expelled.[42] Asian countries obviously differ, as have as the types of migrants (traders, laborers, and so on) they have received. In Thailand, the Chinese constitute a substantial proportion of the population, and share in political power, while in Malaysia or Indonesia they are an assimilated but distinct minority. The so-called "Chinese diaspora," established throughout Southeast Asia, is often said to be a privileged channel of corruption within the region, because they are the wealthiest group and own the majority of the assets in countries like Thailand or Indonesia.[43] However, if they are vectors of corruption, it is linked to their status as "visible capitalists". Since they contribute considerably to the dynamism of the economies, one can find among them, as everywhere else, corrupt and non-corrupt entrepreneurs. Furthermore, depending on the country in question, non-Chinese constituencies and voters often maintain collusive relations with the political leaders who in turn favor them in their economic policies and political strategies.

The coalescing of governments and private entrepreneurs has been an important feature in Asian development.[44] Borrowing from the Japanese model, a characteristic of the Northeast Asian "developmental" state has been the influence of the state on the behavior of firms, its support of high levels of savings and investment, the incentives it provided to stimulate the country's competitiveness,[45] and the "embedded autonomy" characterizing business-government relations.[46] The close association between governments and the private sector also included a third and necessary partner, the financial sector, linked to the interests of the state, politicians and businesses. Firms relied more on the financial intermediation of the banking system than on capital markets, and on their relationships with the banks; the Korean *chaebols* are a well-known example. Cronyism has even been said to reduce transaction costs when a small group of actors leads to a situation of "mutual hostages" in government-business relations, as in Korea. The different effects of cronyism in other countries may be explained by the fact that either too few or too many actors increase deadweight losses from corruption, as in Indonesia and the Philippines.[47] Countries are obviously not identical. Governments have granted privileges to a number of large financial and industrial conglomerates in countries like Indonesia, Malaysia and Thailand that are often run by families of Chinese origin. In Suharto's Indonesia, routine collusion and nepotism were well-known facts, as were the favors dispensed by him to his relatives and allies. A similar co-extension of politics and business interests exists in the Philippines, which has been described as an example of "booty capitalism" or the "sick man of Asia".[48] Such practices cannot be said to have contributed to the growth of these countries, even if growth actually occurred.

The point is that the promotion of the private sector has been the focus of support by governments for a variety of possible reasons, be it increasing the national cake, which can be profitable for its rulers and managers, or permitting political patronage by placing relatives and clients in the firms. Clientelism and corruption, as in Thailand, did not prevent competition between firms, thus suggesting a "competitive clientelism" that explains why economic growth was not affected to a greater extent.[49] However, destabilizing events, such as financial liberalization and openness to foreign capital, have highlighted the intrinsic risks of collusion and rent-sharing among, firms and politicians, which appeared *ex post* as detrimental to the economies. This has revealed the fragility of the economic bases and led to a series of bankruptcies.

Productive vs. dissipative rents

As in many developing countries, growth in Asia has been based, among other factors, on the exploitation of rents: natural resources, exploitation of monopoly positions in trade or state-owned enterprises, revenues from the export of commodities, and so on. In this regard, a clear distinction should be made between Northeast Asia and Southeast Asia. The former has promoted developmental states through proactive public intervention and industrial policies aimed at becoming internationally competitive. In contrast, growth in Southeast Asia has been grounded on foreign direct investment (FDI). This has built up a private sector of a different type than in Northeast Asia, which is of a more *rentier* nature for the large firms and conglomerates. The latter have been primarily financial and secondarily industrial, as they have been protected by government policies and privileged political connections.[50] Capital accumulation has been based historically on finance and trade, and later on manufacturing activities, which were boosted by foreign firms through FDI. Many prominent entrepreneurs in Southeast Asia were traders (and smugglers) during the Second World War who later invested in the financial and industrial sectors, creating conglomerates with heterogeneous activities revolving around a family.[51]

Rents, especially from the exploitation of natural resources, are often considered a crucial determinant of corrupt regimes and administrations, as well as international corruption. They also induce the so-called "Dutch disease" whereby the non-tradable sector (generally agriculture) becomes unprofitable and shrinks, while the economy depends increasingly on the export sector. This is the well known "natural resources curse." However, Asian states such as Indonesia and Malaysia, initially exporters of natural commodities, were able to overcome the natural resources constraint and became exporters of manufactured goods.[52] Initially comparable to Nigeria, and also an oil exporter, Indonesia overcame the Dutch disease syndrome and fostered an agricultural sector, contrary to Nigeria[53]. Political regimes play a strategic role here. The well-known example of Botswana, with an economy entirely based on the extraction of a single natural resource—diamonds—shows that appropriate policies of rent distribution and institution building can manage and even transform the "curse" into a source of growth. Botswana has had the longest continuous growth in the world.[54]

One of the specificities of South-East Asia has been the ability of its political regimes to shift the rents towards productive ends. This issue is the core of debates over the description of Asian capitalism and "miracle" as genuinely developmental vs. an "ersatz capitalism" fuelled by cronyism and corruption.[55] For some studies, the latter has been one of the factors of the Asian financial crisis of 1997-98, while for others, the crisis had external causes (for example, the liberalization of the capital account, excessive inflows of foreign capital, the volatility of the "sentiments" of international investors).[56] This debates aim at disentangling the effects of the local political structures and collusive practices between politicians and businessmen[57] from the effects of the volatile behavior of international capital markets and financial liberalization on the countries' otherwise sound economic fundamentals. The relationship between firms and banks has been described more as an "alliance capitalism" that turned out to be a powerful motor for growth in Asia than a "crony capitalism".[58] Likewise, a "crony capitalism" that is based on profit-sharing may indeed have positive economic outcomes, in contrast with rent-creating corruption.[59]

State-private sector relationships in Africa: antagonism or straddling

In SSA, by contrast, colonization was of an "extractive" type. The objectives of the colonizers were not to build or reinforce existing institutions. Equally, the combination of the colonization institutions with the existing ones may have produced new types and outcomes that have been deleterious in terms of development. This issue of institutional combination—"productive" or destructive" for growth—is a more complex argument than the well-known studies explaining the differences of economic outcomes resulting from the various types of colonization that did or did not create institutions.[60] After independence in the 1960s, many political regimes did not try to promote, or even exhibited an overt hostility, towards their national private sectors, as they were confronted with political instability, state building, arbitrary borders and centrifugal forces competing for political power.

Different variants in the behavior of political rulers have been possible. One is open hostility, accompanied by measures taken to close private firms or push them to bankruptcy, as in the case of Ghana and the well-known antagonism felt by Kwame Nkrumah towards Ashanti politicians who, historically, owned the private wealth derived from cocoa. Another variant is the predatory behavior, especially through taxation.[61] Yet another example is the "buying" of individuals, i.e. potential opponents, by giving them state resources as rewards for political submission, and thus converting them into "entrepreneurs," as in the Côte d'Ivoire.[62] Local firms are, therefore, strongly tied to a political regime and to a specific person and his political links. As a result, the firm rarely survives after the death of the founding entrepreneurs. Likewise, local firms have difficulties in surviving changes of political regimes.

Even now, this antagonism between governments and an "autonomous" but barely existing private sector persists. One example is the recurrent difficulty of setting up enterprises because of years of cumbersome paperwork, compared to a couple of hours in some industrial countries. The promotion of the private sector is therefore pushed mainly by external aid agencies, with initiatives such as the creation of export processing zones, various tax exemptions and schemes aimed at attracting foreign investors, micro-credit projects and the promotion of small local enterprises. It is remarkable that even after years of functioning, many of these initiatives are still in the initial stage. The "internalization" of these reforms by governments and civil servants has not occurred, external aid has often become a new form of rent, and the incentives are absent. Liberalization and trade openness are now justified not by their intrinsic virtues for development but by their possible capacity to attract foreign investors, presumed to represent a solution to economic stagnation.[63] It is hardly surprising that individuals have a different and negative perception of these economic reforms as being prescribed from the outside and corresponding to external interests.

Governments did not do much to promote the local elites, in particular the educated class. SSA has the highest level of brain drain and expatriation of university graduates of any region.[64] At the end of the 1980s it was estimated that 30 percent of the skilled manpower had left SSA for developed countries.[65] Moreover, SSA governments do not appear to encourage these skilled emigrants to return to their home countries because no labor market can provide them with the type of employment that would meet their expectations. Furthermore, governments do not seem to consider this type of employment as a priority in their policies. This creates a typical vicious circle: the missing skills are filled through costly external aid, and often paid for by public borrowing from the Bretton Woods institutions and by expatriate technical assistance with disproportionately high wages compared to local standards of living.[66] The results include the perpetuation of aid dependence and indebtedness, deficits in skills and knowledge (and their positive externalities), and disorganization and tensions within the civil service due to the various salary scales and projects arising out of the multiplicity of donors. Yet another effect is the creation of enclave markets for luxury goods to satisfy expatriates, which induce social tensions and envy in countries that are generally characterized by high inequality. These elements give a specific connotation to the corrupt behavior of local civil servants.

V. The Role of Economic Reforms

External dependence and corruption

The poorer they are, the more developing countries depend on external financing. Since the debt crisis of 1982, SSA countries have relied increasingly on official development assistance, both bilateral and multilateral (mainly from the Bretton Woods institutions) for their financial needs because private international investors stopped their flows towards the continent. Thus, the IMF and the World Bank, bilateral donors, mainly European, and in French-speaking Africa, the former colonial power, France, became the pre-eminent providers of funds.

This financing was public, from state to state, owing to the absence of private flows resulting from the general distrust towards SSA. At the beginning of the 1980s, the crisis of commodities prices induced severe budgetary difficulties in SSA countries and dried up private lending flows, thus leading the Bretton Woods institutions to launch stabilization and adjustment programs.

Stabilization programs are aimed at balancing budgets and containing their deficits through contractionary policies, downsizing the civil service, and freezing public wages, among other measures. The objectives of adjustment programs are to promote market mechanisms in SSA economies, to "get the prices right," and to tip the weight of the public sector in favor of the private sector through the privatization of state-owned enterprises, price liberalization, trade openness, and the suppression of public marketing boards for commodities. However, after two decades the mixed results of these reforms have seriously undermined both their credibility and that of the BWIs. Foreign investment failed to materialize, and integration of SSA into the global economy and its competitiveness remained low—around 1 percent of global trade.

Thus begins a vicious circle in which SSA countries become increasingly dependent on international financial institutions that are unable to stimulate growth by themselves. Sub-Saharan Africa does not attract international capital flows because of this dependence, and because poor economic performances is viewed as a negative signal. From the 1960s to the 1990s, aid represented an increasing part of the GNP (around 15 percent in the 1990s[67]) and public budgets of SSA. Governments were therefore heavily dependent on these flows, loans or grants, and the conditions attached to them led to inevitable problems of local resistance and policy reversals. This in turn aggravated the ineffectiveness of economic reforms and increases dependence on external donors. At the same time, in the 1990s Asian countries were the biggest recipients of international private capital flows. Certain Asian countries ceased to depend on international public assistance. These trends, however, were not entirely beneficial, as they created intrinsic risks and negative effects revealed during the Asian crisis of 1997-98.

This situation had a series of consequences in terms of the behavior of governments and civil services, including corruption. The stabilization programs of the first generation had a negative impact on the morale of civil servants. Colonial history and the formation of African states, before and just after independence, were based on the centrifugal collection of heterogeneous groups, focused more on political unification than on effective public service. Equally, the rare status of the educated class and civil servants was highly valued since colonization. Corruption and clientelism, which were already present at independence, often increased under stabilization programs. Civil servants had even less incentive to work, owing to their feeling that the prescriptions came from foreign donors and not from their own governments, and they tended to maintain their standard of living by increasing bribery and diverse levies on administrative transactions. Consumers paid the price of this corruption. The main effect was increased poverty: already-poor individuals pay more and thus get poorer, with this vicious circle lowering their likelihood of getting out of the poverty trap. Furthermore, the most competent people left the civil service since they were the only ones who were able to do so without excessive personal costs. Confronted with this situation, donors launched so-called second-generation civil service reforms designed to enhance incentives for civil servants, such as pay according to merit.[68] However, these reforms remain within the apolitical conceptual framework of administrations and public institutions, and thus condemn them to failure. In view of the historical politicization of administration—and in some countries, the existence of corruption that has become pervasive and routine in a "stabilized equilibrium"—these incentives often proved ineffective.

Unrealistic hypotheses on private sectors, privatization, and corruption
In the 1980s, SSA states were considered the main culprits of economic stagnation and cause of distortions, under the influence of the public choice and the rent-seeking theories.[69] The necessary attributes and functions of states were considered to be minimal, consisting mainly in providing regulations and facilitating the functioning of markets. Asian countries, being less dependent on BWI financing and backed by Japan, which owed its success to public intervention[70] and the model of the "developmental state", had more room of maneuver.[71] In the 1990s, information asymmetries and market failure theories, as well as institutional economics, attenuated the minimalist vision of states,[72] although the latter are still confined to a limited number of functions (provision of stable expectations, predictable macroeconomic and regulatory framework), with little reflection on the intrinsic political dimension of the activity of governing. The BWIs indeed considered the Asian crisis as a proof of the negative effect of state intervention and the intrinsic corruption, cronyism, and bad corporate governance associated with it.

In Sub-Saharan Africa, economic reforms in the 1980s aimed at transferring functions previously executed by states to the private sector, according to the orthodox economic paradigm. The problem is that the historical trajectories of African states before and after their independence gave specific features to the local private sectors. The colonizers left tiny local private sectors composed mainly of traders and rarely of industrial entrepreneurs. The formal private sector, both its trading and its industrial components, was overwhelmingly foreign and dominated by the colonizing country. At the time of independence in West Africa, there were no local private firms and banks. The theories of the "big push," as well as the political necessities of providing consumer goods and clientelist rewards, obliged the leaders to build up national private sectors quickly from almost nothing. By definition, they could only use public resources, since there were almost no local private resources, or they could nationalize or resort to external borrowing. The reimbursement of these debts was intrinsically compromised due to the low profitability of the public service infrastructure.

Two broad options were available, depending on the local situation, i.e. political stability or instability. In stable authoritarian regimes like Côte d'Ivoire, the local private sector was created by the political power as clients, with rewards such as the management of state-owned-enterprises (SOEs). Some of these clients became industrialists. In addition, trading may have been in the hands of different groups, according to local historical traditions (for example, the Sahelian traders).[73] In unstable political regimes, the private sector was also a creation of the state, but each new political regime brought in its own class of entrepreneurs-clients, and weakened the group of entrepreneurs linked to the previous regime. This has induced many bankruptcies and much instability among local private firms. In all cases private sectors that were not of their creation were seen as threats by weak rulers, i.e. as independent sources of wealth and redistribution that they could not control via the usual channels of patronage. These entrepreneurs were the only individuals in a position to join the expensive game of politics, usually firmly controlled by the power in place *via* privileged access to, and use of, public resources.

This means that private business was not developed much in West Africa outside crony practices. When in the 1980s the BWI programs assigned the mission of replacing the failing state to the local private sectors, they found the latter had different routine behavior, habits and expectations, and were also very small. There was an overlapping with the state in terms of individuals, networks, resources, captive markets and outlets, in public procurement, the building sector, etc. The share of states in the formal economy was still pre-eminent. Thus, privatization led to oligopolies, cartels and hidden agreements, as in the marketing circuits (rice being an example) that were inefficient and costly for the consumer. They led to the buying of SOEs by political cronies, the only individuals who had accumulated sufficient resources for large-scale acquisitions.[74] Through the pressure of donors, and sometime political calculations, utilities and firms were also given to foreign investors, often from developed countries, more rarely from other SSA or developing countries. Autonomous institutions free of the arbitrary decisions of leaders are absent even though they are the necessary prerequisites for a genuine private sector. This absence prevented the allocation to the private sector of economic activities, previously carried out by states, that could have effectively fostered growth.

In Asia, particularly after the 1997 crisis, recommendations for increased reliance on the private sector were also criticized. There too effective laws and their enforcement are necessary prerequisites, as well as reliance on markets mechanisms, prices and contracts. However, the reforms assumed "British-American" style contracts, which were absent. Transactions continued to be based on personal relationships and unwritten agreements, with special links to banks. This system was effective during the growth period, despite studies warning against its intrinsic risks and fake economic successes—the famous "ersatz capitalism". Banks, firms and politicians worked in collusion, which was economically efficient and productive. However, financial liberalization weakened this personal relationship model that, when placed in a global context, exhibited its negative side effects—clientelism and cronyism—and highlighted the financial weaknesses of the firms and the banking systems.

VI. Social Networks: The Relevance of the Concept
Networks and trust

Corruption may have different channels and uses that strongly influence its economic impact. There are many options. Its products can end up quickly in private pockets or they can be channeled to numerous other people, according to patronage and redistributive networks. They can be invested for productive purposes or immediately consumed. These investments or consumption practices can occur within the region in a broad sense, or else they can be exported to remote places or offshore financial centers for reasons of secrecy. They can be given without any compensation, e.g. work or allegiance, or they can imply a return. Obviously, the products of bribes that are channeled to many individuals through networks for productive use, with expectations of compensation, are more economically positive than those diverted to private consumption abroad. This is why the structure and features of networks, as well as the nature of the private sector, and their relationships with political regimes shape the consequences of corruption. In all these respects, Asian and SSA networks reveal contrasting features.

For the concept of network to be useful, it has to be clearly defined. Transitivity is one of its attributes, meaning that individuals belong to a network and act at different points without necessarily having personal links between themselves. This requires common mechanisms, i.e. shared norms, trust, incentives for co-operation and reputation effects. These common norms are crucial for constraining members of a network to fulfill their commitments, and for avoiding free riding effects. For instance, a borrower in some location may reimburse its loans in another place. In this case shame, a typical shared norm that may affect the entire membership group of the individual at fault, can be an efficient mechanism to enforce co-operative rules. These norms can be of many kinds: traditionally, religion, kinship and occupational groups are good candidates for constituting common norms and strong sources of obligations.[75]

Here, the extension and size of the networks appear to be essential. In small societies, where few people share common norms, enforcement is difficult and free riding and cheating become attractive as soon as an individual decides to migrate. Defections may occur rapidly, and the communities have no instrument to prevent them. Hence markets are limited, transactions risky and transaction costs high. These traits have been recurrent in "traditional" societies, and have contributed to limiting their potential economic efficiency.[76] These networks may be considered as "short," and their character as genuine networks may even be questioned. This is the case of many societies in SSA, often characterized by fragmentation, manipulation and instrumentalization of the ethnic idiom by the colonizers. Local politicians may thus exhibit little "ethnic capital". A few large groups have developed diaspora-type networks founded on common norms, trust and co-operation, with compliance based on reputation, e.g. the Hausa, Dyula or Wolof. Short networks, by definition, restrain the extent of redistribution and legal rents, as well as bribes, whether they are for investment or consumption purposes.

As embodied by the Chinese modes of organization, Asian networks are "long" and involve large groups sharing common norms and mechanisms of contracts enforcement, even on an international scale.[77] The extension of Chinese networks has not only been a matter of size but also of economic sectors, as banks, also owned by Chinese individuals, have provided the capital for many activities. This has been an important aspect of their economic efficiency and their international reach, which can be metaphorically described as having a fractal shape: the form is the same at a very local scale and at a very extended and global one, and the networks operate both within and among many countries. That extended scale improves efficiency, for there is no capital flight or leakage outside the local region—as in SSA—since their global extension permits both local and global assimilation.

Asia and SSA differ in terms of ethnicity and ethnic capital. A recurrent explanation of SSA's poor economic performance is its high ethnic fragmentation, which is considered more prone to producing civil wars and conflicts than in more ethnically homogeneous countries in Asia.[78] This thesis, based on cross-country regressions, concludes that a few ethnic groups may be even more detrimental than many, and could even increase the likelihood of unstable competition and conflicts. While this argument is attractive, it is too broad and superficial. Ethnic groups are difficult to define and isolate, they are subject to continuous processes of assimilation, fusion and division, and they can have infinite sub-levels. Depending on the particular situation, they can split and enter into civil conflict with each other as easily as with other ethnic groups—the "segmentary" systems analyzed by anthropology. Moreover, many African countries have few ethnic groups and are close to homogeneity, as in Senegal. On the other hand, many countries constituted by differentiated ethnic groups have had remarkable economic performances, such as Singapore and Malaysia in Southeast Asia. Although it can be argued that they are not ethnic groups, strongly multicultural societies like Canada and the US are among the most developed in the world. The determining factor in terms of economic outcomes is again the political management of this situation and the relevance of the policies.

Asian and African networks: structure and political economy

Following the Japanese and Korean structure of networks of firms, strongly established internally and flexible externally in their exporting capacity, Asian growth has been grounded on the economic model of networks of firms. An important feature of Asian networks, unlike those in SSA ones, is already present in Japanese and Korean business networks, i.e. they are embedded both in their societies, following the norms of kinship and community, and in the wider political economy of their countries, hence in their export strategies. The networks developed in the Chinese world, Taiwan, and Hong Kong were organized in different ways, based on structured relationships among families and friends, with value given to co-operation within and between families,[79] and usually specialized in manufactured products. An extensive literature has been devoted to the transnational production networks that have been one of the main ingredients of Asian industrialization. Japanese firms played an essential role in Northeast Asia, where efficient vertical production chains and distribution networks of firms operating across countries have been created.[80] In Southeast Asia, growth has been based on FDI on the one hand, and networks of local firms on the other. Business networks developed beyond the national borders. Another important feature is that business networks have been rooted simultaneously in their own economies, for instance, Chinese traders operated in the countryside, and also extended far beyond, on a regional or global scale. This has rarely been the case in SSA, where local networks tend to be short and regional. Comparable networks were of foreign origin without a local anchor, such as the Lebanese in West Africa and the Indians in East Africa.[81]

The extensive literature on the Chinese diaspora and its global economic efficiency[82] questions the tension between forces pushing towards identity and assimilation.[83] East Asia has been conceived as a single space (*nanyang*), and the first generations felt they were still linked to their areas of origin in China. Most of them now feel like citizens of their countries, while at the same time retaining some elements of identity. Relying on the family model and referring to common regions of origin in China, Chinese networks are typically long and transitive with common norms and mechanisms of trust that do not necessarily require written contracts. In such a large space, networks are in some sense at home everywhere, pursuing strategies of diversifying assets in the various countries belonging to the same space. There is no need to secure assets abroad in capital flight, in sharp contrast to SSA.

The family metaphor of organization is efficient and has led to large and highly concentrated firms. Sino-Thai wealth, for example, is concentrated in five key families.[84] Whatever happens to the owner of heterogeneous conglomerates, familial collective action ensures that firms survive and do not fall apart, which is rare in SSA. Due to their visibility and entrepreneurship, Chinese business networks are often accused of corruption. The important point here is that this capacity of accumulation does not stem from intrinsic features of "Chineseness" but from political economy mechanisms. These mechanisms link the structure of the developmental state and the existence of networks:[85] the appropriate norms for building long and effective networks, and the use of capital for productive and not consumption ends, whether it is the product of corruption or not.[86] An essential feature is the close linkage, sometimes on the patronage model, of Chinese business networks with the political leaders and indigenous elites.[87] In SSA, with a few exceptions, local social networks did not contain these features, being short, fragmented and subject to permanent internal problems of collective action and free riding, while businessmen faced the external hostility of rulers if they were not actually their political instruments.

Social norms, labor and reciprocity

Another important trait that distinguishes the Asian and African settings are the norms relating to labor and labor markets, the obligations associated with wealth accumulation, and the use of savings for consumption and ritual obligations instead of production. In Asian contexts, there is a norm of reciprocity involving the protection of the extended network in exchange for work. There are informal markets, as in SSA. However, in Asia, the informal workforce is put on the family labor market or any other labor market. In SSA, the individuals forming part of this informal sector can survive, and being underemployed, their "host" cannot expel them. This strong social norm is not a contractual relationship. It is not negotiable, even in urban settings, and it maintains a vicious circle of low productivity.

In Asia, wealth and power are not necessarily associated with external signs, such as houses, luxury goods, etc. In SSA, the link between social status and conspicuous consumption has frequently been noted: if an individual becomes rich, he has to spend money in ceremonies and entertain parasitic groups without any provision of labor or goods in exchange, for this is precisely what legitimizes his status as a "big man".[88] The products of corruption are therefore not used in the same circuits. Broadly speaking, they are reintegrated into the production circuit in Asia, while they are dissipated in the consumption circuit in SSA, be they local or deterritorialized through capital flight, consumption of foreign goods and real estate investments in developed countries.

Poverty plays a crucial role in sustaining petty corruption. It shortens the network effects because deep poverty intensifies the individual dimension of urgency and coping strategies for survival. Moreover, it shapes the time frame of individuals for it is widely accepted that the time horizon of subsistence standards of living tends to be extremely short: the present, the duration of "today". The calculations of individuals on the future effects of corruption, cheating on rules or fraud, are therefore irrelevant. These malpractices can either involve their own production tool (often consisting of their labor force only, i.e. their health or bodies), or the collective production tools (bribes relating to the maintenance of machines, etc.), or even the health of other people (bribes relating to food, medical drugs, the maintenance of collective transportation, etc.).

An essential point is the role of norms or "community pressure" relating to exchange, rights and obligations, especially work obligations. When helped by a wealthier relative, there is no norm of reciprocity for the assisted person. Another related aspect is the absence of social security. Social security is not provided by a third party such as the state, and individuals are therefore obliged to "acquire" networks and use them as an insurance to cover future risks and hazards through offers of services, time, effort, work, money, and so on—especially by receiving, feeding or housing people. This can be very costly in terms of time, money, or the personal acquisition of education or human capital. An individual who does not comply with this nexus of norms incurs the risk of being excluded from society, and in the event of misfortune, will not receive any help. The assisted person does not have to provide work in return, unlike other settings in Asia where family ties are associated with the productive activities of each member, their integration in labor markets, and savings for the purpose of setting up a new firm, the network acting as a "performance-based group".[89] In

SSA, assistance is not an implicit contract consisting of reciprocal rights and obligations between two persons, but rather an asymmetrical norm with the dimension of obligation weighing on only one individual. This makes networks in SSA vectors of consumption rather than production, and of impoverishment rather than growth.

VII. Conclusion

Corruption has generally been considered as a factor of poor economic performance, and is widely used as a major explanation for the current Sub-Saharan Africa economic stagnation, in academic research as well as in the literature of aid agencies. It has been shown in this paper that corruption is a complex, derived and inclusive phenomenon.

Its economic effects are not *ex ante* predictable; both legal and illegal rents can be channeled into productive activities. Consequences depend on a series of other determinants: colonial history; the developmental nature of the states; the style, time frame and legitimacy of the political regimes; the modes of the state-business relationships, which can be alliances or antagonisms; the structure of social networks that are the vectors for the transfer of money, goods and work, accompanying corruption when it is redistributed through patronage relationships or other types of networks; the norms relating to co-operation, reciprocity and labor; and finally, the political economy and the links of these networks to the political classes.

The aim has not been to make a thorough analysis of all cases but rather to isolate the main questions and the possible levels of comparison between the various expressions of corruption in Sub-Saharan Africa and East Asia. It is striking to see that both regions can be contrasted at each level. This contributes to an understanding of their divergence in terms of economic performance, of the causal role of institutions or the effect of corruption on them, and of the orientation towards production or consumption ends.

ENDNOTES

1. Sindzingre, Alice. 2001. "Economie illégale et drogues en Afrique sub-saharienne: crédibilité des Etats et réformes économiques." *CEMOTI* (*Cahiers d'Etudes sur la Méditerranée Orientale et le Monde Turco-Iranien*, special issue "Drugs and Politics"), n°32, July-December, pp. 117-137; and Sindzingre, Alice. 2003. "Contracts, Norms, and Political Economy: Sub-Saharan State Credibility and the Microeconomic Foundations of Developmental Taxation." *Cambridge Review of International Affairs* 16:1, pp. 89-103.

2. Khan, Mushtaq H. 2000. "Rent-Seeking as a Process." In Khan, Mushtaq H., and K. S. Jomo (eds.). *Rents, Rent-Seeking and Economic Development: Theory and Evidence in Asia.* Cambridge: Cambridge University Press.

3. Sindzingre, Alice. 1997. "Corruptions africaines: éléments d'analyse comparative avec l'Asie de l'Est." *Revue Internationale de Politique Comparée* 4:2 (September), pp. 377-412; Sindzingre, Alice. 2002. "A Comparative Analsyis of African and East Asian Corruption." In Heidenheimer, Arnold J., and Michael Johnston (eds.). *Political Corruption: Concepts and Contexts. Third Edition.* New Brunswick, NJ: Transaction Publishers; Sindzingre, Alice. 2004. "Economic Reforms, The State, and Corruption: Some Insights From Sub-Saharan Africa." In Jain, R. B. (ed.). (forthcoming), *Towards a Corruption-free Sustainable Development: Challenges of Good Governance in the New Millenium.* New Delhi.

4. In an analogy with the analysis of entrepreneurship by Baumol; see Baumol, William J. 1990. "Entrepreneurship: Productive, Unproductive, and Destructive." *Journal of Political Economy* 98:5, pp. 893-921.

5. Przeworski, Adam, Michael E. Alvarez, José Antonio Cheibub and Fernando Limongi. 2000. *Democracy and Development: Political Institutions and Well-Being in the World, 1950-1990.* Cambridge: Cambridge University Press; Rodrik, Dani. 2001. "Institutions, Integration, and Geography: In Search of the Deep Determinants of Growth." Conference on the Analytical Country Studies on Growth. Cambridge, Mass.: Harvard University, Center for International Development (August), mimeo.

6. Rodrik, Dani. 1997. "Democracy and Economic Performance." Harvard University, mimeo.

7. Mauro, Paolo. 1995. "Corruption and Growth." *Quarterly Journal of Economics* CX:3 (August), pp. 681-712; Campos, Nauro F. 2000. *Context is Everything: Measuring Institutional Change in Transition Economies.* Washington D. C.: The World Bank, policy research working paper 2269.

8. Wei, Shang-Jin. 2001. "Domestic Crony Capitalism and International Fickle Capital: Is There a Connection?" *International Finance* 4:1.

9. On "growth without governance, see Kaufmann, Daniel and Aart Kraay. 2002. *Growth Without Governance.* Washington D.C.: The World Bank, policy research working paper 2928; see also Dearden, Stephen J. H. 2000. "Corruption and Economic Development." Manchester, Manchester Metropolitan University, Department of Economics, Development Studies Association European Development Policy Study Group discussion paper n°18.

10. Auty, Richard M. (ed.) 2001. *Resource Abundance and Economic Development.* Oxford: Oxford University Press; Sachs, Jeffrey D. and Andrew Warner. 2001. "The Curse of Natural Resources." *European Economic Review* 45:4-6 (May), pp. 827-838; Leite, Carlos and Jens Weidmann. 1999. *Does Mother Nature Corrupt? Natural Re-*

sources, Corruption and Economic Growth, Washington D. C.: International Monetary Fund working paper WP/99/85.

11. UNCTAD. 2003. *World Investment Report 2003: FDI Policies for Development: National and International Perspectives*. Geneva, UNCTAD.

12. Rodrik, Dani. 2001. "Institutions, Integration, and Geography: In Search of the Deep Determinants of Growth." Conference on the Analytical Country Studies on Growth. Cambridge, Mass.: Harvard University, Center for International Development (August), mimeo.

13. Niles, Kimberly. 2001. "Indonesia: Cronyism, Economic Meltdown, and Political Stalemate." In Horowitz, Shale, and Uk Heo (eds.). *The Political Economy of International Financial Crisis: Interest Groups, Ideologies and Institutions*. Lanham, MD: Rowman and Littlefield Publishers.

14. Gomez, Edmund Terence ed. 2002. *Political Business in East Asia*. London, Routledge; Johnson, Simon and Todd Mitton. 2001. *Cronyism and Capital Controls: Evidence from Malaysia*, Cambridge Mass: NBER working paper 8521; Kang, David C. 2002. *Crony Capitalism: Corruption and Development in South Korea and the Philippines*. Cambridge, Cambridge University Press.

15. The author thanks Hugo Stokke for many seminal discussions, and for having suggested this comparison.

16. West African Economic and Monetary Union.

17. BCEAO. 2001. *Situation du système bancaire de l'UEMOA à fin septembre 2000*. Dakar: Banque Centrale des Etats d'Afrique de l'Ouest.

18. Over the period 1996-2000, see Debrun, Xavier, Paul Masson and Catherine Patillo. 2002. *Monetary Union in West Africa: Who Might Gain, Who Might Lose, and Why?*, Washington D. C.: International Monetary Fund working paper WP/02/226, Table 3.

19. For example, very undesirable acts like the public execution of corrupt rulers, as in Ghana.

20. Besley, Timothy and John McLaren. 1993. "Taxes and Bribery: The Role of Wage Incentives." *Economic Journal* 103 (January), pp. 119-141.

21. Stiglitz, Joseph E. 1999. "*Quis Custodiet Ipsos Custodes?* Corporate Governance Failures in the Transition." Paris, Conseil d'Analyse Economique and the World Bank, Annual World Bank Conference in Development Economics.

22. Collier et al. (1998) estimate capital flight in SSA at 39 percent of private wealth, vs. 6 percent in East Asia; Ndikumana and Boyce (2003) show its correlation with external borrowing as well as the large differences between SSA countries, the countries with the highest levels (i.e. above 200 percent of GDP over the period 1970-96) being Angola, Nigeria, Côte d'Ivoire and the RD Congo. See Collier, Paul, Anke Hoeffler and Catherine Patillo. 1998. *Capital Flight as a Portfolio Choice*. Washington D. C.,: The World Bank, Development Research Group, and Policy Research Working Paper 2066; and Ndikumana, Leonce and James K. Boyce. 2003. "Public Debts and Public Assets: Explaining Capital Flight from Sub-Saharan African Countries." *World Development* 31:1, pp. 107-130.

23. Fieldhouse, D. K. 1999. *The West and the Third World: Trade, Colonialism, Dependence and Development*, Oxford, Blackwell, Ch. 11; Kohli, Atul. 1994. "Where Do High Growth Political Economies Come From? The Japanese Lineage of Korea's Developmental State." *World Development* 22:9, pp. 1269-1293; also appears in Woo-Cumings, Meredith (ed.). 1999. *The Developmental State*. Ithaca: Cornell University Press.

24. Brautigam, Deborah. 1995. "The State as Agent: Industrial Development in Taiwan." In Stein, Howard (ed.). *Asian Industrialization and Africa: Studies in Policy Alternatives*

to Structural Adjustment. New York: St. Martin's Press; Brautigam, Deborah. 2000., *Aid Dependence and Governance.* Report, Ministry of Foreign Affairs, Division for International Development Cooperation. Stockholm.

25. Cho, Yoon Je. 1996., "Government Intervention, Rent Distribution and Economic Development in Korea." In Aoki, Masahiko, Hyung-Ki Kim and Masahiro Okuno-Fujiwara (eds.). *The Role of Government in East Asian Economic Development: Comparative Institutional Analysis.* Oxford: Clarendon Press.

26. Lall, Sanjaya. 2000. *Selective Industrial and Trade Polices in Developing Countries: Theoretical and Empirical Issues.* Oxford: Queen Elizabeth House Working Paper n°48.

27. Fieldhouse, D. K. 1999. *The West and the Third World: Trade, Colonialism, Dependence and Development,* Oxford: Blackwell.

28. Young, Crawford. 1994. *The African Colonial State in Comparative Perspective.* New Haven: Yale University Press.

29. Hopkins, A. G. 1973. *An Economic History of West Africa.* London: Longman.

30. See Fieldhouse, D. K. 1994. *Merchant Capital and Economic Decolonization: The United Africa Company, 1929-1989.* Oxford: Clarendon Press, for an account of the history of the United Africa Company (UAC) in Nigeria.

31. Forrest, Tom. 1994. *The Advance of African Capital: The Growth of Nigerian Private Enterprise.* Charlottesville: University Press of Virginia.

32. Yeats, Alexander. 1991. "Do African Countries Pay More for Imports? Yes." In Chhibber, Ajay, and Stanley Fisher (eds.). *Economic Reform in Sub-Saharan Africa.* Washington D. C.: The World Bank; Sindzingre, Alice. 2000. *Competitiveness, Trade Arrangements and Political Economy: the Case of ECOWAS.* Oslo: University of Oslo, Centre for Development and the Environment Working Paper.

33. Cheng, Tun-Jen, Stephan Haggard and David Kang. 1999. "Institutions and Growth in Korea and Taiwan: The Bureaucracy." In Akyüz, Yilmaz (ed.). *East Asian Development: New Perspectives.* London: Frank Cass; on the political-cum-developmental strategies of the authoritarian regimes in Korea see Kwon, Huck-Ju. 1999. *The Welfare State in Korea: The Politics of Legitimation.* London: Macmillan.

34. Robinson, James A. 1996. "When is a State Predatory?" Los Angeles: University of Southern California, Department of Economics, mimeo.

35. Yoshihara, Kunio. 1994. *The Nation and Economic Growth: the Philippines and Thailand.* Oxford: Oxford University Press.

36. Ekeh, Peter. 1975. "Colonialism and the Two Publics in Africa: A Theoretical Statement." *Comparative Studies in Society and History* 17:1 (Fall), pp. 91-112.

37. Berkowitz, Daniel, Katharina Pistor and Jean-François Richard. 2000. *Economic Development, Legality and the Transplant Effect.* Cambridge Mass,: Harvard University, CID working paper 39.

38. See, on Korea, Chang, Ha-Joon and Peter Evans. 2000. "The Role of Institutions in Economic Change." Venice, the "Other Canon in Economics" workshop (January), mimeo.

39. Shleifer, Andrei and Robert W. Vishny. 1993. "Corruption." *Quarterly Journal of Economics* CVIII:3 (August), pp. 599-618.

40. As highlighted by the title of Berry, Sara. 1993. *No Condition is Permanent: the Social Dynamics of Agrarian Change in Sub-Saharan Africa.* Madison: University of Wisconsin Press.

41. On Kenya, see Fafchamps, Marcel. 1996. *Ethnicity and Markets: Supplier Credit in African Manufacturing.* Washington, D. C.: The World Bank, RPED Discussion Paper, October.

42. Brown, Rajeswary Ampalavanar. 1994. *Capital and Entrepreneurship in South-East Asia.* New York: St. Martin's Press.

43. Depending on the period, they are estimated to represent 4 percent of the Indonesian population and own 70-75 percent of the nation's privately-held assets; in Thailand, they account for 8-10 percent of the population and own 90 percent of assets in the commercial and manufacturing sector, and half the capital of banks, *The Economist*, "The Overseas Chinese." July 18th, 1992. In the Philippines, they would represent 1 percent of the population, but own 40 percent of corporate equity. In Malaysia, in the mid-90s, despite the affirmative policies favoring the Malays, they were 28 percent of the population and owned 41 percent of total corporate equity. On the Philippines, see Yoshihara, Kunio. 1994. *The Nation and Economic Growth: the Philippines and Thailand.* Kuala Lumpur, Oxford University Press; for Malaysia, see Gomez, Edmund Terence. 1999. *Chinese Business in Malaysia: Accumulation, Accommodation and Ascendance.* Richmond: Curzon Press.

44. Haggard, Stephan. 2000. *The Political Economy of the Asian Financial Crisis.* Washington D. C.: Institute for International Economics.

45. Singh, Ajit. 1999. "Savings, Investment and the Corporation in the East Asian Miracle." In Akyüz, Yilmaz (ed.). *East Asian Development: New Perspectives.* London: Frank Cass.

46. According to the well-known model in Evans, Peter. 1995. *Embedded Autonomy: States and Industrial Transformation.* Princeton, Princeton University Press.

47. Kang, David C. 2003. "Transaction Costs and Crony Capitalism in East Asia." *Comparative Politics,* 35:4 (July).

48. Hutchcroft, Paul D. 1998. *Booty Capitalism: The Politics of Banking in the Philippines.* Ithaca: Cornell University Press; Hutchcroft, Paul D. 1999 "Neither Dynamo nor Domino: Reforms and Crises in the Philippine Political Economy." In Pempel, T. J. (ed.). *The Politics of the Asian Economic Crisis.* Ithaca: Cornell University Press.

49. Doner, Richard F., and Ansil Ramsay. 1997. "Competitive Clientelism and Economic Governance: The Case of Thailand." In Maxfield, Sylvia, and Ben Ross Schneider (eds.). *Business and the State in Developing Countries.* Ithaca: Cornell University Press; Doner, Richard F. and Ansil Ramsay. 2000. "Rent-Seeking and Economic Development in Thailand." In Khan, Mushtaq H., and K. S. Jomo. (eds.). *Rents, Rent-Seeking and Economic Development: Theory and Evidence in Asia.* Cambridge, Cambridge University Press.

50. As shown by the country studies of 'political business' in Gomez, Edmund Terence. (ed.). 2002. *Political Business in East Asia.* London: Routledge.

51. This is shown in a series of biographies presented in Paix, Catherine and Michèle Petit. 1986. Itinéraires et stratégies d'une bourgeoisie: le cas de Singapour, *Strates*, n°1, Université Paris I, pp. 49-119.

52. Chirathivat, Suthiphand and S. Mansoob Murshed. 2001. *Globalization and Openness.*Helsinki: United Nations University, WIDER discussion paper n°2001/35.

53. On Indonesia, see McIntyre, Andrew. 2000. "Funny Money: Fiscal Policy, Rent-seeking and Economic Performance in Indonesia." In Khan, Mushtaq H., and K. S. Jomo (eds.). *Rents, Rent-Seeking and Economic Development: Theory and Evidence in Asia.* Cambridge: Cambridge University Press; and Temple, Jonathan. 2001. *Growing into*

Trouble: Indonesia After 1966. Cambridge, Mass.: Harvard University, Centre for International Development, Analytical Country Study on Growth Conference.

54. An annual rate of 7.7 percent between 1965 and 1998, according to Acemoglu, Daron, Simon Johnson and James A. Robinson. 2003. "An African Success Story: Botswana." In Rodrik, Dani (ed.). *In Search of Prosperity: Analytical Narratives on Economic Growth.* Princeton: Princeton University Press.

55. Yoshihara, Kunio. 1988. *The Rise of Ersatz Capitalism in South-East Asia.* Oxford: Oxford University Press; Bello, Walden and Stephanie Rosenfeld. 1990. *Dragons in Distress.* London: Penguin Books; Chang, Ha-Joon. 2000. "The Hazards of Moral Hazard: Untangling the Asian Crisis." *World Development* 28:4 (April), pp. 775-788.

56. See, for example, Stiglitz, Joseph E. 2001. "From Miracle to Crisis to Recovery: Lessons from Four Decades of East Asian Experience." In Stiglitz, Joseph E., and Shahid Yusuf (eds.). *Rethinking the East Asian Miracle.* Washington, D. C.: The World Bank, and Oxford: Oxford University Press.

57. McIntyre, Andrew. 1998. "Political Institutions and the Economic Crisis in Thailand and Indonesia." *ASEAN Economic Bulletin* 15:3 (December).

58. On "alliance capitalism" see Wade, Robert. 2000. *Governing the Market: A Decade Later.* London: London School of Economics, LSE Development Studies Institute working paper n°00-03, and Suehiro, Akira, with Nate-Napha Weilerdsak. 2001. *Family Business Gone Wrong? Ownership Patterns and Corporate Performance in Thailand.* Tokyo: Asian Development Bank Institute, working paper n°19.

59. According to the distinction developed by Bhagwati, Jagdish. 2000. *Crony Capitalism: Rent-creating versus Profit-sharing Corruption.* New York: Columbia University, http://www.columbia.edu/~jb38/crony_cap.pdf (viewed 6 August 2004).

60. Acemoglu, Daron, Simon Johnson and James A. Robinson. 2000. *The Colonial Origins of Comparative Development: An Empirical Investigation.* Cambridge Mass, NBER working paper n°7771.

61. Evans, Peter. 1997. "State Structures, Government-Business Relations and Economic Transformation." In Maxfield, Sylvia, and Ben Ross Schneider (eds.). *Business and the State in Developing Countries.* Ithaca, Cornell University Press.

62. On the comparison between Ghana and Côte d'Ivoire see Sindzingre, Alice. 1996. *Industrie, ajustement et « entrepreneurship » en Côte d'Ivoire et au Ghana.* Leipzig: Leipzig University papers on Africa n°2.

63. Rodrik, Dani. 2001. "Trading in Illusions." *Foreign Policy* (March-April).

64. Haque, Nadeem Ul and M. Ali Khan. 1997. *Institutional Development: Skill Transference Through a Reversal of "Human Capital Flight" or Technical Assistance.* Washington, D. C.: International Monetary Fund, working paper WP/97/89; Hatton, Timothy and Jeffrey G. Williamson. 2001. *Demographic and Economic Pressure on Emigration Out of Africa.* Cambridge Mass, NBER working paper 8124.

65. *Le Monde*, September 25, 2001, relying on studies of the International Organisation for Migration; See also Carrington, William J. and Enrica Detragiache. 1998. *How Big Is the Brain Drain?* Washington, D.C., International Monetary Fund working paper WP/98/102.

66. Berg, Elliot J. 1993. *Rethinking Technical Cooperation.* New York, UNDP, DAI.

67. Azam, Jean-Paul, Shantayanan Devarajan and Stephen A. O'Connell. 1999. *Aid Dependence Reconsidered.* Oxford: Centre for the Study of African Economies, working paper 189.

68. Sindzingre, Alice. 2001. "Dimensions économiques des réformes de l'Etat en Afrique sub-saharienne." In Toulabor, Comi, and Dominique Darbon (eds.). *Réforme de l'Etat : reconstruction institutionnelle et modes de régulation, L'Afrique Politique.* Special issue: "Reform of Sub-Saharan African States." Paris, Karthala.

69. See, for example, Krueger, Anne O. 1974. "The Political Economy of the Rent-Seeking Society." *American Economic Review* 64:3, pp. 291-303, and Tollison, R. D. 1982. "Rent-Seeking: A Survey." *Kyklos* 35:4, pp. 575-602.

70. See the well-known account of the role of MITI in Japan in Johnson, Chalmers. 1982. *MITI and the Japanese Miracle.* Stanford: Stanford University Press.

71. A well-known example was the World Bank analysis of the Asian miracle in World Bank. 1993. *The East Asian Miracle.* New York: Oxford University Press, and the fierce controversies surrounding it; on the latter, see, for example, Wade, Robert. 1994. "Selective Industrial Policies in East Asia: Is *The East Asian Miracle* Right?" In Fishlow, Albert, Catherine Gwin, Stephan Haggard, Dani Rodrik and Robert Wade (eds.). *Miracle or Design? Lessons from the East Asian Experience.* Washington, D.C.: Overseas Development Council.

72. On the "Post-Washington consensus" see, *inter alia,* Stiglitz, Joseph E. 1998. *More Instruments and Broader Goals: Moving Toward the Post-Washington Consensus.* Helsinki: The 1998 WIDER Annual Lecture (January).

73. Sindzingre, Alice. 1996. *Industrie, ajustement et « entrepreneurship » en Côte d'Ivoire et au Ghana.* Leipzig: Leipzig University papers on Africa n°2.

74. Tangri, Roger. 1999. *The Politics of Patronage in Africa: Parastatals, Privatization and Private Enterprise.* London: James Currey.

75. For an analysis of the concept of networks in the context of Benin see Sindzingre, Alice. 1998. "Réseaux, organisations et marchés: exemples du Bénin." *Autrepart (Cahiers des Sciences Humaines)* 6, pp. 73-90 (Special issue "Cross-border trade and regional integration in Sub-Saharan Africa").

76. Platteau, Jean-Philippe. 1994. "Behind the Market Stage Where Real Societies Exist: Part1: The Role of Public and Private Order Institutions." *Journal of Development Studies* 30:3, pp. 533-577; Part 2: "The Role of Moral Norms." *Journal of Development Studies* 30:4, pp. 753-817; Fafchamps, Marcel. 1992. "Solidarity Networks in Preindustrial Societies: Rational Peasants with a Moral Economy." *Economic Development and Cultural Change* 41:1 (October), pp. 147-174.

77. Comparable with the medieval guilds analyzed by Greif, Avner. 1989. "Reputation and Coalitions in Medieval Trade: Evidence on the Maghribi Traders." *Journal of Economic History* XLIX:4 (December), pp. 857-882.

78. Using Easterly, William and Ross Levine. 1997. "Africa's Growth Tragedy: Policies and Ethnic Divisions." *Quarterly Journal of Economics* 112, pp. 1203-1250; Collier, Paul. 1998. *The Political Economy of Ethnicity.* Oxford: Centre for the Study of African Economies, working paper WPS/98-8; and Collier, Paul. 1998b. *The Economics of Civil War.* Oxford: Centre for the Study of African Economies, Nottingham, CREDIT 10th Anniversary Conference (September).

79. See Hamilton, Gary. 1999. "Asian Business Networks in Transition: Or, What Alan Greenspan Does not Know about the Asian Business Crisis." In Pempel, T. J. (ed.). *The Politics of the Asian Economic Crisis.* Ithaca: Cornell University Press; and for a sociological view, Redding, S. Gordon. 1993. *The Spirit of Chinese Capitalism.* Berlin, De Gruyter.

80. Ernst, Dieter. 1992. "Network Transactions, Market Structure and Technology Diffusion: Implications for South-South Co-operation." In Mytelka, Lynn K. (ed.). *South-

South Cooperation in a Global Perspective. Paris: OECD Development Centre; for an analysis of their transformation see Ando, Mitsuyo and Fukunari Kimura. 2003. *The Formation of International Production and Distribution Networks in East Asia.* Cambridge, Mass.: NBER working paper 10167.

81. These arguments have been analysed in depth in Malaizé, Vincent and Alice Sindzingre. 1998. "Politique économique, secteur privé et réseaux en Asie du sud-est et en Afrique de l'Ouest." *Revue Tiers-Monde* 39:155 (July-September), pp. 647-672.

82. Among others, see Cheung, Henry Wai-chung and Kris Olds (eds.). 2000. *Globalization of Chinese Business Firms.* London: Macmillan, and New York: St. Martin's Press; Chan, Kwok Bun (ed.). 2000. *Chinese Business Networks: State, Economy and Culture.* Singapore: Prentice Hall, and Copenhagen, Nordic Institute of Asian Studies.

83. For example, see Wang, Gungwu. 1981. "A Short History of Nanyang Chinese." In *Community and Nation: China, Southeast Asia and Australia.* Sydney: Allen and Unwin; Reid, Anthony (ed.). 1996. *Sojourners and Settlers: Histories of Southeast Asia and the Chinese.* Sydney: Allen and Unwin.

84. Gomez, Edmund Terence. 1999. *Chinese Business in Malaysia: Accumulation, Accommodation and Ascendance.* Richmond: Curzon Press.

85. Moon, Chung-In, and Rashemi Prasad. 1994. "Beyond the Developmental State: Networks, Politics and Institutions." *Governance* 7:4 (October), pp. 360-386.

86. Khan, Haider A. 1999. *Corporate Governance of Family Businesses in Asia: What's Right and What's Wrong?* Tokyo: Asian Development Bank Institute, working paper n°3, analyses the potential risks of the family business model in terms of corporate governance.

87. See Gomez, Edmund Terence. 2000. "In Search of Patrons: Chinese Business Networking and Malay Political Patronage in Malaysia." In Chan, Kwok Bun (ed.). *Chinese Business Networks: State, Economy and Culture.* Singapore: Prentice Hall, and Copenhagen, Nordic Institute of Asian Studies; Searle, Peter. 1999. *The Riddle of Malaysian Capitalism: Rent-seekers or Real Capitalists?* Honolulu, Allen and Unwin, and University of Hawai'i Press.

88. There are obviously many exceptions, as shown for instance by Warnier, Jean-Pierre. 1993. *L'esprit d'entreprise au Cameroun.* Paris: Karthala; see discussion of Bamileke entrepreneurship in Cameroon.

89. Yoshihara, Kunio. 1994. *The Nation and Economic Growth: The Philippines and Thailand.* Kuala Lumpur, Oxford University Press.

4

The Cultural Dimensions of Corruption: Reflections on Nigeria

Donald R. Sherk

Any reform effort aimed at mobilizing sustained social opposition to corruption will have to take into account the ways people understand the problem. Too often, discussions of cultural aspects of corruption concentrate only on mitigating factors, or on customs and traditions that seem to contribute to corruption problems. But cultural also involves limits and standards; moreover, people who have lived with extensive corruption and whose countries retain significant traditional values have little trouble understanding the problem and its implications for their lives. Donald Sherk, in this chapter, draws upon his extensive work in West Africa to examine social conceptions of corruption, and to suggest ways of combating the problem that might be both workable and consistent with social values. The case in question is that of Nigeria, but the cultural views, and the views of culture, discussed here will suggest similar ideas relevant in other social settings.

I. Introduction

From May through October, 2000, I worked in Nigeria on a macro-economic policy project sponsored by the United States Agency for International Development (USAID). This was one of a series of extended stays in Africa, totaling several years in all, that has enabled me to look closely at corruption and related problems. In this chapter I will consider African corruption as an obstacle to economic growth, but will place that analysis in the context of the culture and society of one of Africa's most important countries—Nigeria.

This was a particularly propitious time to be in Nigeria and to examine its corruption problems. First, it was during this period that Transparency International (TI), the widely respected non-governmental organization monitoring governance throughout the world, published its 1999 Corruption Perception Index. TI announced that for 1999 Nigeria ranked number one on its list of ninety countries evaluated. The impact of this widely publicized announcement on the Nigerian "man in the street" was one of noticeable frustration. This was because shortly before the TI pronouncement the National Assembly, Nigeria's national legislative body, had debated and passed the President Olusegun Obasanjo's Anti-Corruption Act. In fact Obasanjo, in summing up his first year in office, called this his "most important piece of legislation." No mention was made of this act in the TI report, which had Nigeria moving from its place as the twenty-seventh worst offender in 1998 to first place in 1999. Nor was mention made of the anti-corruption drive sponsored by President Obasanjo, nor of the more than $1 billion of public contracts that were cancelled or re-negotiated as the result of the newly established Commission of Inquiry for the Review of Contracts, Licenses and Appointments. The Commission reviewed all contracts that had been approved between January 1 and May 28, 1999; 1,684—or 41 percent—were cancelled. The sentiment most often expressed was, "What does a country have to do?" to begin to shake off the reputation of being a very corrupt country.

The second reason why this was a particularly important time stems from the fact that civilian government was still a relatively recent phenomenon in Nigeria. Prior to May, 1999, the country had been ruled by a series of corrupt military dictatorships that not only enriched themselves in massive proportions but also, almost daily, suppressed human rights. The internationally-monitored elections that brought Obasanjo to power and breathed life back into the country's moribund legislative and judicial arms of government touched off dramatic changes in the country.

In addition to being in the right country at the right time, the nature of my assignment was also ideal from the standpoint of getting a good exposure to the ideas and views of some very articulate Nigerians. I had the good fortune to work with about forty mid-level government officials from both the executive branch and the country's legislature, the National Assembly. Working daily with such a dedicated and highly motivated group of Nigerians gave me a unique opportunity to explore the topic of corruption at some depth. I am grateful to the trainees for their willingness to speak openly and with candor of the plight of Nigeria, and of the day-to-day impact of corruption on individual Nigerians living in the country that Transparency International ranked as the most corrupt country in the world.

I will argue that the Nigerian model of corruption, although not identical in every respect to others found across the continent of Africa, is sufficiently similar to be useful to our understanding of the topic. Moreover it is my core contention that, unless we focus on the cultural underpinnings of corruption, we will continue to concoct half-way measures and short-term solutions that are unlikely to remain in place for any significant period of time. Worse, they will only serve to deepen the cynicism rife in the country, and will threaten the nascent instruments of democracy being developed in a "hot-house" environment.

II. The Roots of Nigerian Corruption

The work I undertook for USAID, under its capacity-building strategy, consisted primarily of training mid-level Nigerian bureaucrats drawn from both the executive and legislative branches of government. The training courses concentrated on project appraisal, economic analysis, financial analysis and welfare economics. USAID's specific goal in funding such a program was to help develop a cadre of governmental officers that could make sensible decisions as to what kinds of economic projects were in the country's best interests. The inclusion of staff members from the National Assembly was seen as a necessary compliment to the training given to the executive branch officials. USAID hoped that they could stimulate a constructive economic dialogue across the federal government concerning the proper utilization of scarce resources and growth-generating public investments.

The trainees in the classes all had records of substantial public service and experienced earlier authoritarian regimes. The subject of corruption came up frequently, especially when failed projects, and the reasons for their failures, were discussed. The trainees were very quick to become involved in the courses. They were a bright and articulate group that would frequently stay beyond the appointed quitting hour to carry on with an intense debate over some aspect of the day's teaching. Nor were they especially shy about stating their own opinions about the topic of corruption. The openness and candor of the trainees was undoubtedly enhanced by the press of Nigeria. The daily newspapers were as critical and unrestrained as any I had ever seen anywhere. It would not be an exaggeration to say that no day went by during my stay in Nigeria that I didn't read at least three or four stories on past and present corruption in the country.

I asked both classes to set down on paper their own thoughts and attitudes about Nigerian corruption. I gave no instructions about how to prepare the statements except to say that they were to be voluntary and could be submitted unnamed. In this way I hoped to get the trainees to speak more candidly about the subject of corruption in Nigeria. Roughly one third of the two classes responded to my plea to give me their own personal views on "what corruption means to me" and submitted statements. By way of explanation for why I needed the statements, I told them how helpful it would be to have some personal statements from people who had lived through the military dictatorship of the Abacha years.

To underscore the importance of that point, as a corruption issue, I would add that while I was in Nigeria the press was reporting almost daily on an estimated $4 to $5 billion that the previous ruler had siphoned out of the country and placed in secret bank accounts in Europe and North America. The fact that a number of reputable and respected western financial institutions had assisted in this process was certainly not lost on the students. According to the *Financial Times,* "Banks in London played a key role in enabling former Nigerian dictator Sani Abacha to launder more than $4 billon looted from the country during his four and a half year rule…".[1]

For my part, I tried to approach the subject with the degree of seriousness it deserved. I asked myself what it would be like if I lived in a society so corrupt that people from other countries would not bother to get to know me as a person, but simply lumped me into a category of corrupt individuals and gave me no opportunity to set the record straight regarding my own family situation. As a husband, father, and soon-to-be grandfather, I thought of what I personally had tried to instill in my children in terms of values and mores. It came as a staggering realization to fully understand that my behavior had little effect on how I would be viewed in another country. I came to realize that my good name would be stolen from me by individuals who had no idea who I was, and who would care little about what their actions caused me to lose.

It was only then that I began to recognize the true social dimensions of Nigeria's corruption problem, and at the same time, be able to grasp what would be required to rescue the good name of the average Nigerian. In spite of the country's immense poverty (with 70 percent of the population living on $1 per day), the robbery of a country's good name was in many respects a far greater hardship.

III. Tribal Loyalties, Social Values, and Corruption in Daily Life

Most Nigerians can trace their roots back to small villages characterized by a single ethnic grouping. Frequently, four generations of a family live side by side. The typical Nigerian village was "undemocratic" in the modern sense of the word, being led by a chief with lifetime tenure. The chief might head a village council of elders or wise men. Village tasks such as farming, hunting, carrying, cooking, child-care, and the like were usually well established and performed by a sub-group of the village population. Special events in the life of an individual or family were often honored with the involvement of the entire village. Major problems or needs in the lives of villagers were brought to the doorstep of the village chief, or to one of the elders. A sense of obligation based on ethnicity and village standing carried with it an unwritten understanding that the most well-off among the villagers were obliged to help the least well-off among them. This sense of village or tribal loyalty has often been admired and respected far beyond the borders of the village community.

But it is precisely this sense of loyalty and obligation that provides the starting point for much of Nigeria's corruption when individuals move out of the village and onto a larger stage—for example, to a district, state or federal government position. It was widely acknowledged by the majority of trainees that local and ethnic loyalties remain strong in the new locale. Jobs, contracts, inside information, are all recognized as being dependent upon special relationships that were often nurtured at the village level. Consequently, removing these relationships as a basis for corruption requires the difficult task of saying that behavior that is strongly valued and admired in one setting is unacceptable and illegal in another.

That sort of "re-education" is extremely difficult to achieve in a short period. The public remains extremely cynical about the ability of the Nigerian administration to make much of a dent in the corrupt behavior that has plagued the country for years. Some Nigerians have argued that, in spite of the showpiece anti-corruption legislation promoted by the President and passed by the National Assembly, the public at large is cynical, and will remain so until a few individuals known to be close to the President and/or the National Assembly are actually sent to prison with stiff prison terms.

Living with corruption

Why corruption, as a proper subject for discussion in the context of development, took so long to come out into the public arena is unclear. Perhaps the Cold War, which forced the super-powers to compete with each other for allies, friends, or just countries willing to remain neutral, caused the aid donors to look the other way or not to raise sensitive subjects. Then too, for three decades beginning during the 1950s it was generally considered not only impolite, but a violation of national sovereignty, if the subject of corruption was raised. In the mid-1980s, for example, the United States Treasury felt that it had to raise the distasteful subject of President Ferdinand Marcos of the Philippines, and his tendency to reward his "cronies" with monopoly concessions in the sugar and coconut sectors, with the International Monetary Fund (IMF). At the initial meeting between U. S. Treasury and IMF officials, the latter professed complete ignorance about such issues in the Philippines, saying that it traditionally left them to the World Bank.

For those and other reasons, discussions of corruption in countries like Nigeria can be very difficult, and are often open to misunderstanding. Nigeria's experience with an elected civil government is so recent, by contrast, that much of the anti-corruption drive is still in significant flux. The President has stated that the anticorruption law that he promoted, and that was passed by the National Assembly, was the most important legislation of his first year in office. Yet it is essential to build reforms on a solid base of social values. As Keith Henderson has pointed out,

> [D]rafting and passing reforms without building a public consensus for them usually means they will not be implemented or enforced. This kind of non-participatory process leads to more public cynicism.... Experience tells us that even if strong, independent legal institutions and well-crafted laws and hotlines exist, they will do little to expose corruption if people and society are generally unwilling to report on the misdeeds of their colleagues or fellow citizens. Toward this end, developing public trust, respect for governmental institutions and the rule of law through concrete action is a fundamental first step in the overall reform process.[2]

It is one thing to say that laws and their enforcement must reflect social values. But what are those values, and how do people come to terms with corruption both as a national problem and as a part of daily life? The following remarks were offered by my trainees, with the understanding that they need not identify themselves. Several did identify themselves, but none will be named here.

> "Corruption is as old as man. The only difference is the degree or intensity of involvement. In Nigeria it has been elevated to a state act."

> "Corruption has been perpetrated in various ways and forms: inflation of contracts, as patronage, in political appointments, over-invoicing of procurements and services, over subscription of welfare packages, elevation of a culture of graft and nepotism into normative patterns of official conduct, in the lopsided recruitment of a section of the country into the various arms of the military, localization of public institutions, tribalism, ethnicism, obvious neglect of some sections of the country in terms of development and appointments into the public and civil services, sharp and shady deals among others."

> "The fall from a high moral pedestal is disturbing to many Nigerians still with conscience who believe that there is still hope for the new renaissance and democratic Nigeria."

> "To fight corruption is invariably to offer good governance. Good governance is defined to include respect for the rule of law and human rights, enhanced accountability, both in the public sector management and public environment, transparency through information disclosure, public expenditure reviews, capacity in public policy expenditure reviews and capacity in public policy, analysis and dissemination. Other vital areas include a credible legal and regulatory system/ these are the vital building blocks for sustained economic growth."

> "There should also be reforms both in the public and civil service and there should be capacity building in all tiers of governance. Anti-corruption laws must be adequately enforced, the key 'watchdog' institutions made strong and sufficiently funded, and corrupt practices visibly punished."

> "To reduce corrupt practices, a fully adequate salary level, adequate pensions and a higher degree of accountability are a must for the civil service. The absence of these features creates a strong pressure for petty corruption at the lower level of the wage scale and grand corruption at the top."

> "The Judicial arm of the government needs to be adequately paid, well staffed and well qualified, otherwise, a weak and corruptible judiciary can not enforce contracts and property rights, and prosecute wrong doers."

"It is unfortunate to state that today, Nigeria is one of the most corrupt countries, if not the most corrupt, in the world. That does not give cause for pride. It has seeped and soaked [into] all facets of Nigerian life, and irrespective of the Anti-Corruption Act recently passed, it would be a hard fight to try to eradicate it. The reasons for this include:

          1) The tradition of being one's brother's keeper has made some Nigerians, once in a public office, accord undue advantages to one's brothers, kin, including ethnic members.

          2) Once in a public office, there are unjustifiable advantages one is expected to extend to one's family, friends and others close to the one appointed/elected.

          3) The primitive acquisition tendencies have not been expunged from the life of an average Nigerian, after all there is the saying 'you pass this way only once' that is common in Nigeria."

"As of today, most, if not all, of the political public office holders are products of the military entrenched corruption because the cost of getting into the political public office limited it only to those who could buy the offices. Consequently upon the above, these public office holders have to ensure the recovery of the money spent in getting into such offices. One has to recall the frequent saying of some of them, 'I did not get elected to now become poor'."

"Lack of the political will or moral justice to get the past perpetrators of corruption to account or atone for their deeds is perhaps the greatest obstacle to the eradication of corruption."

"Before independence in 1960 there was little corruption but there were elements of it. With the incursion of the military, corruption became insti tutionalized and reinforced. The military, not only corrupted itself, it also corrupted other segments of society, namely: civil service, the judiciary and the traditional people. The traditional structure had been an important element, which held our social values in tact. Having corrupted this segment of our society other segments fell apart. Corruption was also rooted in our social family structure. Family values were let loose as corruption crept into our schools and universities. Merit and standards were downgraded in favor of mediocrity."

"...to the human race and especially African communities, corruption is embedded in the natural life."

"Corruption to all intents and purposes is a global phenomenon and is a product of the absence of 'good governance' and is a feature of most countries of the world, especially Africa."

Clearly, these comments resist any simple summary or categorization. But what is striking is the importance of *both* traditional values *and* the key ideas of good, accountable government to these observers. It is also worth noting that even in the so-called "most corrupt country in the world" at the time, there was still optimism among some that corruption could be checked, and that democracy might flourish. At the very least it seems safe to say that there are opportunities for reform in Nigeria, but that such reforms must involve public participation and debate—Henderson's point, as noted above—and must integrate traditional social values of society with intended practices of good government within the modern state. What might such ideas look like? In the following section I take up one example that emerged from my discussions with the executive and legislative trainees.

Coping with Corruption

With those issues in mind, I asked my trainees, "Is it enough to simply institute laws and procedures that will stop corruption in the present and future but let bygones be bygones and forget about past corruption?" Those who commented were nearly unanimous in saying that allowing officials to hold on to their ill-gotten gains and to simply agree not to violate the law in the future was unacceptable. They believe that some way must be found to bring past perpetrators to account and to impose some type of punishment.

It was during these discussions that a proposal was considered that might meet two critical tests: first, it would be workable; second, it would likely be seen, and socially accepted, as a kind of rough justice. Borrowing from the concept of the recent South Africa Peace and Reconciliation Commission, it was proposed that a grace period of from three to six months be established during which time individuals could come forward and account for their ill-gotten gains. The accounting would need to be confirmed by a reputable accounting firm as a fair recording of the wealth derived from illicit activities. Once this confirmation was received, the individual (from the public or private sectors) or the business establishment would be expected to contribute a significant percentage of the wealth to the federal treasury. This percentage would need to be low enough to serve as an encouragement for people to come forward, but also high enough so that the average citizen would understand that a significant penalty was being exacted from the corrupt official. For sake of argument we might choose a figure between 30 and 40 percent. The remaining balance would then be declared to be part of the individual's own wealth holdings and free from any further government action. After the grace period had expired, any individual found to have engaged in corrupt acts going back for a reasonable, administratively manageable, period of time—say, ten years—would be subject to prosecution. Those convicted would forfeit one hundred percent of their ill-gotten wealth to the state, and would be given stiff jail terms.

Understandably this proposal would need to be subject to certain refinements, but it should emerge roughly in this form. Most of the trainees would settle for nothing less. They felt that to do anything less would dishonor the bulk of the Nigerians who had tried to live moral and upstanding lives only to have their country's reputation besmirched by the acts of a few selfish individuals who thought only of themselves.

IV. Conclusion

Nigeria's success or failure in its efforts to rid the country of the blatant corruption that earned for that country the title, "the most corrupt country in the world" will depend on a number of factors. Partly it will depend upon the country's ability to implement an effective strategy for economic growth. Raising national income will be essential to help reduce the country's abysmal level of poverty at the grassroots. Programs to empower the poor can be politically risky, and meaningful social safety nets are hard to maintain in a stagnating economy. To that end the developed countries of the world may choose to support a meaningful debt reduction program for the country with assurances that the freed-up foreign exchange can be directed into effective anti-poverty programs (see, for an extended discussion of such proposals, Arvind Jain's Chapter 7 of this volume).

But in the final analysis, it will be the country's own efforts to re-educate the public about the importance of ethical and honest government and business procedures, and to integrate reform policies with social values, that will make the difference. I have tried to convey above just how difficult such a re-educational program will be if it is to prove successful, but also to show that there are opportunities for creative approaches to succeed. It is safe to say that such efforts, if they are to succeed, will require a number of years. Donor nations, in a time of "aid fatigue" and tight budgets, are not known for their patience. Expecting this very difficult and entrenched problem to be solved in the near term will doom the effort to failure. For that reason Nigeria will have to demonstrate that it has earned the patience of the donors; and the evidence to date, while reassuring, remains limited. The jury is still out on Nigeria.

ENDNOTES

1. *Financial Times*, Oct. 19, 2000.
2. Henderson, Keith. 2000. "Draft Background Paper Prepared for the Organization of American States." October. Presented at a Brookings Institution Corruption Workshop, Washington, D.C.

Part II

Building a Reform Presence:
Leadership, Participation, and Incentives

5

The Big Picture: Building a Sustainable Reform Movement against Corruption in Africa

Sahr J. Kpundeh

Anti-corruption strategies are most effective when they are participative and inclusive of all stakeholders in society, including government, civil society, the private sector, non-governmental organizations (NGOs), and the media, among others. Such inclusiveness requires sustained cooperation among stakeholders—government, civil society, and NGO—-in order to ensure the sustainability of reforms. The international community also has a role to play in supporting committed reformers who are likely to generate challenges to their country's regimes. In this chapter, Sahr J. Kpundeh draws upon his extensive work with reform and civil society groups in Africa to examine the practical issues involved in minimizing corruption. He argues that reforms are more likely to succeed when major segments of society are involved from the beginning in the design and implementation of an anti-corruption strategy. Such an approach can create the necessary consensus for reform as well as a sense of participation in improving the quality of governance.

I. Introduction

Building a sustainable reform movement against corruption in Africa requires building coalitions among stakeholders (government, civil society actors, non-governmental organizations, the private sector, the media, and other key players in society) whose input is essential in the development and implementation of an action plan that is inclusive of the views of citizens in both urban and rural areas. In a majority of African countries, citizens have rarely held their governments accountable primarily because the fundamental mechanisms of accountability are either not available or are not functioning well. This has resulted in a general problem of not incorporating civil society's concerns and general involvement into sustained anti-corruption actions, which may in turn have impeded action against corruption.

Such problems result mainly in systems where there is a general lack of accountability, coupled with pervasive corruption. Using Schedler's two-dimensions of accountability—*answerability*, the obligation of public officials to explain what they are doing; and *enforcement*, the capacity of accounting agencies to impose sanctions on power builders who have violated their public duties—a case can be made that the lack of accountability as it relates to both answerability and enforcement has contributed to corruption in Africa.[1]

In quite a few African countries, the negative impact of corruption has been translated into political instability and frequent regime changes. The overthrow of governments in countries such as Sierra Leone, Mobutu's Zaire, Moussa Troare's Mali, and Samuel Doe's Liberia are a few examples of countries where high-level and systemic corruption have been highlighted as factors that contributed to the denunciation and overthrow of these governments. More recently, civil unrest in a number of African countries, such as Liberia under Charles Taylor and Robert Mugabe's Zimbabwe, has been associated with increasing levels of systemic corruption and the lack of effective leadership necessary to deal with this persistent problem. In short, Africans have continued to hold their states responsible for economic hardships in large part because of widespread abuse in official circles. Paradoxically, this abuse fostered democratization in several countries in the early 1990s by forcing civil society to take matters into its own hands and demand more transparent and accountable systems of government.[2] Furthermore, in many of these African countries, a real political process and legitimate links have yet to grow. Corruption is at the core of this dilemma.

Until recently, citizens and donors have rarely held African governments accountable. But the globalization of markets has dramatically highlighted developmental inequities in these countries. Citizens want economic reforms such as liberalization and privatization, but questions remain about whether these initiatives, including structural adjustment have made it easier to build accountability, or perhaps much more difficult because they have allegedly disregarded the role and potential of the state in more general terms. The focus on the economy has also renewed attention to more democratic forms of governance. Internal stakeholders and the international community are beginning to insist on transparency, creating a dilemma for those leaders who resist their countries' move to more inclusive and participatory governments. The demand for increased transparency, accountability, integrity, political and economic competition, and the involvement of civil society in the broader governance of the country have highlighted the importance of addressing corruption, which has contributed to impeding development in the continent.

This chapter asks why so little progress has been made in the fight against corruption in Africa. It focuses on the practical, yet critical, issue of participatory governance that has been absent in anti-corruption reform initiatives, and argues that reform strategies are more effective when they are participative and include all stakeholders. Coalition building (see also Chapter 9 of this volume) is essential to sustaining an anti-corruption strategy and these coalitions must be reflective of all the stakeholders at the national and local levels including government, civil society, NGOs, and community-based organizations (CBOs).[3] The first section will briefly examine the various anti-corruption strategies that have been adopted in African countries, to understand some of the specific issues holding back reform in the continent. I will argue that of four key strategies—national efforts; local or citizen level efforts; populist initiatives; and international efforts—local or citizen level initiatives against corruption have received the least effort and fewest resources. Additionally, this section will also discuss the significance of utilizing grassroots knowledge and experience in corruption. The second part of the chapter will analyze the role of political will in the fight against corruption. The argument here is that if political will is looked at as an outcome of coalitions rather than an input, the chances of sustaining reform movements become greater, especially so if the issue of incentives for coalition members are addressed.[4] The third part of the chapter will make the case for an inclusive strategy, giving examples of countries that have adopted such a strategy. The final section will discuss the role of the international community in terms of the kinds and level of support they can provide to countries.

II. Anti-Corruption Strategies in Africa

Numerous strategies have been adopted by African countries to address corruption. However, when one examines the "report card" of these strategies, it becomes apparent that there has not been much success in quite a number of them, and such assessments raise questions about whether expressed commitments have been genuine and whether they have focused on addressing priority areas. Some of these strategies have included *national campaigns* which focus on corruption inquiries, training, capacity building, and anti-corruption agencies; *local or citizen level campaigns*, which emphasize community oversight, investigative reports from the media, and private sector efforts, which include local chapters of Transparency International (TI); *populist initiatives* such as military coups, moral campaigns, and civil servant purges, and *international efforts* by the World Bank, IMF, TI, OECD, and other bi-lateral donors. Table 5.1 explains the categorizations in detail:

Table 5.1:
Types of Anti-Corruption Strategy:
General Characteristics

National Efforts	Corruption inquiries; training within state and public institutions; Islands of Integrity; legal approaches; Anti-corruption agencies; Auditor General and Parliamentary Oversight Committees; Police and Inter-Agency Cooperation; Capacity Building, Codes of Conduct for Public Officials, and Declaration of Assets.
Local or Citizen Level	Community Oversight, Media, coalitions with stakeholders, Ombudsman—complaints and redress; local chapters of TI promoting "pillars of integrity"; decentralization and deregulation; protection against arbitrary nature of the state; service delivery surveys on public services; business enterprise surveys on corruption.
Populist Initiatives	Military coup d'etats; moralization campaigns; civil servant purges; public humiliations and executions; quasi-official tribunals; property seizure, heavy fines, and imprisonment.
International Efforts	World Bank and IMF policies; OECD efforts to criminalize transnational bribery; TI interventions; bilateral donor efforts.

Source: Compiled by the author, drawing upon Riley, 1998.[5]

National efforts

National efforts to fight corruption have been fundamentally government-driven without much involvement from other stakeholders. Too often, only minimal attention has been paid to local or citizen-level initiatives to address the problem. The most common examples are national anti-corruption efforts led by institutions such as the Inspector General of Government in Uganda, the now disbanded Kenya Anti-Corruption Authority, the Prevention of Corruption Bureau in Tanzania, the Commission on Human Rights and Administrative Justice, and the Serious Frauds Office in Ghana, the Anti-Corruption Bureau in Malawi, to mention but a few. While their levels of authority vary from country to country, their general purpose has been to change the attitudes of public officials through awareness campaigns, investigating allegations of corruption, and prosecuting those who have violated the public's trust. These institutions have produced mixed results due to a combination of factors including their vulnerability to regime changes, lack of sufficient autonomy, lack of support from the political leadership, and more importantly, a lack of resources. In Uganda, for example, the Inspectorate of Government has uncovered corruption cases, demanded severe punishment, and constructed a new strategy that focuses on grassroots awareness. Despite these accomplishments, the Inspectorate continues to be constrained by insufficient funding; inadequate staff; and a shortage of vehicles, computers, photocopiers, and investigative equipment.[6]

Parliamentary oversight committees have had little, if any, impact. Only a few countries such as Uganda, Kenya, and Ghana have effectively utilized legislative committees. For example in Uganda, the Public Accounts Committee (PAC) has vigorously demanded proper accountability of government expenditures from ministries and government agencies. Many senior officials have been prosecuted and dismissed as a result of its efficient work. The PAC has exposed malfeasance in all areas of the Ugandan Government, forcing some government ministers out of office and censuring others. To ensure its continued success, some of its functions have been decentralized and are now handled by the District Accounts Committees.[7] This has strengthened the auditing function at all levels of government and society. In countries such as Sierra Leone, Nigeria, and Kenya under former President Daniel arap Moi, where this kind of institutional strategy has not contributed to the fight against corruption, it is arguably the institutional arrangements, and the dominance of the ruling party in Parliament, that are the obstacles. In Tanzania, for example, members of its public accounts committee are often rotated, prohibiting continuity in policies. In Moi's Kenya the ruling Kenya Africa National Union (KANU) used its majority in Parliament not only to ignore the annual recommendations of PAC but also, in 2002, to shelve the recommendations of a Parliamentary Select Committee on corruption that had called for the prosecution of senior government and party officials.

Codes of conduct for senior government officials and civil servants have been introduced in Tanzania, Uganda, Mali, Malawi, and recently in Kenya. Top government officials and high-level civil servants are required to adhere to a leadership code of conduct, which in most cases includes provisions for declaration of assets, income, and liabilities. While these procedures are productive and necessary, they are usually ineffective because they are not enforced. For example, less emphasis is placed on the monitoring of declarations, drastically reducing its utility to prevent illicit enrichment. Furthermore, the information declared is kept secret from the public. The lack of capacity and political will to verify declarations also has been a major factor in its ineffectiveness. Several countries influenced by organizations such as TI and other donors have adopted integrity pledges and "islands of integrity" commitments to introduce integrity in governance and in public administration.

National strategies can make inroads when they are supported by strong political will at all levels of government. However, the constraints identified above have led to a general cynicism from the populace about the level of sincerity to address the problem at the national level. In some countries, usually the "small fry" are prosecuted for wrongdoing while the "big fish" go untouched. Such behavior in Uganda, Sierra Leone, Ghana, Tanzania, Kenya, and Nigeria may have led citizens to assume the pattern to be the rule rather than the exception. One of the greatest dangers to the preservation and development of a society is the loss of trust and faith not only in government, but also in its institutions. Selective law enforcement, focusing mainly on small fry and opposition members has undermined public outreach and awareness raising campaigns that preach about the evils of corruption. People recognize that the benefits of corruption outweigh the costs, and consequently find the awareness messages inconsistent with reality. It is difficult to sustain a reform program without a credible messenger and strong political will, especially from critical areas such as enforcement.

Local or citizen efforts

The influence of TI has raised the stakes in the political economy of addressing corruption. Several countries including Ghana, Uganda, Tanzania, Nigeria, Zambia, Kenya, and Zimbabwe have established local chapters that continue to push for reform. Between 1996 and 1999, TI in partnership with the World Bank Institute (WBI), organized National Integrity Workshops in Tanzania, Malawi, Uganda, and other countries in an attempt to raise awareness about the costs of corruption. Additionally, this collaboration conducted investigative journalist training aimed at improving journalists' skills and confidence, and cultivated a renewed commitment to the fight against corruption. More recently, with the assistance of the WBI's Core Course Program on Anti-Corruption, several countries have formed coalitions. For example, the Ghana Anti-Corruption Coalition was organized by a variety of stakeholders, including representatives from government, to implement a national strategy. In Tanzania, civil society, media, and private sector representatives formed the Tanzania Civic Monitor (TACIMO) to monitor the implementation of the National Anti-Corruption Action Plan.

Establishing civil society organizations to perform the function of community oversight is encouraging. It is a homegrown strategy, which demonstrates ownership and improves chances for sustainability. A strong civil society is essential for the kind of structured political competition that can remedy problems inherent in systems where there is a lack of civil liberties, political freedoms, and incentives. More importantly, it can reinforce the political will needed for reform.[8] However, civil society in African countries traditionally has been weak and divided, and consequently, its contributions to improving governance sporadic. In the early 1990s, the pro-democracy movements in Africa drew large numbers of people into political debate and organization. The leaders of Benin's public employees union, for example, opposed privatization and criticized structural adjustment measures. They contended these measures placed the burden of reform on the lower grades of civil service rather than the "plunderers and corrupt ones" who initiated the program.[9] In Cote d'Ivoire, the *Syndicat National de*

Recherché et d'Enseignement Superieur, the teachers union, demanded that "the immense fortunes illicitly acquired and stashed abroad should be brought back, and that personalities who obtained huge loans through state guarantees should be summoned to repay them".[10] Several African countries have not been able to build on the momentum of the pro-democracy movements due to repressive laws that squash the media and organized citizen protests; or governments do not encourage *genuine* political competition and/or citizen participation.

More important, civil society organizations have been ineffective because few have the support of government in their efforts. In addition, civil society organizations are plagued with resource scarcity and capacity weaknesses. Institutions such as Ombudsmen in Malawi, the Commission on Human Rights and Administrative Justice (CHRAJ) in Ghana, Public Complaints Commission in Nigeria, and other organizations that address complaints from citizens and/or protect them against the arbitrary nature of the state, have been in constant conflict with government officials. Although many are constitutionally established institutions, most governments view them as adversaries and attempt to stifle their progress through intimidation of their officials and control of their budgets. In Ghana, for example, former President Rawlings was very condescending towards the Director of CHRAJ, which did not help the morale of the organization. Although the existence of the Commission is guaranteed in the constitution, it becomes difficult for the organization to be effective when the government considers it as an adversary. Additionally, budgetary constraints due to Government reductions in support led to a higher level of dependence on the support from both bi-lateral and multilateral donors. Some of these organizations have also taken on the role of civic monitor by conducting service delivery surveys designed by local experts to help public managers and policy makers determine the effectiveness of government services and its delivery system.

These surveys have been useful in countries such as Uganda, Tanzania, Ghana, and Zimbabwe, allowing consumers an opportunity to conveying strong messages to service providers. The results have been used as a mandate to design specific strategies to improve service delivery, give reform a solid base of legitimacy in society, as well as provide real political incentives to public officials to support these reforms. However, despite the contributions some of these efforts have made, they continue to receive the least backing from bilateral and multilateral financial institutions, contributing to their lack of effectiveness.

The ineffectiveness of local or citizen efforts can be explained primarily as a function of the ruling elites' capture of state and governmental institutions. This capture has intensified systemic corruption because political leaders and/or other powerful forces are not constrained by the society's institutions. National resources are monopolized, patronage and political cronyism are rampant, and the government dominates all facets of the economy. Such domination creates a climate for systematic exploitation of illegal income and rent-seeking opportunities by public officials. Recent empirical evidence suggests that corruption thrives where the state is unable to protect property and contractual rights, or to provide institutions that support the rule of law.[11] These governments repress citizens and NGOs and muzzle the press.

Reformist citizens in democracies may face disappointment, but those in Africa may face intimidation or worse. Anti-corruption agencies lack the independence to be effective; political competition is stifled and vocal opposition politicians are prevented from making valuable contributions to the governance of the country. Such actions undermine political development and stability as well as threaten the democratic experiment, and consequently national development. Long-term strategies for national development and improved governance in these countries are difficult because the citizens who are critical to "owning" the long term strategies have distanced themselves from contributing to government-led reform programs due to intimidation and cynicism. Citizens need to see more credible anti-corruption action which is inclusive of their views as well as effectively demonstrating government's commitment to promote notions of vertical and horizontal accountability.

Populist initiatives

Populist initiatives such as civil servant purges, arrests, detention, and public humiliations of senior government officials are more prevalent following military coups and civil unrest. In some countries, corrupt officials have received very harsh punishments including executions in Ghana under Rawlings in 1979 and in Liberia under Samuel Doe in 1980. Some military regimes have confiscated the property of public officials as in Sierra Leone after the military coup in 1992. It is characteristic of military governments to institute commissions of inquiry to investigate deposed government officials for embezzling and mismanaging government funds. After the military coup in Sierra Leone in 1992, the government of Valentine Strasser immediately established three commissions of inquiry. These inquiries were charged with the investigation of former senior government officials in the Momoh and Stevens regimes, and all public officials, members of the board and employees of parastatals, the armed forces, and the police force.[12]

In the Sierra Leone case, and in others such as Gambia, Ghana, Liberia, etc., quick-fix measures, anti-corruption purges, and moralization campaigns instituted by military regimes to deal with corruption have not been successful primarily because these campaigns do little to mobilize civil society or the sort of lasting, legitimate political process mentioned at the outset. In other words, each round of coups weakens the fragile civil society, which in most cases is the military's prime target after the politicians they have overthrown. Olowu[13] argues that "the existence of political will to genuinely tackle corruption must not be assumed on the basis of policy pronouncements by political leaders. Those most vocal often turn out to be the ones who aid and abet corruption most". Military regimes in most African countries have got away with this sort of charade because they are not really accountable to anyone. This observation proved true in Sierra Leone. Despite the military's stated mission to eradicate mismanagement and institutionalized malfeasance, the administration was plagued with accusations of corruption. Its own members ignored its policies aimed at infusing morality and discipline. Senior military personnel including Head of State Strasser lived luxurious lives, probably better than those of the politicians they kicked out of office. The public's trust dissipates when people witness widespread abuse, disrespect for human rights, and a blatant lack of transparency and accountability.[14]

In general, populist initiatives have not been successful in Africa. They have mainly focused on quick-fix measures and meting out punishment to deposed government officials. The record of failure is exceedingly high for measures that use the blunt instrument of prosecution (or the fear of it) as their principal tool of compliance. Corruption and other crimes are based upon motive, opportunity and means, and how these elements are built into the relationship between private citizens and government agents. A general lack of understanding and appreciation of the institutionalization of corruption by military governments have largely been responsible for their focus on individuals. For military officials, it seems corruption is viewed as a problem of individuals with excessive ambition and greed. But if this were the case, then a quick-fix strategy of throwing out the "rotten apples" ought to work. However, when this action has been taken, for example in Ghana, Sierra Leone, Gambia, and Nigeria, corruption has persisted and sometimes flourished. Exposure, humiliation, prosecution, and/or disciplinary action against corrupt officials, removes the offender, but fail to eliminate the offense.[15] Corruption has continued unabated in these countries. Institutional weaknesses have not been addressed and the culture has remained unchanged. Consequently, the circumstances that produced the corruption still subsist in most cases, recur, and are now entrenched in the system.

International efforts

Efforts at the international level highlight the seriousness of addressing malfeasance as integral on the new development agenda to reduce poverty. This new agenda involves helping developing and transitioning countries to enable market economies, and liberal democratic political systems to grow. Additionally, it emphasizes the interests of the poor and marginalized within the context of higher ethical standards in donor programs and the state.[16] Based on this agenda, international organizations such as the World Bank, the International Monetary Fund, the UNDP, OECD, and bilateral donors have developed new policies. Through technical and other forms of assistance, multi- and bilateral donors are helping African governments in the implementation of reform measures that reduce opportunities for corruption, build capacity, reform the public sector, and strengthen institutions that may contribute to improving the quality of governance.

Recent regional initiatives have promoted good governance. For example, the African Governance Forum, a deliberative process that includes sub-Saharan African countries and their external partners, is an opportunity for regular dialogue and interaction on good governance. The Forum held its first meeting in July 1997 in Ethiopia, focusing on governance, and its second in Ghana, June 1998, focusing on accountability and transparency. The Africa Development Bank (AFDB) has adopted governance and corruption as performance factors in credit worthiness when considering loans to regional member countries. Under the auspices of the Global Coalition for Africa (GCA) ministers and senior officials from Benin, Botswana, Ethiopia, Ghana, Malawi, Mali, Mozambique, Senegal, South Africa, Tanzania, and Uganda have adopted a set of twenty-five anti-corruption principles demonstrating a concerted and collaborative effort to combat corrupt practices.

However, international and regional initiatives to address corruption will meet with little success unless they are coordinated with effective action against domestic issues.[17] Switzerland, for example has made some strides in helping to discourage the laundering of ill gotten and embezzled funds by agreeing to freeze and return stolen wealth deposited in its banks. For example, in 2000, at the request of Nigeria's Obasanjo Government, about $650 million was frozen in 140 accounts throughout Switzerland. The Clinton Administration and some European governments also pledged support.[18] In April 1997, Swiss authorities agreed to return US$2.2 million to Mali as repatriated funds of the former President Troare. They were responding to claims by the successor government that embezzled funds had been illegally deposited in Swiss Banks. In May 1997, Switzerland also agreed to freeze assets of former Zairean President Mobutu, which were found in the country. Authorities subsequently announced that they had been able to identify US$3.4 million in bank accounts belonging to Mr. Mobutu and his relatives.[19]

This concerted international effort to deal with corruption is a far cry from the Cold War days when despots like Mobutu often had Western backing. Because kleptocrats like Mobutu resisted Communism, the developed world condoned their schemes to get rich fast by plundering national treasuries and shipping the money to banks in the United States and Europe. The battle against corruption is now becoming a priority for Western powers trying to bring stability and prosperity to global markets. In the United States, for example, at least three legislative initiatives were proposed to make the handling of corrupt money a crime. The Treasury Department also announced a proposal to give the government more power to battle money laundering of all types.[20] Recent international agreements on money-laundering may be the most important developments of all in this area.

III. The Significance of Political Will in Fighting Corruption

Reform efforts are often unsuccessful due to a combination of inadequate strategies, political resistance, poor participative approach, failure to develop sustainable efforts, and the inability to construct appropriate tools to establish systemic change. Political will is another particularly critical component for sustainable and effective anti-corruption strategies and programs. Without it, governmental efforts designed to improve civil service, strengthen transparency and accountability, and reinvent the relationship between government and private industry may prove to be ineffective.[21] However, neither its presence nor absence can be presumed in any single initiative. Instead, political will is evident by the level of participation that is built into reform initiatives, incorporating a range of political actors and civil society. In other words, unwavering determination to fight corruption is not only a problem for leaders and bureaucratic reformers. The private sector, too, may lack the will to overcome corrupt systems. Citizens face the problems of mobilizing for collective action and turning their convictions into changes in public administration.

The growing pressures to address issues of corruption from both domestic and international stakeholders have also shown strong commitment from top leadership, both in the opposition and civil society organizations. Opposition figures have made corruption a major issue while those in government have formed new anti-corruption agencies as a response. The desire to change the culture of corruption can reside in many locations. Numerous examples illustrate reform efforts that have arisen from each branch of government, the political opposition, civil society, international organizations, and private sector institutions. Each group has different motives and goals, and consequently defines success differently. But political will neither originates nor manifests in a vacuum. Rather, it is the reflection of complex circumstances that incorporate the aspirations of individual leaders, a calculation of the benefits that can be derived from changes in rules and behaviors, and a belief in the ability to muster adequate support to overcome resistance to reforms.

While these measures are platforms for change, they often do not incorporate comprehensive strategies for remaining sustainable. In many cases, anti-corruption campaigns are political, rather than ideological, in motivation, scope, and objectives.[22] As such they are political instruments employed to delegitimate the previous regime, purge the opposition, or legitimize the current regime by temporarily decreasing corruption. Alternatively, they may be a tactical response to challenges from a counter-elite, popular discontent arising from socioeconomic conditions, or adverse publicity or investigations. Even when the anti-corruption campaigns are not just political instruments, the strategies may be too broad-based to have any impact or may create disequilibria, by overfortifying the powers of the head of state or, instead, undermining his effectiveness.[23]

Johnston describes political will as that point "where the analytical and practical aspects of the corruption issue meet, recognizing that active political processes and strong leadership are necessary parts of any effective response to malfeasance".[24] But what has been lacking in several African countries is the demonstration of a credible intent by political leaders to attack the perceived cause or effects of corruption at a systemic level—translating policy pronouncements into sustainable action. Additionally, disregard for the input of the citizens at the grassroots has also led to problems in creating and sustaining political will. Perhaps through periodic surveys of citizens in the rural areas, by incorporating their views in the reform process, and providing incentives such as access to health care, electricity, water, good local schools, and other basic necessities, African governments can persuade citizens at the grassroots to join the reform process.

In several countries, the leadership has taken steps to demonstrate a commitment to reform by either disclosing their assets and/or seeking aid and technical assistance from international and bilateral donors. In Tanzania, for example, President Benjamin Mkapa disclosed his assets and those of his wife after he assumed presidency in 1995. In 2003 the Administration of Kenya's President Mwai Kibaki made asset declaration a legal requirement for all public employees, members of Parliament and the President himself. In Ghana, Benin, Sierra Leone, Nigeria, Malawi and a few others, the various Heads of State have requested assistance directly from the World Bank to help with addressing corruption. With the assistance of the WBI, diagnostic surveys are either underway or have been completed as first steps to understanding the causes and consequences of corruption and poor service delivery in these countries, prior to developing a reform strategy. The critical question then is, what are the political and institutional requirements needed for a serious assault against corruption in Africa?

Remedies should be country specific, based on sound analytical work that delineates the vulnerable areas and the reasons for lack of progress. "One size fits all" kinds of suggestions are ineffectual. Initial political and institutional requirements can be divided into governmental actions and civil society programs. The former is a variety of legal, administrative and organizational responses executed by a system of incentives; the latter engage the forces and interests of society in anti-corruption efforts, providing sustainable support. Neither strategy is likely to be sufficient alone. Both government and civil society programs work best in partnership, where public opinion and social interests support reform, and anti-corruption efforts in civil society enjoy the protection and encouragement that only government can provide.[25]

Government actions fall into four broad areas: legal reforms, public administration and regulation, financial management and control, and intra-governmental accountability and oversight. All countries have laws against fraud and corruption, and rather than create more laws, it is important to review and, if necessary, strengthen existing legislation. Modernizing the penal code to increase the costs of corruption include criminalizing bribery and strengthening laws against illicit enrichment, protecting whistle-blowers, financial disclosure, freedom of legislation, watchdog agencies, supreme audit institutions, financial management systems, etc. Aggressive enforcement of existing laws in African countries remains one of the missing links in supporting reform.

As discussed in the previous section, some countries have chosen to create special agencies that have the primary responsibility for change. For example, the Inspector General of Government in Uganda, the Kenya Anti-Corruption

Authority (now Kenya Anti-Corruption Commission), the Prevention of Corruption Bureau in Tanzania, the Commission on Human Rights and Administrative Justice, and the Serious Frauds Office in Ghana, the Anti-Corruption Bureau in Malawi, the Directorate for Control of Economic Crimes in Botswana, the Anti-Corruption Bureau in Zambia were all created to lead their countries' reform efforts. Most of these bodies have been modeled on the successful operations of the Independent Commission Against Corruption (ICAC) in Hong Kong. Unfortunately, the Hong Kong model cannot easily be transferred to African countries because it is an expensive operation.[26] Aside from its abundant resources and highly qualified staff, neither of which is always available in African countries, the ICAC operates within a relatively well-regulated administrative culture, alongside a well-equipped police force, and within a supportive political and legal framework.[27]

Civil society programs raise awareness, increase citizen participation, civic monitoring, and political competition. Political competition—how people win and lose power, has been an issue that has received less attention. The absence of genuine political competition in elections—winner take all politics and the notion of a zero-sum game still continues to be a common feature in a majority of African elections. Until recently, violence and intimidation usually overshadowed elections and consequently, few competent citizens participated. Campaign finance abuse is also becoming a critical element. Because the cost of running for office is high, aspiring politicians obtain funds from the private sector and other backers with promises of huge contract awards and senior-level political appointments. Where there is no effective monitoring of political contributions and/or contribution limits, financing elections has become a way of supporting dictators or incumbents with the hope of reaping the illegal benefits of elected office. Proposals for reform include limitations and regulations on donations, and full and immediate disclosure of contributors.

A serious assault against corruption becomes difficult in an environment where there is an absence of political will. Additionally, the fight against corruption has to be part of broader reforms affecting the civil service, financial management, supreme audit institutions, watchdog and oversight mechanisms, judicial and legal institutions, and the climate of incentives affecting citizen and official conduct. This is not to imply that without political will, the reform process is doomed. But political will can be nurtured by involving a variety of stakeholders in the reform process—building a constituency that recognizes the value of reform and dedicates itself to monitoring and defending a reform strategy. Such a constituency—its interests not always aligned with those of the leadership—can check on political actors' abuse of power.

IV. The Need for an Inclusive Strategy

The thesis that anti-corruption approaches are most effective when they are participative and inclusive of all stakeholders has found support in the preceding discussions. Such inclusiveness requires the building of coalitions among stakeholders—government, civil society, NGOs, etc., to ensure that reforms are sustainable. Coalition building in Africa has not been a common practice. What we have witnessed in several African countries is separate reform efforts—government driving their anti-corruption reform agenda with no involvement from civil society and civil society accusing government of a general lack of commitment. This relationship has been adversarial and has driven a wedge between the various stakeholders, consequently resulting in a lack of a cohesive strategy.

A participative approach to confront issues of accountability, especially at the community level, has been a historical tenet in African societies. In Botswana, for example, John Holm[28] argues that democratic accountability draws upon long traditions of openness in the rural society. He highlights the *"Freedom Squares"*, the *"Kgotla"*, and the role of traditional authorities in institutionalizing accountability in the country. Politicians first established Freedom Squares during the first national elections in 1965. They needed a local venue to engage in dialogue with a population that was almost totally illiterate and had few radios. Community members of all political beliefs were allowed to question the rally's speakers. In most rural areas, freedom squares are the primary means the citizenry uses to obtain information about party politics. The *Kgotla* meetings are the traditional gatherings chiefs have used for centuries to correspond with local communities. This remains an important part of the democratic accountability process in rural areas as government ministers visit *Kgotla* meetings to seek community approval for local development projects.

According to Holm[29] these visits were not only integral to standard bureaucratic needs-assessment activities, but also were opportunities for senior officials to convince politicians and foreign donors that the government was accountable to the people when policies were implemented at the grassroots level. In other words, the need to obtain *Kgotla* approval has become a mandatory part of the initiation of projects in the rural areas. More important, civil servants develop program, knowing they must be prepared to defend their proposals at the community level and not just order their implementation. *Traditional Authorities* have also played a role in ensuring that issues affecting their local communities are on the local agenda. For example, chiefs and headmen have defended their districts or communities against actions proposed by government ministries. Community involvement has ensured that the people participate in the governance of their local areas and, in some cases, local resources have been utilized to accomplish their goals.

A participatory approach to governance—where locals are involved in designing and implementing programs—means that the people participate in establishing priorities and in rewarding or penalizing leaders who do or do not follow through. In some African countries, the government has ignored the voice of the rural areas. However, the desire to improve governance has introduced new actors seeking to defend and further their interests in the policy process. Politicians who have practiced the policy of exclusion by monopolizing the benefits of state resources find it more difficult now to appropriate the benefits of governance for their own private interests. Decentralizing powers can be tricky, particularly if there is no real delegation of authority including authority to generate and reserve a portion of local revenues. The African Development Foundation (ADF) and the World Bank are currently supporting participatory development projects that give group members both control over the design and implementation of projects and the resources needed to implement them. This simply means that individuals participate in the decision-making process, including identification of the problem, project design, implementation, distribution of benefits, and evaluation of impact.

Two examples of projects supported separately by the World Bank[30] and the ADF[31] are examples of ways to promote inclusive and participatory governance. First, in Tanzania, with support from the ADF, the Songambele Fishing Society—a forgotten population of twelve thousand people in the island of Tumbatu, near the larger island of Zanzibar, off the coast of Tanzania—sets its own priorities and strategy. Twenty-nine individuals organized the Songambele Fishing Society in 1988. With contributions from members engaged in lime-making and petty trading, they managed to acquire one fishing boat. Eventually, they were able to buy another boat from their earnings although they still had to rent expensive nets from other more prosperous fishermen. Despite these efforts, many of Songambele's members could not fully engage in fishing nor earn enough money to meet basic survival needs. The society's attempt to obtain a bank loan failed. However, support from the ADF, which included funds for building three new boats and a work shed, purchasing four outboard engines and fishing gear, and technical and management training, enabled the Songambele to compile an impressive record of accomplishments. They constructed new boats and started open sea fishing operations; increased members' income from $10 per month to $45 per month; increased daily, marketable fish supply by 200 percent per boat; fully employed all twenty-nine members; employed eight community members part-time as net makers, boat repairers and watchmen; completed 85 percent of the work shed construction; and realized a gross profit of $1,000 every two weeks from the four boats.

Second, building on previous WBI work in selected countries a "pilot" core course on curbing corruption was launched in June 1999. A diverse group of stakeholders from seven countries—Benin, Ethiopia, Ghana, Kenya, Malawi, Tanzania, and Uganda—presented a program of action at the 9th International Anti-Corruption Conference in Durban, South Africa. The course was based upon a participatory approach that produces an integrated action oriented framework. The process empowers the participant country teams as they lead in the preparation of their own rigorous action programs, explicitly stating and requesting from WBI and the Africa Region staff at each stage their highest priorities for technical advice or assistance. Participants, selected from their countries to represent key governmental, private sector, and civil society organizations dedicated to anti-corruption, work together through the process of action program design, then discuss and review the challenges of integrating the participatory process with concrete institutional reforms. The ultimate objective of this process is to conduct anti-corruption institutional reforms formulated and "owned" by the participant country teams.

The program has demonstrated that an inclusive and participatory approach backed by empirical knowledge and rigorous analysis is critical to success. As a result of this initiative participants in the various teams have become catalysts in their home countries. They are working to build coalitions among various stakeholders (e.g. the Ghana Anti-Corruption Coalition was formed after the Durban workshop; TACIMO has been formed in Tanzania to monitor the implementation of the National Anti-Corruption Action Plan), and are now taking concrete steps to address the problem of corruption. The major output of the course was a series of national anti-corruption strategies[32] developed by the teams; the outcome was a national action plan supported by a broad coalition including, in many instances, the Head of State, Parliamentarians, key members of the Executive, civil society leaders, journalists and business people.

These two examples demonstrate that a participative approach helps generate local "ownership" of reforms, put people in the driver's seat, and harness their capabilities. The strategies for countries should be home grown, not donor-driven. Even when they are locally developed, they should not be central government-driven lest local communities become dependent upon the center. When the people own reform programs, it goes a long way in preventing social exclusion and the capture of programs by politicians and urban elites. However, the international community still has a role to play in the fight against corruption. In the next section, several suggestions will be made on the role of the international community.

V. The Role of the International Community

This section builds on the argument that sustainable reform in Africa must be integral to the domestic agenda and not driven by international donors. Kenya and Sierra Leone, where the constituency for reform is weak, illustrate the obvious danger of dealing with the perennial problem of whether the reform efforts are genuine or simply attempts to appease donors.

Corruption is an intricately woven set of circumstances that occur as a result of the actions of domestic as well as international actors within the political, economic and social sectors of a country. Consequently, collaboration and coordination among the members of the international development community are crucial to an effective campaign to reduce corruption. A solid commitment from the government, the private sector and civil society along with institutional changes are required to develop and enact concrete solutions—solutions that include both preventive and punitive measures that address accountability, transparency and system inequities, both politically and economically.

International donors have taken several steps to address corruption both within their own organizations and in their policies for granting loans and grants to developing countries. Multilateral institutions such as the World Bank, IMF, and UNDP, and several bilateral donors have all instituted new policies to either prevent corruption in their projects and/or support international efforts such as the OECD convention that seeks the criminalization of bribery in international business transactions. However, international efforts, especially from multi and bilateral donors have to support and compliment domestic strategies. If a particular country does not make public sector reform a part of its governance policy process, international remedies will be ineffective. Sanctions can be imposed, as in 1997 when the World Bank and IMF withheld multi-million-dollar assistance to Kenya and suspended a number of investments.[33] Similar action was taken against Tanzania in 1994, when the donor community suspended aid and conditioned future assistance on the government's commitment to recover evaded and exempted taxes and to initiate legal action against corrupt officials.[34]

Donors can continue to support the domestic agenda in countries genuinely struggling with reform. First, they may want to consider putting additional pressure on countries with invasive persistent fraud and mismanagement. Countries requesting help may be required to demonstrate their commitment in their country budgets by increasing the support allocated to anti-corruption efforts. Perhaps the idea of matching funds from donors should be considered—donors promise to match whatever the country has in their budget for anti-corruption measures.

Second, bilateral donors should ensure that political corruption is a priority in their policy agenda, especially since the mandate of multilaterals such as the World Bank limits this activity. Political corruption is a fundamental problem that needs to be addressed—campaign financing; checks and balances; civil liberties, and structured competition in both political and economic realms are all factors that are important in the fight against corruption. For example, political competition can place a check upon arbitrary political interference in the bureaucracy, encouraging genuine oversight in its place and can maintain healthy opposition to political attempts to compromise judiciary and regulatory agencies.

Third, donors may want to encourage collective action to deal with corruption and, more important, target additional support to programs that promote such action among various stakeholders in developing and implementing anti-corruption reforms. An inclusive and participatory approach involving government, civil society, private sector, media, and so forth to designing and implementing anti-corruption reforms helps to sustain the process. However, given the mutual suspicion that exists between governments, anti-corruption agencies and civil society, it is unclear whether government reformers genuinely attempt to involve civil society and the private sector in anti-corruption activities. Coalition building between civil society and the government continues to be one of the foci in future reform strategies, and support for this process is crucial to its sustainability as well as strengthening political will. The World Bank has recognized that civil society organizations play an especially critical role in helping to amplify the voices of the poorest people in the decisions that affect their lives, enhance the poverty impact of Bank-funded projects, and improve development effectiveness and sustainability. According to a 1999 survey of Bank assisted projects in seven countries, nearly $900 million was approved to support activities involving civil society organizations and community-based organizations between fiscal years 1985 and 1997.[35]

A fourth suggestion is for donors to encourage countries to adopt long-term strategies. "Quick wins" are important in the early stages of any anti-corruption program, but a long-term vision and strategy are equally important. The mission is to tie political security and/or insecurity of political leaders to the way power changes hands. For example, when leaders believe they are secure in office, they are more likely to view corruption as a long-term fight. Leaders whose positions are tentative may be more inclined to concentrate on immediate or short-term solutions as a way of staying in power. Adopting short-term approaches opens society to more abuse, which ultimately erodes the strength and legitimacy of the reigning regime. Donors should encourage and help borrower countries to design long-term strategies that can be prioritized into short, medium and long-term goals.

Another suggestion is for donors to consider providing more support to NGOs or CBOs that provide practical initiatives, especially at the municipal level. This support would be in addition to any they provide to NGOs presently working through policy instruments. For example, the USAID-funded Americas' Accountability and Anti-Corruption (AAA) Project coordinates the Donor Consultative Group (DCG) on Accountability and Anti-Corruption in Latin America and the Caribbean. The DCG is composed of six bilateral and twelve international donors and uses the bilingual (Spanish/English) newsletter *Accountability* as its communication vehicle. As the Tanzanian example demonstrated earlier, community-based programs have a higher rate of success and provide the "neglected" people in the rural areas the opportunity to participate in their governance. Additionally, supporting such projects provides an opportunity for citizens to articulate their needs, establish their priorities, and monitor service delivery effectively.

However, it is important to note that some of the groups in African societies are cynical about international assistance because they have not established built-in safeguards in their assistance that prevents the kind of abuse witnessed by dictators such as the late Sani Abacha in Nigeria and late Mobutu in Zaire. Despite the misrule and high-level corruption in some of these countries, international assistance continues to flow to them. What may be seen as credible action on the part of the donors is much more transparency in demanding accountability from countries. The actions by the IMF and World Bank in denying assistance to Kenya can be a good example for others, if it is replicated with the same standards in other countries. What breeds the cynicism so often seen regarding international assistance is the lack of application of similar standards to corrupt governments. The level of alleged corruption and misgovernment in

Ethiopia is at least equal that in Kenya, but the international donors continue to support the regime in Ethiopia with more donor funds.

Reform must to be seen to come from within, and donors must recognize this reality in their program design. They can do appraisals to satisfy their project demands, but rather than provide government options of what to do, they should demand or help the government come up with strategies, and then fund programs within those strategies. Fragmentation will be a non-issue if donors support programs within an overall strategy that they have worked with the government to develop. Uganda, for example, has moved towards this type of arrangement. The Government has approved an anti-corruption plan for the next few years, with an aim to improve coordination and implementation. The Ministry of Ethics and Integrity convenes an inter-agency forum on corruption and coordinates all activities. Several public institutions are involved including the judiciary, the Director of Public Prosecutions, the Inspectorate of Government, Parliament, and the Police. They meet regularly with donors and this has been useful in encouraging joint planning as well as improving the coordination among donor programs.

Finally, and most important, donors should provide support to nurture political will in countries where it is either weak or totally lacking. The presence of political will is important in any reform efforts, but its presence cannot always be assumed. Reformers face resistance from groups that benefit from corruption in any society, and coupled with their insecurity in office about how power changes hands, their political will to pursue reform is threatened. The risk involved in this pursuit is real and there are numerous examples of well-intended regimes that have engineered their own downfall through inept and or ineffective strategies. Johnston[36] reminds us that the will to fight corruption has as much in common with the will to pursue any other goal. It must be given space to grow from within a political system and eventually to ensure its effectiveness and sustainability, become an integral part of basic social and economic processes.

ENDNOTES

1. Schedler, Andreas. 1999. "Conceptualizing Accountability." In Andreas Schedler, Larry Diamond, and Marc F. Plattner (eds.). *The Self-Restraining State.* Boulder, CO: Lynne Rienner, pp. 13-28.

2. Kpundeh, Sahr (ed.). 1992. *Democratization in Africa: African Views, African Voices.* Washington, D.C.: National Academy Press.

3. Johnston, Michael, and Sahr Kpundeh. 2002. "Building a Clean Machine: Anti-Corruption Coalitions and Sustainable Reforms." *WBI Working Paper* SN37208. Washington, DC: The World Bank.

4. *Ibid.*

5. Riley, Stephen. 1998. "The Political Economy of Anti-Corruption Strategies in Africa." In Robinson, Mark (ed.). *Corruption and Development.* London: Frank Cass.

6. Kpundeh, Sahr John. 2002. "The Institutional Framework for Corruption Control in Uganda."
In Heidenheimer, Arnold J., and Michael Johnston (eds.). *Political Corruption: Concepts and Contexts. Third Edition.* New Brunswick, NJ: Transaction Publishers, pp. 425-440.

7. *Ibid.*

8. Johnston, Michael. 1998. "Fighting Systemic Corruption: Social Foundations for Institutional Reform." In Robinson, Mark (ed.). *Corruption and Development.* London: Frank Cass; Kpundeh, Sahr. 1998. "Political Will in Fighting Corruption." In Kpundeh, Sahr, and Irene Hors (eds.). *Corruption and Integrity Improvement Initiatives in Developing Countries.* Paris: UNDP/OECD.

9. FBIS Daily Report. 1991. "Sub-Saharan Africa." (Nov.22). Washington, D.C.: FBIS, p.25.

10. Harsch, E. 1993. "Accumulators and Democrats: Challenging State Corruption in Africa." *Journal of Modern African Studies* 31:1, pp.31-48.

11. Hellman, Joel, G. Jones, and D. Kaufmann. 2000. "Seize the State, Seize the Day: An Empirical Analysis of State Capture and Corruption in Transition." Paper presented at the World Bank's 12th ABCDE 2000 Conference, April 2000. Online at http://papers.ssrn.com/sol3/papers.cfm?abstract_id=240555 (viewed 8 August 2004).

12. Kpundeh, Sahr. 1994. "Limiting Administrative Corruption in Sierra Leone." *Journal of Modern African Studies* 32:1, pp. 139-157.

13. Olowu, Dele. 1993. "Roots and Remedies of Governmental Corruption in Africa." *Corruption and Reform* 7:3.

14. Kpundeh, Sahr. 1999. "Controlling Corruption in Sierra Leone: An Assessment of Past Efforts and Suggestions for the Future." Hope, K.R., and B. Chikulo (eds.). 1999. *Corruption and Development in Africa: Lessons from Case Studies.* Basingstoke: Macmillan.

15. Kpundeh, Sahr. 1993. "Prospects in Contemporary Sierra Leone." *Corruption and Reform* 7:3.

16. Riley, Stephen. 1998. "The Political Economy of Anti-Corruption Strategies in Africa." In Robinson, Mark (ed.). *Corruption and Development.* London: Frank Cass.

17. Johnston, Michael. 1998. "Cross-Border Corruption: Points of Vulnerability and Challenges for Reform." In Kpundeh, Sahr, and Irene Hors (eds). *Corruption and Integrity Improvement Initiatives in Developing Countries* Paris: UNDP/OECD.

18. Masland, Tom and J. Bartholet. 2000. "The Lost Billions." *Newsweek,* March 13, pp.38-40.

19. E. Harsch, quoted in Hope, K.R., and B. Chikulo (eds.). 1999. *Corruption and Development in Africa: Lessons from Case Studies.* Basingstoke: Macmillan.

20. Masland, Tom and J. Bartholet. 2000. "The Lost Billions." *Newsweek,* March 13, pp.38-40.

21. Kpundeh, Sahr. 1998. "Political Will in Fighting Corruption." In Kpundeh, Sahr, and Irene Hors (eds.). *Corruption and Integrity Improvement Initiatives in Developing Countries.* Paris: UNDP/OECD.

22. Gillespie, K., and Gwen Okruhlik. 1991. "The Political Dimensions of Corruption Cleanups: A Framework for Analysis." *Comparative Politics* (October), pp.77-95; Riley, Stephen P. 1983. "The Land of Waving Palms: Political Economy, Corruption Inquiries and Politics in Sierra Leone." In M. Clarke, ed. *Corruption: Causes, Consequences, and Control.* London: Frances Pinter.

23. Gillespie, K., and Gwen Okruhlik. 1991. "The Political Dimensions of Corruption Cleanups: A Framework for Analysis." *Comparative Politics* (October), pp. 77-95.

24. Johnston, Michael. 1997. "Political Will and Corruption." Washington, D.C.: Paper prepared for the World Bank, PREM Division.

25. Kpundeh, Sahr, Michael Johnston, and Robert Leiken. 1998. "Combating Corruption in Developing and Transitional Countries: A Guidelines Paper for USAID." Silver Spring, MD: Development Alternatives, Inc.; Dininio, Phyllis, Sahr Kpundeh, and Robert Leiken. 1998. *USAID Handbook for Fighting Corruption.* Washington, D.C.: Center for Democracy and Governance, U.S. Agency for International Development, Technical Publication Series.

26. Doig, Alan. 1995. "Good Government and Sustainable Anti-Corruption Strategies: A Role for Independent Anti-Corruption Strategies?" *Public Administration and Development* 15:2, pp. 151-165.

27. Kpundeh, Sahr, Michael Johnston, and Robert Leiken. 1998. "Combating Corruption in Developing and Transitional Countries: A Guidelines Paper for USAID." Silver Spring, MD: Development Alternatives, Inc.

28. Holm, John D. 1998. "Curbing Corruption through Democratic Accountability: Lessons From Botswana." In Hope, K.R., and B. Chikulo (eds.). 1999. *Corruption and Development in Africa: Lessons from Case Studies.* Basingstoke: Macmillan.

29. *Ibid.*

30. The Africa Region of the World Bank has funded several Community-based projects. Analysis shows that 75 percent of African projects with some level of community participation have been rated satisfactory by the Operations Evaluation Department (OED) of the World Bank, against 60 percent for all African projects in 1994-1997.

31. For more details on the Songambele project and others supported by the African Development Foundation, refer to African Development Foundation. 1997. "Participatory Development: Report on ADF Funded Projects, Fiscal years 1994-1996." Washington, D.C.: African Development Foundation.

32. For details on the seven country programs:
http://www.worldbank.org/wbi/governance.

33. *Washington Post.* 1997. (August 12), p. A. 15.

34. *The Executive* (Dar Es Salaam). 1995 (August).

35. For more information on the "World Bank and Civil Society":
http://www.worldbank.org

36. Johnston, Michael, 1997. "Political Will and Corruption." Washington, D. C.: Paper prepared for the World Bank, PREM Division.

6

Language, Culture, and Reform in Hong Kong

Jenny C. Y. Chan

Hong Kong's Independent Commission Against Corruption (ICAC) is the world's best-known and, arguably, most successful anti-corruption agency. For nearly thirty years it has engaged in public education on corruption as an equal counterpart to its investigation and prevention functions. As a result it has transformed major elements of Hong Kong culture. Deep-rooted tolerance for, or resignation to, corruption has become strong public resistance, and reluctance to file reports of cases has given way to broad-based citizen participation. As Jenny C. Y. Chan makes clear in this chapter, none of this could have been accomplished without a detailed understanding of popular values and responses to corruption, both as aspects of history, language and culture, and as facts of daily life.

I. Introduction

To many residents of Hong Kong the name and symbols of the Independent Commission Against Corruption—ICAC—are synonymous with credibility: credibility of the anti-graft agency to properly handle corruption cases. To others they may represent fear—the fear of getting caught on the wrong side of the law. In the agency's early days, however, the meaning might have been "I Can Accept Cash", for the agency's credibility and respect had to be earned, both through aggressive enforcement activities and sustained efforts to link anti-corruption policies to social values and cultural traditions. The diverse and ambitious community education efforts undertaken by the agency helped change perceptions of corruption as a social problem and affected the culture itself, in-

teracting with the semantics and vocabulary of corruption as a personal experience. In this chapter I will illustrate, through a focus on linguistic issues, a
"quiet revolution" in Hong Kong's outlook on corrupt practices: one that replaced acceptance of corruption with a new refusal to tolerate it.

Background

Hong Kong, six times the size of Washington, DC and located in south-east
China, was ceded to Britain in 1842. It was a British Crown colony, ruled by an
appointed governor, until 1997. Its legal system is based on the British common
law system. Hong Kong became the Hong Kong Special Administrative Region
(SAR) of China on July 1, 1997, as a result of a British-Chinese agreement
signed in 1984. China promised that, under a "one country, two systems" for-
mula, China's socialist economic system will not be practiced in Hong Kong
and that Hong Kong will enjoy a high degree of autonomy in all matters except
foreign and defense affairs for fifty years. Policies and budgets are set by an
Executive Council made up of both appointed and elected locals. The law-
making Legislative Council is made up of elected locals, even though the British
did not introduce elections until the 1990s. Economically, Hong Kong has a free
market economy highly dependent on international trade, with a GDP per capita
in excess of $27,200 in 2002. The population is over sevem million, 94 percent
of whom are literate (defined as aged 15 and over and have attended school); 95
percent of the population are ethnic Chinese.[1]

As early as 1898, rampant corruption led to the enactment of the first anti-
bribery law, the Misdemeanors Punishment ordinance. In 1948, the Government
passed the Prevention of Corruption Ordinance, and in 1952, the Anti-
Corruption Branch was set up within the Criminal Investigation Department of
the Police Force. During this time, however, the Hong Kong police, customs
officers, and Inland Revenue officers were notorious for their corrupt practices.
Paying bribes for passing a driving test, for a successful public housing application, or for a restaurant license was generally accepted as a part of life.

In 1962 it was estimated that roughly one-third of the population (then
around 3.5 million) were refugees who had entered Hong Kong after the communist takeover in China in 1949.[2] The majority had no assets other than hope
and the determination to work in order to survive and to send remittances back
to China to keep their relatives from starvation. Non-English-speaking working-
class people—the greatest part of the population—suffered from corruption but
accepted bribery as a way of life. As Christopher Patten, the last Governor of
Hong Kong said: "To be fair, until the late 1970s ... people were too occupied
making their way in the world—earning a living, getting a roof over their head,
putting their children into school, finding the security that stormy times had so
far denied them."[3]

For those Hong Kong Chinese not in official positions, offering gifts to get
things effectively done through a connection (or *guanxi*) was a cultural ploy.
And many who were in power positions dispensed favors left and right, even

when unsolicited, so that they could build up a bank of obligations they could call upon later if needed.[4] Many found it acceptable, or even a daily ritual, to pay "tea money" or "convenience money" to government servants. That kind of connection was a way to get benefits that were otherwise difficult to obtain, partly because of the language barrier which added to the obfuscation of government procedures. Nonetheless, it is also a long-standing Chinese custom to pay "tea money" out of genuine kindness and an appreciation for hard work. In those days, "tea money" or "convenience money", as the names suggest, were just something one paid for what he/she got, while the concept of "bribes" or "illegal proceeds" in the common-law sense was quite alien. As a result, Civil service corruption was serious, and syndicated corruption in the police force, with its law-enforcement power and extensive contact with the public, was almost expected. Bribery, thus, became a second tax that working-class people, such as hawkers, cab drivers, had to pay to survive.

Economic growth between 1960 and 1970 doubled wages, on average, and cut the share of people living in acute poverty from over 50 percent to less than 16 percent.[5] In the early 1970s the economy took off; the port and the local stock exchange flourished, and banks multiplied. The children of the refugees who fled China in the 1950s and 1960s, given a chance at education through the labor of their parents, started to join the work force. The rise of this new generation, which altered the fabric of the society, could not be ignored: while ethnically Chinese, they were literate, and were raised and educated in the colony's Western-influenced social setting which marked them out from their reserved and conservative refugee parents.

Independent Commission Against Corruption

Sir Murray MacLehose, who became Governor of Hong Kong in 1971, launched significant reforms addressing a variety of major social issues: for example, Chinese was made an official language of the colony. Socially, corruption was one of the central concerns. In 1971 the outdated Prevention of Corruption Ordinance was replaced by the Prevention of Bribery Ordinance, which widened the investigative powers of the police. A Commission of Inquiry, led by Justice Alastair Blair-Kerr, was charged with a number of tasks, notably to probe the case of Peter Godber, a Chief Police Superintendent who had fled the colony while under investigation by the then Anti-Corruption Branch of the police. Godber's flight sparked a series of street demonstrations, especially by students and young people, demanding reform. The slogan "Fight Corruption, Catch Godber" (*fan tanwu; zhuo Gebo*) was heard and seen on all the streets of Hong Kong; public outcry against corruption had never been stronger in the colonial history of Hong Kong. Justice Blair-Kerr proposed an independent anti-corruption body manned by agents of absolute and unquestioned integrity. Against that social background, the Independent Commission Against Corruption Ordinance created the ICAC on February 15, 1974.[6]

From its inception the ICAC adopted a unique three-pronged attack on corruption. The Operations Department is the investigative arm of the Commission. The Corruption Prevention Department aims at eradicating corruption opportunities, while the Community Relations Department's duty is to educate the public against the evils of corruption and to foster public support. One long-term goal was to develop a new public consciousness and a clean and honest culture. It was recognized that prevention was as important as deterrence and prosecution, and that the battle against corruption could only be won by changing social attitudes, i.e. by winning the hearts and minds of the people. This strategy remains the ICAC's guiding principle today.

II. A New Culture for the Society

Human beings communicate what is meaningful to them within the context of their cultures. Whether or not the communication process succeeds depends, *inter alia*, on the effectiveness of the message, in both spoken and printed language, upon how it is delivered, and—critically—upon whether or not the receiver identifies with what the sender meant to send out and gives the desired kinds of feedback. The ICAC believes that treating the symptoms but not the disease will not systematically wipe out corruption. In other words, mere prosecution is not enough. Thus, the ICAC strategy has relied extensively on interactive communication, introducing to society across the board a new clean and honest culture in place of the old corruption-tolerant one.

"The era of awakening" (1974-1979)

ICAC posters for the "teething years" of 1974-1979 focused on disseminating the evils of corruption; urging the public to report corruption at ICAC regional offices all over Hong Kong, and advising residents not to engage in corrupt doings. ICAC posters during these years bore slogans such as "Walk Tall, Report Corruption, 5-266366" (the ICAC public "hotline" number); "Report Corruption, Write to P O Box 1000, All Information Will Be Treated In Strict Confidence"; "Report Corruption Right Away"; "Both Offering & Accepting Bribes Are Offences." These bilingual posters were comprehensible to residents to all walks of life.

Mobilizing the public to speak up was something novel in a predominantly Chinese society. Most Chinese had been ignorant of colonial government affairs, owing partly to the language barrier, and tried not to get involved. To the majority, face-to-face contacts with government officials such as ICAC Community Relations officers to discuss corruption complaints were novel in both the Chinese culture and in the colonial experience. The early ICAC posters appealed in particular to the low-income residents such as hawkers and taxi-drivers who were most vulnerable to abuses, urging them to change their own culture and to participate in keeping order in their own society by lodging complaints. The Chinese are accustomed to a Confucian-oriented social system, based on vertical relationships between people, government, a high degree of paternalism, and trust founded on mutual obligations and reciprocity. "Whistleblowers" historically have often been deemed betrayers, and have been seen as disrupting harmony in personal or hierarchical relationships; no body of law on earth could be relied upon to protect them. Accordingly, the Chinese, by culture, were reluctant to report wrongdoing to the authorities. In the late 1960s, for example, the imagery of "riding on a bus" was adopted to describe corruption inside the Hong Kong Police: "Some get on the bus, others run alongside it, yet very few stand in front of it." For these reasons, the Hong Kong people had tolerated corruption even though they suffered from it. Posters—many of them aimed at lower-income residents such as hawkers and taxi drivers, and featuring slogans such as "All Information Will Be Treated in Strict Confidence," by contrast raised possibilities of equality and human rights (within a colonial setting, to be sure).

Even the ICAC logo shown above, a Chinese seal (usually in red) bearing the agency's name in Chinese and its English acronym underneath, uses traditional themes to underline the government's strong commitment to fight corruption. A Chinese seal signifies that someone claims responsibility for his or her own work. In the Imperial Chinese courts, the ruler held the official seal of the Middle Kingdom (i.e. China); to the civilians in the old days, stamping of seals carried the effect of a signature. Even now both in Mainland China and Taiwan, government offices and officials use such seals or stamps to certify letters, records and documents. The four characters of the Chinese name for the agency appear in the "seal" script, evoking a feeling of dignity and power. Such a logo for a governmental department was novel in the colonial history of Hong Kong. And yet such design, symbolic of credibility and a powerful weapon, succeeds in appealing to the feelings and emotions of the majority population rooted in its own traditional culture.

Between 1974 and 1979, face-to-face contacts with ICAC officers, mass media messages, legal convictions of corrupt individuals irrespective of background (and of government servants in particular) gradually awakened the public to a law-abiding culture and a firm belief in the virtue of integrity and fair play in the community. Police Superintendent Godber was extradited from the United Kingdom, tried and sent to prison. The indictment of many "big tigers", the mass-media term for high-ranking government officials, showed that the government was serious and determined in addressing the corruption problem. The public responded with reports of its own. In its first year, the ICAC received

3,189 reports of alleged corruption, more than double the 1,457 reports received by the Police Anti-Corruption Office the previous year.

"Level playing field" (1980-1989)

During "The Era of Awakening", syndicated corruption in the civil service was virtually eradicated. The ICAC then focused on private sector corruption during the economic boom of the 1980s. The government did not want to practice a double standard—i.e., that corruption was sinful in the civil service but not in the private sector. Up until then, the small local Chinese firms, unlike international enterprises or foreign incorporations, still relied on payment of commissions and kickbacks to secure business in local markets and to compete for business. To help evolve the colony into an international market of free trade and finance, the ICAC had to persuade the local Chinese businessmen to break with such business traditions. "Level Playing Field" thus became the theme of ICAC publicity campaign in the 1980s. The main message for this period, with the local businessmen as the main target, was "Whichever Way You Look At It, Corruption Doesn't Pay." Other messages in the television commercials and posters included "There are many ways to get ahead. Corruption isn't one of them", "Keep Hong Kong Beautiful. Report Corruption", and "Ignorance is No Defence". Compared with the slogans of "The Era of Awakening", the messages for this period (1980-1989) was more subtle—partly because the audience was better educated and refined, and partly because the anti-graft agency had already secured a place in the hearts and minds of the public. The change in tone and manner of the ICAC mass media messages reflected changes in the formerly corruption-tolerant culture of the people.

A shift in corruption reports concerning the private sector in the 1980s suggests that the ICAC was persuasive in breaking with the traditional Chinese business culture of commissions and kickbacks. In 1985, corruption reports involving the police accounted for 28 percent, other government departments and bodies 32 percent, while the private sector alone came to 40 percent. By 1991, private sector corruption reports accounted for 57 percent of all recorded corruption, an all-time high since the ICAC's inception. One of the high-profile cases handled in this period involved the indictment of Ronald Li, former chairman of the Hong Kong Stock Exchange, and other Stock Exchange officials for taking bribes. Li was found guilty and sentenced to four years' imprisonment in 1990. When the case was over, the Hong Kong Stock Exchange ceased to be a private club for a handful of Chinese brokers, and became more "transparent" in administration.

Between 1983 and 1988, the ICAC received some eighty corruption allegations against the legal profession. In the Stock Exchange case, three of the nine indicted were lawyers. In those years, two partners of Deacons, the territory's second largest solicitors' firm, were indicted for fraud. In 1988, a lawyer of Simmons and Simmons was found to have stolen $1 million from his clients' accounts. A commissioned clerk system, though outlawed in 1986, was still common in Hong Kong law firms. The clerks, acting as touts or go-betweens for lawyers and offenders in need of counsel, often solicited kickbacks from the legal fees. Such practices had become so pervasive that some law firms were rumored to be run by clerks who were responsible for picking lawyers for their clients and setting their legal fees. To address corruption in the legal field, the ICAC set up an exclusive hotline for public reports. During this period, the ICAC also successfully handled a number of bank and financial institution frauds where the majority of the victims were of the grassroots class. The collapse of the Overseas Trust Bank, Ka Wah Bank, and Carrian Investment Ltd. were found to be caused by corruption-related frauds which lost much of the life-long savings of the working class and general shareholders.

In 1986, Yuen-long Yang, a full voting member of the Royal Hong Kong Jockey Club and a local textile tycoon who had businesses in nine countries with an annual turnover of around $52 million, was arrested and indicted by the ICAC for conspiracy to cheat at horse-racing gambling. Yang maintained punting relationships with some jockeys and was a ringleader of a race-rigging syndicate. The syndicate, by manipulating race results, caused tens of thousands of ordinary bettors to lose their hard-earned wages. In the same race-rigging scandal, two businessmen and three jockeys were also indicted for conspiring to cheat at gambling. As a result of the ICAC investigation, both expatriate and local jockeys were heavily disciplined.

By working hard on such private sector corruption cases and emphasizing their impact upon the grassroots class, the ICAC was, indeed, hammering home its message of this "Level Playing Field" period. The public at large had come to believe that ICAC anti-corruption messages meant what they said, and were not mere propaganda. Not only were the businessmen, in particular those who practiced the Chinese business tradition, persuaded that a "Level Playing Field" was proper, lawful and beneficial, the grassroots class was convinced that the same anti-corruption laws applied to all strata of the society. Public complaints, which account for 13 percent of ICAC cases in 1974, rose to 37 percent of the caseload in 1984. The "quiet revolution" in Hong Kong society was gaining momentum.

"The 1997 syndrome" (1990-1999)

By the 1990s, Hong Kong had overtaken the average GDP-per-head figures of many of the world's richest nations, and had become one of the four "tiger economies" in South East Asia (along with South Korea, Singapore, and Taiwan.). Along with Singapore, Hong Kong became known for its clean and honest business environment—one well protected and regulated by legislation. To the grassroots class, economic progress, coupled with justice and fairness, was not only expected but guaranteed. But in the run-up to 1997, the public viewed the notion of "one country, two systems" with trepidation. Some saw it as a deadline for making good money, while others seized the chance to scramble for money by any means possible before migrating to other countries. Therefore, there was a general concern that the Hong Kong migrant community, as always, was busier than ever in making "quick-bucks".

During this period, a great majority of the local workforce grew up along with the ICAC. In other words, while they learned their ABCs they were also being taught in school, and through the mass media, not to be corrupt. Many, however, were ignorant of the bad old "rotten apple" days when the public suffered because of corrupt law enforcers and improper business practices. Would the new generation of the workforce unscrupulously attempt to make quick and big money facilitated by corruption and then flee Hong Kong? To assure the public that the ICAC would be as committed as ever to fight corruption and to refresh the public of its past success, the agency send out an unprecedented, perhaps even rather arrogant slogan: "Hong Kong's Advantage is the ICAC". Posters of this period read "Tea Money Totally Forbidden"; "Tips Forbidden"; "Report Corruption Right Away"; and "Agonies Go with Corruption", for example.

Prior to the establishment of the ICAC two decades before, "Tea Money" and "Tips" were deemed acceptable awards for favors acquired from government officials, or as lubricants in business dealings. Two decades on, "Tea Money" and "Tips" were socially regarded as "bribes", the offering *or* acceptance of which were punishable under the law. The ICAC poster messages during this period served to ring a reminder bell to those who witnessed the old "Rotten Apple" culture, and to warn the new generation who were raised in the new clean and honest culture. Two such posters carried the setting of traditional Chinese New Year greetings which, on top of being just a poster design, can be interpreted as symbolizing law-abiding, clean, and honest values and culture advocated by the ICAC.

During this period, successful indictment of "1997 Syndrome" cases demonstrated the government's commitment to fight corruption and that "Hong Kong's Advantage is the ICAC". On July 15, 1996, a senior Immigration & Naturalization Service officer of the U.S. Department of Justice attached to the U.S. Consulate in Hong Kong was arrested by the ICAC for possession of five forged Honduras passports. In March, 1997, another senior Immigration & Naturalization Service officer of the U.S. Department of Justice was detained, along with his wife, by ICAC for interrogation for providing passports to Chinese mainlanders in return for bribes. This officer was subsequently released under diplomatic immunity. In March 1999, a senior Customs and Excise Department inspector arrested in an undercover investigation was prosecuted for helping a Russian businessman acquire Brazilian passports at $32,500 each by unlawful means, and for conspiracy in money laundering. The senior inspector was finally given a three-year sentence.

District Board (the lowest administrative level) elections were introduced in the 1980s, but a fully-elected Legislative Council, the law-making body in Hong Kong, did not exist until the 1990s. Democratic elections and voting for politicians to represent their individual human rights and interests was another innovation for the community of Chinese refugees and their descendants. Election scandals, such as vote-rigging, take place in all societies, breeding undesirable government and compromising the well-being of citizens. Therefore, clean elections creating representative government for and by the people are a critical goal. With that in mind the ICAC, to tie in with new changes in the political system, urged the public during the 1990s to back up a fair and clean election and voting culture: "Money Can Buy What You Want But Not Justice". The public was also reminded that anti-corruption laws covered election and voting procedures, and that those engaging in election malpractices would be indicted.

The ICAC made good on those pledges, exposing political scandals as they arose under the new democratic representative government. On June 1, 1993, Legislator Kam Ho Leung was convicted for offering bribes for votes in the 1991 Legislative Council election. In September, 1994, Barrister Y.Y. Chi and her lieutenant in her election campaign were arrested by ICAC officers for offering advantages to her voters in the District Board election. In November, 1995, Lawyer K. F. Yeung was arrested by ICAC officers for vote-rigging in his own Regional Board election. With these moves the ICAC gained further public confidence that the anti-corruption messages sent out by the ICAC were not white-washes, and the anti-corruption agency was not a month-piece of the government.

In the run-up to 1997, various types of election-related corruption complaints continued to arise. Prior to the Legislative Council election of August 1995, the ICAC set up a special team of investigators in the Operations Department ready to handle election-related corruption complaints and a forty-member Community Relations team to educate the public on the election-related anti-corruption ordinances. The ICAC Community Relations Officers also approached the candidates and their campaign agents to elaborate on the related ordinances, while the public was warned not to compromise their own democratic rights for "advantages" offered by any of the candidates.

"New millennium" (2000-)

The new millennium is the cyber era and belongs to the younger generation. That generation was brought up in a comparatively well-off, clean and honest environment, without experiencing or witnessing the endemic corruption of the bad old days. The ICAC now targets this young generation for probity education. The ICAC reaches them through the Internet, popular among the youths, and a youth website called "Teensland"[7] has been set up for them. In less than six months the youth website scored more than one million hits, which reflects its popularity and its efficacy. The agency, in its messages to this young generation, stresses the importance of continuing the battle against corruption, which has been bringing fruitful results. The culture of lawfulness and integrity has to be sustained to make Hong Kong one of the cleanest cities in the world, and it is of prime importance that the younger generation, the future hosts of the territory, shares that view.

The new anti-corruption culture

The ICAC's success in building a new anti-corruption culture is reflected in survey figures on public confidence and support. In 1974, when the agency was newly established, only 35 percent of the complainants reporting corruption were willing to identify themselves, but in 2002 this figure stood at almost 72 percent. In 1993, 36.7 percent of respondents said they would not tolerate corruption in both the private and public sectors; the level of intolerance rose to about 80 percent in the late 1990s and stood at 90 percent in 2002. In 1993, 44.5 percent of respondents expressed tolerance of private sector corruption, a figure that fell to 13 percent in 2002. Respondents indicating "willingness to report" corruption stood at 54.4 percent in 1993 but rose to 64.7 percent in 2000, and 67 percent in 2002, as Table 6.1 shows:

Table 6.1:
Trends in Corruption and Social Attitudes

Year	**1974**	**1993**	**2000**	**2002**
Identified corruption reports	35%		70%	72%
Intolerant of corruption		36.7%	83.7%	90%
Tolerant of private sector corruption		44.5%	11%	13%
Willing to report corruption		54.4%	64.7%	67%

Source: ICAC Annual Reports.

III. Linguistic, Cultural, and Legal Dimensions of Corruption

Such successes are possible because Hong Kong residents trust the ICAC and identify with its messages and appeals. That in turn has much to do with language and cultural values, and with the agency's long-term efforts to link such traditional elements of Hong Kong society to the policies it pursues. A semantic analysis of concepts such as "advantage", "bribery", and "corruption" reveals a complex interplay and interaction of legal (common-law) and social definitions central to the "quiet revolution" that changed opinions on corruption from acceptance to intolerance.

As noted above, the Hong Kong legal system is based on the British common-law one. In the former British Crown colony, statutes and ordinances are clearly defined and spelt out to protect people against unreasonable, arbitrary, or capricious acts of law enforcers. The people, in other words, are given due process protection. Common-law definitions refer to a register distinguishable from other registers for the purposes of law enforcement. Social definitions are primarily culture-based, i.e. the pattern of values, beliefs, perceptions, norms and behaviors shared by the ethnic Chinese accounting for over 95 percent of the Hong Kong population.

"Advantage" in common-law definition

Under the Prevention of Bribery Ordinance, Laws of Hong Kong,[8] "advantage" is defined as:

a)   any gift, loan, fee, reward or commission consisting of money or of any valuable security or of other property or interest in property of any description;

b)   any office, employment or contract;

c)   any payment, release, discharge or liquidation of any loan, obligation or other liability, whether in whole or in part;

d)   any other service, or favor (entertainment), including protection from any penalty or disability incurred or apprehended or from any action or proceedings of a disciplinary, civil or criminal nature, whether or not already instituted;

e)   the exercise or forbearance from the exercise of any right or any power or duty; and

f)   any offer, undertaking or promise, whether conditional or unconditional, or any advantage within the meaning of any of the preceding paragraphs (a), (b), (c), (d) and (e).

A few cases will illustrate the common-law definition of "advantage":

1.   Policeman X accepts "tea money" (legally defined as an "advantage") for not arresting a hawker selling stolen goods (i.e. "forbearance from the exercise of any power or duty").

2.   Government Mortuary Staff Y obtains (i.e. "from the exercise of any power or duty") carnal knowledge of female dead bodies (an "advantage").

3.   Chinese Restaurant Owner Z offers free buffet coupons (an "advantage") to License Inspector A during Chinese New Year for showing favors in license renewal.

4.   Bank Executive B accepts "tea money" (an "advantage") from a firm for authorizing unsecured loans from his bank.

5.   Legislator C offers "tea money" (an "advantage") to his constituents in exchange for his votes.

6.   Government Architect X is given a free overseas tour (an "advantage") in return for approving construction tenders.

7.   Policeman Y accepts "tea money" (an "advantage") for tipping off a drug den operator on upcoming police raids.

Though the "advantages" in these cases take various forms, the public is certain of the well-defined and clear legal definitions of "advantage". The people know that offering and accepting bribes, with the intent to obtain certain favors, will be punished under the law. They now trust that the law applies to all, irrespective of background, because of years of successful investigations and indictments.

"Advantage" in social definition

To the Chinese, with their history of thousands of years, "advantage" is a catch-all word that includes justified privileges, benefits, tips, service charges, tokens of appreciation, well-meaning tea-money, convenience, and expressions of friendliness and respect. But it can also include privileged personal connections or social credits (*guanxi*), favors, preferences, bribes, or the acquisition of stolen goods. Some day-to-day social situations illustrate these meaning of "advantage" in a typical Chinese community:

1.   Policeman X sends New Year's gifts, i.e. crates of first-class whisky, to his supervising officer during the Chinese New Year as a sign and expression of respect.
2.   Citizen Y sends his friend, Principal Z, of a renowned high school a gold Rolex right after his son has applied to the school for admission.
3.   Supervising Driving Examiner A and his subordinates were given a lavish meal by a friend just before the friend was due to take his driving examination at his center.
4.   Prosecutor B accepts an apartment from a businessman friend right after the police hand over an investigation file to him to decide whether or not to prosecute his businessman friend, who is seeking his professional advice at the same time.
5.   Policeman C accepts Hawker X's "tea money" in return for not arresting the latter for illegal hawking.

Such social situations, common in Hong Kong before the establishment of the ICAC in 1974, bred discontent among the Chinese community when the inequality and privilege of personal relationships and connections (*guanx*i) grew out of proportion. The "advantages" obligated to be paid to civil servants and the police heavily taxed the scanty resources of the grassroots class. The society was condemning corruption, and the street demonstration of the Godber Incident saw the climax of pent-up grievances and social disapproval. At that juncture, the social definition of an "advantage" perfectly locked in with the common-law one spelt out in the new anti-graft legislation when an "advantage" was socially perceived and interpreted as a bribe in the legal sense. By tracking down and jailing Godber, the ICAC made critical connections between the legal and social conceptions of "advantage", and showed its willingness to uphold basic, widely shared values.

Under the ICAC, Policeman X in Case 1 will be charged with bribing his senior for possible favors. Citizen Y, in Case 2, will also be charged with bribing an influential individual for favors. In Case 3, Supervising Driving Examiner A and his subordinates will be charged with accepting an "advantage" for using their official powers to show favors while the friend will also be charged for offering bribes. Prosecutor B in Case 4 will be charged for accepting bribes using his official powers and his businessman friend will also be charged with offering bribes. Policeman C in Case 5 will be charged for accepting bribes for not carrying out his official duties and Hawker X will be charged for offering bribes at the same time.

The grassroots class was thus awakened from a culture of acceptance of corruption. The once acceptable ploy of offering gifts to get things done through a connection (or *guanxi*) began to lose its legitimacy. Meanwhile, successful arrests, indictments and prosecutions of the ICAC during that "Era of Awakening" were unprecedented powerful unspoken language to the general public that the then new legislation was mighty, the agency committed to its mission, and the anti-graft messages meant what they said. The people in the colony for the first time tasted the contrast between the western concept of equality and well-defined laws and the Chinese one based on partial judgments, personal relationships and the Confucian one of presumed benevolence.

"Corruption" in common-law definition

Under the Prevention of Bribery Ordinance "corruption" is not expressly defined, but "corrupt" transactions with agents are defined as:

1)   Any agent who, without lawful authority or reasonable excuse, solicits or accepts any advantage as an inducement to or reward for or otherwise on account of his

i)   Doing or forbearing to do, or having done or forborne to do, any act in relation to his principal's affairs or business; or

ii)   Showing or forbearing to show, or having shown or forborne to show, favour or disfavour to any person in relation to his principal's affairs or business,

shall be guilty of an offence.

b)   Any person who, without lawful authority or reasonable excuse, offers any advantage to any agent as an inducement to or reward for or otherwise on account of the agent's

i)   Doing or forbearing to do, or having done or forborne to do, any act in relation to his principal's affairs or business; or

ii)   Showing or forbearing to show, or having shown or forborne to show, favour or disfavour to any person in relation to his principal's affairs or business,

shall be guilty of an offence.

2)   Any agent who, with intent to deceive his principal, uses any receipt, account or other document

i)   In respect of which the principal is interested, and

ii)   Which contains any statement which is false or erroneous or defective sin any material particular; and

iii)   Which to his knowledge is intended to mislead the principal,

shall be guilty of an offence.

3)   If an agent solicits or accepts an advantage with the permission of his principal, being permission which complies with subsection (5), neither he nor the person who offered the advantage shall be guilty of an offence under subsection (1) or (2).

3)   For the purposes of subsection (4) permission shall
i)   Be given before the advantage is offered, solicited or accepted; or
ii)   In any case where an advantage has been offered or accepted without prior permission, be applied for and given as soon as reasonably possible after such offer or acceptance,
and for such permission to be effective for the purposes of subsection (4), the principal shall, before giving such permission, have regard to the circumstances in which it is sought.

The common-law definition of "corrupt" transactions would thus include:
1.   Restaurant Chef X accepts "kickbacks" from flour suppliers without the permission of his employer.
2.   Bank Manager Y, without permission of his employer, accepts "commissions" from his clients for approving unsecured loans from his bank.
3.   Doctor Z offers "commissions" to an insurance agent in return for referring patients to him instead of doctors approved by the agent's insurance firm.

Under the common-law definition, such transactions conducted even by professions or the privileged class without prior approval will be deemed "corrupt" dealings not executed on a "level playing field", and perpetrators will be punished. The standard for measuring whether an offense has committed lies in whether or not permission of one's employer has been obtained. Such a clear-cut standard indicates that personal relationships and connections (*guanxi*) are not acceptable in place of a "level playing field" and bribes are not legitimate lubricants for securing business.

"Corruption" in social definition

Some everyday scenarios illustrate the traditional Chinese social definition of "corrupt" transaction of agents:
1.   Restaurant Chef X accepts "tea money" from flour suppliers without the permission of his employer.
2.   Bank Manager Y, without permission of his employer, accepts "monetary gifts" from his clients for approving unsecured loans from his bank.
3. Doctor Z offers "monetary gifts" to an insurance agent in return for referring patients to him instead of doctors approved by the agent's insurance firm.

To traditional Chinese such *socially* corrupt transactions may not all be crimes in the common-law sense, though evils of corruption have always been condemned in the millennia of Chinese civilization.

In the Chinese-English Dictionary of Chinese Law and Government[9] "corruption" is referred to as "a vague term used to mean any of several offenses committed by an official for his private benefit at the expense of the public benefit, including accepting bribes, embezzling public funds, stealing public properties, swindling, speculative manipulation of public property, and in general serving private ends in the name of official business". Similar usages include "rotten...grasping...greedy...insatiable...avaricious, misuse of law".

For millennia in China, "corrupt", "dishonest" and "rotten" have referred to someone lacking moral integrity—the last thing one expects from an individual, a capable political leader or well-respected professional. The traditional Confucian attitude holds that a government will be in peace and prosperity if the people, free from "corrupt" or "rotten" values or beliefs, are governed by moral integrity, their conduct regulated by rules of propriety and decorum, or by codes of honor under which the sense of shame makes them law-abiding and responsible. If the people are corruption-free and not metaphysically "rotten", the society will be in harmony. A ruler is to act like a ruler, just as a law enforcer is to act like a law enforcer; each is to fulfill his obligations and be mindful of supervision from above. Such submissive attitudes do not encourage the Chinese grassroots class to come forward with corruption reports on government servants or private individuals. Nonetheless, deep inside their hearts and minds, they have a high respect for those who are honest, fair, and "non-rotten" souls, who are, indeed, their heroes. In a traditional Chinese community, law enforcers and judges are nothing but ordinary civil servants rather than special officials independent of political authority.[10]

In Hong Kong, civil servants and individuals, regardless of their backgrounds, were arrested, prosecuted, and sent to jail for "corruption" as defined by the common-law legislation. Once again the laws became identified with the social definition perceived by the Chinese grassroots class. Prior to the establishment of ICAC people could only tolerate corruption; it is easy to understand why the local society supports and endorses the ICAC, which speaks their minds with concrete deeds.

"Bribery" in common-law definition
Under the Prevention of Bribery Ordinance "bribery" is defined as

1)   Any government servant, who, without the general or special permission of the Governor/Chief Executive, *solicits or accepts* any advantage shall be guilty of an offence.
2)   Any person who, whether in Hong Kong or elsewhere, without lawful authority or reasonable excuse, *offers/accepts/solicits* any advantage to and from a public servant as an inducement to or reward for or otherwise on account of that public servant's
i)   Performing or abstaining from performing, or having performed or abstained from performing, any act in is capacity as a public servant;
ii)   Expediting, delaying, hindering or preventing, or having expedited, delayed, hindered or prevented, the performance of an act, whether by that public servant or by any other public servant in his or that other public servant's capacity as a public servant; or
iii)   Assisting, favouring, hindering or delaying, or having assisted, favoured, hindered or delayed, any person in the transaction of any business with a public body,

shall be guilty of an offence.

3)   Any person who, without lawful authority or reasonable excuse, *offers/solicits/accepts* an advantage to/from a public servant as an inducement to or reward for or otherwise on account of such public servant's giving assistance or using influence in, or having given assistance or used in influence in

i)   The promotion, execution, or procuring of

(1)   Any contract with a public body for the performance of any work, the providing of any service, the doing of any thing or the supplying of any service, the doing of any thing or the supplying of any article, material or substance, or

(2)   Any subcontract to perform any work, provide any service, do any thing or supply any article, material or substance required to be performed, provided, done or supplied under any contract with a public body; or

ii)   The payment of the price, consideration or other moneys stipulated or otherwise provided for in any such contract or subcontract as foresaid,

shall be guilty of an offence.

4)   Any person who, without lawful authority or reasonable excuse, *offers/solicits/accepts* any advantage to/from any other person as an inducement to or a reward for or otherwise on account of the withdrawal of a tender, or refraining from the making of a tender, for any contract with a public body for the performance of any work, the providing of any service, the doing of any thing or the supplying of any article, material or substance, shall be guilty of an offence.

5)   Any person who, without lawful authority or reasonable excuse, *offers/solicits/accepts* any advantage to/from any other person as an inducement to or reward for or otherwise on account of that person's refraining or having refrained from bidding at any auction conducted by or on behalf of any public body, shall be guilty of an offence.

6)   Any person who, without lawful authority or reasonable excuse, while having dealings of any kind with the Government through any department, office or establishment of the Government, public body, offers any advantage to any Government servant/public servant employed by that public body, shall be guilty of an offence.

Thus anyone offering, soliciting or accepting an "advantage" for giving assistance in regard to contracts, or for procuring withdrawal of tenders, in relation to auctions and dealings with public bodies will be prosecuted for bribery. The common-law definition prohibits civil servants and individuals from offering, soliciting or accepting an "advantage" for "getting things done" through personal connections or social credits. Here are some cases to illustrate the common-law definition of "bribery":

1.   Police Squad A receives large amounts of money every month for not taking action against drug divans and vice dens in their neighborhood. [Policemen of Squad A will be charged with accepting an "advantage", a bribery offense]

2.   Builder B offers a Housing Authority official a new car to approve his tender application for building a housing estate. [Builder B will be charged with offering an "advantage", a bribery offense in regard to procuring a contract.]
3.   Immigration Officer C solicits a colossal amount of money for approving a passport application from an unqualified applicant. [Immigration Officer C will be charged with soliciting an "advantage" in his capacity as a government servant.]
4.   Building Inspector X accepts money for approving substandard materials used in a construction project. [Building Inspector X will be charged with accepting an "advantage" in his capacity as a government servant, again a bribery offense.]

"Bribery" in social definition

Before the ICAC came into being such common-law definitions of bribery did exist, but the society generally defined the "advantage" as "convenience money" or "tea money" unless the amount was significant and used for serious wrongdoings. At that time, the "tea money" was generally perceived by the grassroots class as a token of appreciation for receiving benefits that went outside the routine—that went beyond the bounds of ordinary friendship and mutual help (i.e. *guanxi* relationships). Some everyday situations illustrating the traditional Chinese social definition of bribery include:

1.   Drug Divan Operator A pays monthly "tea money" to his friends of Police Squad X
who facilitate his drug operation business.
2.   Builder B presents his high-ranking Housing Authority official friend a car in return for procuring a contract for him.
3.   Immigration Officer C asks for undocumented administration fee from an unqualified applicant for doing him a favor.
4.   Building Inspector X takes "convenience money" to save his friend from going through the red tape in a construction project.

Since its inception, the ICAC has urged the public to redefine "tea money" or "convenience money", even of a token amount, to mean "bribes", which are socially and legally unacceptable. The message to the public was simple: if the society did not redefine the terms, they would go on to suffer from injustice and the crimes bribes generate; whether you apply the common-law definitions or the old social definitions, injustice occurs and people with few advantages. Over thirty years with different stages and themes of publicity campaigns from the anti-graft agency, coupled with successful indictments and sentencing, the grassroots class has gradually adopted a social definition of "bribery" as meaning "something offered in order to influence a person illegally or improperly to act in favor of the giver,"[11] an evil both morally and legally unacceptable.

IV. Conclusion

In quantitative terms, the ICAC has been a success. Public reports of corruption by citizens willing to identify themselves have increased, and investigations, prosecutions, and convictions continue. At a more intangible level, however—and underlying the outcomes just noted—success has taken the form of a cultural transformation with regard to corruption. The recipe for ICAC success lies in the orderly interplay and interaction between the common-law definitions adopted by the anti-graft agency and the evolving social definitions disseminated through public education and communication with the people. In other words, the Confucian-Chinese virtues emphasizing honesty, obligations, righteousness, benevolence, and propriety, awakened and rekindled by the ICAC publicity messages among the majority Chinese population, coupled with the vigorous enforcement of the common-law defined anti-corruption legislation, succeeded to win the hearts and minds of the grassroots class . Before the inception of the ICAC in 1974, the local population experienced the injustice and high costs of "getting things done" through personal relationships (*guanxi*) in the government or in the business sector. And they were aware that such relationships, involving human feelings and of course selfish desires, could be easily and arbitrarily abused, creating injustice and undermining government and administration. Upon its being, the ICAC has been seriously operating through clearly-defined legislation which applies to each and every one in the colony, irrespective of their background. Over time, the public saw that the ICAC really meant what it said, and at the same time they were reminded of the deep-rooted Confucian values and beliefs of an "honest", "dutiful", "righteous", "benevolent" and "upright" individual where "rotten" and "corrupt" are never part of the makeup of a Chinese "gentleman". Protected by the due process of the common-law legal system, the people became willing to report wrongdoing and to embrace new social definitions of corruption. This mindset is a marked change from their submissive culture. In short, the ICAC has succeeded in fighting corruption in a rapidly modernizing society by linking its well-defined laws and reforms to rekindled Confucian-Chinese virtues.

ENDNOTES

1. [1]Factbook Online. 2004. "Hong Kong."
http://www.cia.gov/cia/publications/factbook/geos/hk.html. Viewed 9 August 2004.
2. Endacott, G.B. 1964. *Government and People in Hong Kong 1841-1962*. Hong Kong: Hong Kong University Press.
3. Patten, Christopher. 1998. *East and West: China, Power, and the Future of Asia*. London: Times Books.
4. De Mente, Boye L. 2000. *The Chinese Have a Word For It: The Complete Guide to Chinese Thought and Culture*. New York: McGraw-Hill.
5. Dimbleby, Jonathan. 1997. *The Last Governor*. London: Little, Brown and Company.
6. On the origins and history of the ICAC, see (for English-language version) http://www.icac.org.hk/eng/abou/index.html (Viewed 9 August 2004).
7. Online at http://www.icac.org.hk/teensland/default_nf.asp (Viewed 9 August 2004).
8. This and subsequent references to text of the Ordinance draws upon Prevention of Bribery Ordinance, Chapter 201, Laws of Hong Kong.
9. *Chinese-English Dictionary of Chinese Law and Government*. 1981. p. 649.
10. Cohen, Jerome A. 1979. "Due Process?" In Terrill, Ross (ed.). *The China Difference*. New York: Harper & Row Publishers, p. 257.
11. *Oxford American Dictionary*, Avon Books, New York

7

Can We Fight Corruption through Debt Relief?[1]

Arvind K. Jain

Massive accumulations of international debt plague many high-corruption countries. Those debts are not only a drag on developing economies but also do little to advance democratization, development, and reform. Recently proposals have emerged to relieve all or most of the debt of poor countries, by various mechanisms, as a step toward reform. Reduced corruption is often listed as one of the benefits of such a strategy: lower debts would mean more growth, less poverty, and a population less vulnerable to exploitation by unscrupulous regimes. Arvind Jain, however, offers an important cautionary tale. While debt is a huge burden, without better institutional, political, and economic governance in poor countries, debt forgiveness might even make the development and corruption problems of some countries worse, as newly freed-up resources end up in the wrong hands.

I. Developing Countries' Debt Burden—The Challenge
Current debate on debt forgiveness for the highly indebted, low-income developing countries entails a dilemma. On the one hand, grassroots organizers are correct in arguing that external debt burden has created a financial stranglehold on the debtor countries. It is easy to see this. For a group of ten low-income countries, total external debt ranges from three to twenty-five times the country's annual exports.[2] Advocates of debt-forgiveness argue that the poorest sections of the population in the indebted countries bear the burden of debt pay-

ments and they attribute increases in the levels of hunger and poverty, reduction in the levels of education and health services, and worsening conditions of women to increased debt payments.[3] Normally, increases in the levels of debt should have been accompanied by the development of the productive capacity of the economy that should have generated revenues to service the debt. Unfortunately, the circumstances under which these debts were negotiated in most of these countries did not allow such capacities to develop. The burden of servicing the large debt leaves few financial resources for economic development—leading to economic stagnation that serves neither the debtors nor the creditors. This provides the practical reason for debt forgiveness. Moreover, the burden of payments, which must be eked out of whatever resources may be available, may fall on segments of population that never benefited from the debt in the first place. This provides the moral reason for debt forgiveness.

On the other hand the quality of internal governance of some of these countries is such that unconditional debt forgiveness at best will not benefit the poorest sections of these societies, and may even worsen their conditions. "Governance" refers to the quality of decision making at the political and the economic institutions of a society that determines the environment under which individual citizens function and that, eventually, determines the quality of life of ordinary citizens. While there is no agreement on a precise definition of this term, it generally refers to fairness and sophistication of the political elite in devising national policies. The reason for a pessimistic projection of the consequences of unconditional debt-forgiveness is that development requires not only financial and economic resources but also governance structures that will use those resources effectively. Debt forgiveness will certainly make financial resources available. These countries, unfortunately, lack the second, and perhaps the more important, ingredient: a governance environment that results in good government policies that foster development, and especially development that benefits the poorest sections of the society. Good governance becomes all the more important as the world economy becomes globalized. A globalized economy requires nimble and dynamic governance that can respond quickly to the changing global environment. Poor governance and polices are an important reason why these countries ended up with large debt burdens in the first place. If the debt were to be forgiven unconditionally, the ruling elites might usurp the resources thus made available. In the worst scenario, debt forgiveness will make the ruling elite—which would certainly take the credit for negotiating the concessions—even stronger, and would create conditions for increased exploitation of the poorest segments of the society.

Debt relief can help control corruption, and improve living conditions more generally, only if the quality of governance is improved along with, or in advance of, the increased availability of resources. Government policies must be reoriented to benefit large segments of populations, not just the political elite. Since that elite has a vested interest in maintaining the status quo, the pressure for change must come from elsewhere. Promise of debt relief offers one such venue for exerting the pressure. To ensure that the additional resources benefit the largest sections of population, it may be essential that debt forgiveness be accompanied by "conditionality". At the top of these conditions should be a requirement to improve the governance structure of the countries involved. To forgive debt without ensuring that conditions are created for a more efficient use of funds within the countries in the future is at best a waste of resources, and at worst counterproductive.

The objective of this paper is to illustrate that unconditional debt forgiveness, while morally comforting, may for practical reasons not be the best path to follow, either for its own sake or as a strategy for controlling corruption. Section II, below, outlines the origins and the extent of the problem. Section III summarizes the Heavily Indebted Poor Countries (HIPC) initiative. Section IV discusses studies that show the importance of tackling corruption. Section V analyzes the changing nature of governance in view of a globalized economy. I conclude, in Section VI, with points on why debt forgiveness must follow a governance reform in the recipient countries.

II. Petro-Dollars and the Lending Boom: How Did We Get Here?

How did a large number of developing countries end up with such high debt burdens? The origins may be traced, with few exceptions, to the oil price shocks of the 1970s. During that decade the Organization of Oil Producing Countries (OPEC) flexed its muscles and managed a many-fold increase in the price of oil, changing the future economic prospects for most of the world. The income of OPEC countries increased dramatically. This income was partly spent on imports of goods from industrialized countries and partly invested in short-term deposits with international banks—deposits that came to be known as "petro-dollars." Oil-importing countries faced a large adverse shock in their terms of trade.[4] For most industrialized oil-importing countries, however, these effects were cushioned by two factors. First, oil was a small part of their imports. Second, increased income of the oil-exporters created demand for sophisticated consumer and industrial goods—demand that could only be satisfied by exports of the industrialized countries. For the industrialized countries, the recession-inducing impact of a decline in their terms of trade was softened by increased demand for their goods by the now-wealthy-oil-exporting countries. Developing countries, in contrast, faced both large increases in their import bills and decline in the demand and prices of their exports—dominated largely by commodities[5]—due to recession in the industrialized countries. This left them with no choice but to find means to finance their balance of payments deficits.

Larger developing countries became prime targets for lending by private commercial banks flush with "petro-dollars", but the smaller developing countries had to rely to a great extent on extensions of export credits.[6] The industrialized countries' export credit agencies that extended these loans may have overlooked many of the risks in order not to interrupt the levels of exports from their economies as they headed into recessions.[7] Overall debt levels would not have continued to increase had the funds obtained through the loans had been put to productive uses, and had necessary macro-economic adjustments been made. But the "crisis" environment that accompanied the oil-price shocks permitted lenders to overlook the extensive misuse of funds that accompanied, and contributed to, rising debt levels.[8] Such complacency was eventually rewarded by external developments: early 1980s saw phenomenal increases in global interest rates at the same time as the industrialized world was heading back into a recession. When the indebted developing countries failed to pay their debts and led the global economy into what became known as a "debt-bomb" in early 1980s, it was easy to lay the blame for the crisis on factors external to the borrowers' economies and systems of governance.[9]

Whatever the accepted explanation, the result was a series of problems for severely indebted low-income countries (SILICs). First, their ratios of debt to exports increased far more than those of other developing countries. Second, debt levels increased far more than the flow of direct investment capital in these countries. Low ratios of cumulative foreign investment to growth of indebtedness indicate, first, the excessive reliance of these countries on debt as a source of foreign capital and, second, a vote of no-confidence by foreign investors in the investment environment within these countries. Third, SILICs as a group faced stagnating exports from about 1980 onwards. While other groups of countries, especially the middle-income countries, saw export growth resume within a few years after the 1982 debt crisis, the exports of SILICs did not return to 1980 levels till 1996. Fourth, the picture looks even worse when imports are taken into account. SILICs, as a group, had a trade surplus only in one year during the entire twenty-seven-year period. On an average (unweighted value), their exports were only 81 percent of their imports. Not only were these countries carrying an increasing load of debt; their exports could not even pay for their imports—requiring financing of the deficits which in turn led to further increases in external debt.

Clearly, the heavily indebted countries did not make the adjustments or create the economic environments necessary to manage external debt. Whereas the initial phase of the increase in the debt can be attributed to the 1970s oil-price shocks, those responsible for managing domestic economies must share the blame for later increases. It is clear that neither the borrowers within SILICs nor the lenders in the industrialized countries were willing to bite the bullet and force the necessary economic adjustments. By the mid-1990s the SILICs were devoting about one-fifth of their export income to debt-service payments. Given their persistent trade deficits, the debt-service payments created a further drain on these countries' external cash flows that left few resources for long-term development projects. SILICs could exercise little control over their cash flows: their ability to service their debts depended more on international commodity prices than on the internal management or performance of the economies.

III. The Heavily Indebted Poor Countries (HIPC) Initiative

Early signs of difficulties associated with the increasing levels of debt began to appear by the end of 1981, when some middle income countries acknowledged payment difficulties. The financial world received its big shock, however, when Mexico asked for a moratorium on its debt payments in August 1982. Other countries followed soon after that, and a full-scale debt crisis had emerged by the end of that year. After many re-schedulings, innovations like debt-equity swaps and Brady bonds, and some influx of new funds, many developing countries resumed their growth path by the end of 1980s. The group of countries now known as highly indebted poor countries, or HIPC (most SILICs discussed in the previous section belong in this group), however, failed to halt the economic decline that had begun in 1982. In September 1996, the World Bank and IMF launched the HIPC initiative at the urging of the G-8 countries and many concerned grass root organizations in the industrialized countries. The aim of this initiative was to obtain debt relief from multilateral creditors. The initiative involved forty-two HIPCs identified in 1994 as needing help.[10] Thirty-two of those countries had a per capita GNP of US$695 or less in 1993 and high levels of external debt.[11] High levels of debt were defined as either a net present value (NPV) of debt-to-exports ratio of 220 percent or higher, or an NPV of debt-to-GNP ratio of 80 percent or higher. The remaining countries were included because they had received concessional re-schedulings from the Paris Club,[12] an informal forum in which debtor countries negotiate with creditors. By the fall of 2003, twenty-seven countries had reached a "decision point" implying that they ready to receive debt relief.[13]

The HIPC initiative required participation of all creditors–public and private, bilateral or multilateral. In the first stage of the initiative, the debtor countries had to pursue and implement structural and social policy reforms. Countries that established a track record were to have debts rescheduled by their creditors. Countries that entered the second stage of the initiative were to receive relief for up to 80 percent of their debt. Some of the funds for the relief were to come from IMF's Enhanced Structural Adjustment Facility.

Some countries have benefited from HIPC and similar initiatives. From 1988 to 1997, debt reductions totaled $72.3 billion, or 32.2 percent of the value of the debt in 1987.[14] It appears, however, that such debt reductions have not resulted in many benefits for the poor people of those countries. Zambia, for example, had received about $100 million indebt relief as of 2001, an amount equal to about 10 per cent of its total government budget. But this has not translated into higher expenditures on another crisis devastating Zambia–that of AIDS–or into the expenditures on education or social programs demanded by donor agencies. In the words of one activist, "(T)he money . . . does not seem to make it out of Lusaka." Instead, it is spent on presidential vanity projects, such as an expenditure of about 0.5 percent of national income on a summit of the Organisation of African Unity, and on an elite institution of higher studies.[15] In Uganda, another recipient of debt relief, citizens have found it necessary to create their own watchdog agencies, while politicians award construction contracts to their relatives—contracts not fulfilled because the money is pocketed, and justified with the question, "(H)ow can you ask a hungry man to take food to someone?"[16]

IV. Corruption and the Indebted Countries

How does corruption fit into this situation, and why is controlling it so important? While corruption is as ancient as human society, serious academic studies of its impact are of recent origin. Most academicians and policy makers are now convinced that corruption is one of the most serious impediments to economic development. Corruption affects the nature of investments that are made, their efficiency, and the distribution of returns that are earned. Even petty corruption harms the economic activity by creating an environment in which value-creating investments are discouraged while small acts of corruption create demand for more. A belief that corruption can be beneficial is now certainly considered simplistic and incorrect.[17]

It is perhaps helpful, first, to dispel the myth that petty bureaucratic corruption can be helpful. Kaufmann[18] shows that corporate managers spend *more* time with bureaucrats—not less—as the frequency of bribes increases. Petty corruption does not, and cannot, exist in a vacuum–those who accept small bribes have to keep their superiors satisfied by ever-increasing shares of the "take". Wade[19] has shown how unchecked corruption leads to a complete breakdown of government services: small bribes eventually lead to an internal market, in which officials at the highest level benefit from corruption at the lower levels by charging a price for allocating positions that offer a chance to collect bribes. Gupta *et. al.*[20] show that higher levels of corruption are associated with lower-quality government services in the areas of health and education. Higher corruption is linked to lower health outcomes (child mortality, infant mortality, births attended by health staff, immunization, and low-birthweight babies) and lower educational outcomes (primary school enrollment, repeater rates, dropout rates, persistence to grade five, and illiteracy rates).

Mauro[21] first established that corruption leads to lower levels of investments. Tanzi and Davoodi[22] show that countries with higher levels of corruption tend to have lower GDP per capita as well as lower growth rates of per capita GDP. They also show that corruption stifles small and medium enterprises more than larger ones, which may contribute to lower growth rates. Their tests establish that corruption leads to choices of careers away from engineering—a productive enterprise—and into law—which they regard as an unproductive activity. Finally, they provide new evidence that corruption affects tax revenues, with higher corruption countries relying more on indirect taxes. The importance of this finding is that countries with higher corruption fail to collect necessary direct taxes that in turn make it difficult to provide government services.[23]

It is important to recognize that the relationship between corruption, on the one hand, and government services, or investment, on the other, is not just a simple pattern of association, but rather is most likely causal. While formal models that conclusively establish such causation from corruption to services have yet to be built, there is an emerging consensus that just as "bad money drives out the good," corrupt decision makers and processes eventually take over. Gupta *et. al.*[24] and Shleifer and Vishny[25] show that in the presence of bureaucratic corruption, honest bureaucratic activities cannot survive. Dishonest bureaucrats will co-opt their superiors and will ensure that honest bureaucrats are rendered ineffective.

The incidence of corruption and debt

This discussion of the consequences of corruption would not be relevant were it not for the fact that the group of highly indebted countries included in the HIPC initiative contains more than its share of highly corrupt countries. Table 7.1 shows the Transparency International (TI) Corruption Perception Index (CPI) for 2001 and 2003 for the countries for which this index is available. TI reported the corruption index for 132 countries in 2003 including twenty-four HIPCs and for ninety-one countries in 2001, including twelve HIPCs.

The Corruption Perception Index, reported by TI, ranges from ten (no corruption in the country) to zero (the highest level of corruption). In 2003, twelve HIPCs are among the bottom quartile of the 132 countries ranked by TI. The highest rank for any of the HIPCs is for Ghana (seventieth from the "clean" end of the scale). The average CPI for the 24 countries is 2.4 compared to an average of 4.2 for all the 132 countries. The corruption index, moreover, showed very little sign of change from 2001 to 2003. Of the twelve countries for which the corruption index is available for 2003 as well as for 2001, the value of the index worsened (denoted by a negative sign in the column at the right) for seven countries from 2001 to 2003 while it improved for the other five.

The manner in which TI indices are collected may mean that the numbers would be worse if rankings were available for all the HIPCs. A country must receive at least three responses to surveys on corruption around the world from its respondents. Non-inclusion in the TI rankings, therefore, means that the country did not receive at least three surveys. One reason for this lack of information about the country may be that given the high levels of corruption, very few investors take an interest in the country. It is reasonable to assume that corruption is a serious problem in the HIPCs.

Table 7.1:
Corruption within Highly Indebted Poor Countries

Country[1]	2003 CPI[2]		2001 CPI		Chg: 2001-2003
	Rating[3]	Rank[4]	Rating	Rank[5]	
Angola	1.8	124			
Bolivia	2.3	106	2	84	0.3
Cameroon	1.8	124	2	84	-0.2
Congo, Republic of	2.2	113			
Cote d'Ivoire	2.1	118	2.4	77	-0.3
Ethiopia	2.5	92			
Gambia	2.5	92			
Ghana	3.3	70			
Honduras	2.3	106	2.7	71	-0.4
Kenya	1.9	122	2	84	-0.1
Madagascar	2.6	88			
Malawi	2.8	83	3.2	61	-0.4
Mali	3	78			
Mozambique	2.7	86			
Myanmar	1.6	129			
Nicaragua	2.6	88	2.4	77	0.2
Senegal	3.2	76	2.9	65	0.3
Sierra Leone	2.2	113			
Sudan	2.3	106			
Tanzania	2.5	92	2.2	82	0.3
Uganda	2.2	113	1.9	88	0.3
Vietnam	2.4	100	2.6	75	-0.2
Yemen	2.6	88			
Zambia	2.5	92	2.6	75	-0.1

Corruption indices are not available for the following countries:
Burundi, Central African Republic, *Chad*, Comoros, *Congo, DR*, *Guinea*, *Guinea-Bissau*, *Guyana*, Lao, Liberia, *Mauritania*, *Niger*, *Rwanda*, *Sao Tome* & *Principe*, Somalia, Togo.

[1] 27 countries for which debt forgiveness decision point has been reached are identified in ***bold italics***.
[2] CPI: Corruption Perception Index
[3] Rating: CPI can range from 10 (no corruption) to 0 (highest level of corruption).
[4] Rank: in 2003. Transparency International ranked 132 countries.

V. Governance in a Globalizing Economy

There is very little doubt that the world economy has become more integrated than at any other time since the early years of the twentieth century. Developing countries have not always been willing participants in the process of globalization—it being far from clear that globalization benefits all participants, much less that it benefits all equally.[26] Whether a country sees itself as benefiting from globalization or not, there is, however, little it can do to change the direction of developments taking place in the world economy. In the same vein, whether a country "joins" the global economy or not, it has the responsibility to ensure that neither its internal management nor its responses to external events makes it a victim of globalization. Good governance should ensure that the country benefits from opportunities offered by globalization, within the degree of involvement in the global economy that the country chooses.[27]

How have the requirements for good governance changed with globalization? Have the competitive advantages of various groups shifted as the world has moved from a nation-state system to a globalized system? First let us look at where the globalization has had the most impact. It is well recognized that financial markets are more or less globally integrated.[28] Investors with funds to invest are able to scan global markets for investment opportunities. Large users of funds—the multinationals and governments—can tap global financial markets for their funding needs. Small users of funds—individuals and small corporations—by contrast, are confined to their domestic capital markets due to legal and informational restrictions. Markets for technology and intellectual property are also global in that new technological developments now spread very quickly. There is an asymmetry, however, in whose ideas are protected. Large actors that can claim protection from their home country governments have easier time of controlling the spread of their technology than smaller players.[29] The markets for labor, by contrast, remain segmented—due both to legal impediments to movements and to labor's own resistance to movement due to cultural factors.

In this context, two areas of interaction between a country and the rest-of-the world are particularly important: the extent and the distribution of monopoly rents associated with the access to domestic markets, and design of strategic trade and industrial policies that would develop domestic productive capabilities. Globalization has changed the manner in which government policies in these two areas must be made.

In the pre-globalization days, foreign firms were interested in access to domestic markets mainly for two reasons: the markets within a country, and the country as a source of raw materials (including, sometimes, cheap labor). Governments controlled access to the domestic markets. This control allowed a government to negotiate the "rent" associated with the access to the market with the foreign firms that were interested in entry. These rents were negotiated both at the time of entry of the foreign firm, and over the entire life of the investment. A country's bargaining power depended upon the size of the market, the strength of its domestic firms, and the number of foreign firms willing to bid for the right to enter the market.[30] With the globalization of markets, however, bargaining power has shifted to the multinationals for two reasons. First, nationalistic policies that allowed a government to limit access to its markets have become less tenable because that country's access to the rest-of-the-world markets depends upon its willingness to allow access to its own. Second, globalization in the late-twentieth century has been accompanied by high rates of innovation. Innovations tend to strengthen the power of innovator for two reasons. First, a country that closes its markets denies its consumers access to recent technologies. Since a country's competitiveness depends partially upon being able to incorporate the most recent technological advances in its exports, closed-market policies become self-defeating. Second, high rates of innovation lower the number of firms that can offer "credible" alternatives to the host country. Countries have also lost bargaining power against the multinationals if these firms were interested in a country for reasons of cheap labor. With globalization, multinationals have been developing sourcing capabilities in a number of countries. Rising labor costs in one location can be countered by shifting production, at very little inconvenience and cost, to another location. Simultaneously, the proportion of labor costs to the total cost of manufactured goods has tended to decrease; hence, firms do not have to locate their production in the country with the lowest wages, but can afford to pay higher wages if they have to be incurred in an economic environment that offers superior infrastructure.

The second area of government's responsibility relevant to our discussion is the design and implementation of industrial and trade policies. Governments have always believed that it is possible to direct their national economies through appropriate fiscal and tax policies—beliefs worth pursuing if government policies are driven by a desire to overcome market imperfections, or at least to help infant industries meet global challenges. Such policies had a fair chance of success in pre-globalization days since national markets were somewhat protected against global competition. Accordingly, many governments provided tariff and legal protection for domestic industries.

There is growing evidence that such policies are no longer tenable in a globalizing world. Hart and Aseem outline a number of serious objections to such policies—and by extension, to the main justifications for government's role in the economy: "[T]here is a belief that (strategic trade and industrial policies) provide fertile grounds for 'crony-capitalism,' that they are inherently corrupt, that they lack transparency and thus impede democratic oversight of economic policies, and that they impede efficient allocation of resources."[31] Rajan and Zingales[32] identify similar problems that help explain the East Asian debt crisis of the late 1990s: decision making by a close-knit elite led to an environment in which proposals for investments and policies were not subjected to the kinds of scrutiny that normally take place in an open environment. This led to selection of projects that turned out to be economically unviable. This failure of governance took place in the advanced emerging economics of East Asia—economics that had hitherto shown an impressive track record—and led to the severe financial crisis of 1997-98.

To summarize, globalization of the world economy, especially the globalization of financial and product markets, has shifted the balance of power in the direction of those who possess organizational skills and away from those who have control over tangible factors of production. In the pre-globalization days, conveniently labeled as a nation-state based system, the competitive advantage of a developing country rested on access to national markets (high rents), access to cheap labor (low rents), and access to raw materials (low rents). In that system, the competitive advantage of corporations rested in access to technology and technical information (medium rents due to oligopolistic competition among firms within an industry), organizational abilities (high rents due to need to manage risks in a changing environment), access to global markets (high rents due to need for advanced marketing technology—which due to the need to be close to the consumer was difficult to acquire and transfer) and the backing of their home country governments. The globalization of the world economy increased competition between host countries as well as firms, resulting in increased levels of risks. The need to manage these risks increased the rents associated with organizational abilities at the cost of rents associated with technical information, access to domestic markets, and tangible factors of production. With globalization, the premium will be on skills that help recognize changes taking place in the environment and shape effective actions taken in response. Countries that do not want to see the levels of rents associated with their endowments decrease will have to exhibit flexibility in view of changing global conditions.

VI. Conclusion: Governance and Conditionality

Should the debt of the highly indebted countries be forgiven? There is no doubt that the debt burden is excessive. Debt concession will release resources for economic development. But financial resources, unfortunately, are not sufficient by themselves to bring about development or to remove poverty. They must be managed with care if the benefits are to flow to the poorest sections of the society. Are the countries that receive debt-forgiveness likely to benefit from such concessions? What will ensure that debt-forgiveness benefits the poorest segments of the society?

The answers to these questions require an understanding of some of the conditions within the countries that are facing debt problems and some of the developments in the world economy. The rapidly globalizing world economy requires efficient and flexible governance structures. Well-functioning governance structures exclude systems in which those in positions of power make political and economic decisions that serve their own interests rather than those of the public they are supposed to represent. This is especially true in a world economy in which comparative advantages of countries and firms change very quickly. Unfortunately the countries that are facing debt problems are, in most cases, characterized by high levels of corruption. The main problem with a corrupt system is that new resources that are made available are not necessarily directed toward the needs of the society. To ensure that freed-up resources benefit the largest sections of population, it is essential that debt forgiveness be accompanied by reform of the governance systems in the indebted countries.

Reforms of the governance structures have to include, above all, reduction in the levels of corruption. It is well recognized now that corruption at lower levels cannot survive unless those at the top share in the spoils of corruption. Hence reform must begin at the top. Since the present governance structures serve those in power, those in control of the governance structures have no incentives to change them. The pressures for changes have to come from elsewhere. Creditor countries can exercise the influence they have by introducing very strict "conditionality" to debt forgiveness. At the top of these conditions should be a requirement to improve the governance structure of the countries involved. To forgive debt without ensuring that conditions are created for more efficient, less corrupt use of funds in the future is at best to waste resources, and at worst would do further harm.

Donor countries must ensure that political elites in the HIPCs agree both to reforms, and to outside monitoring of the implementation of these reforms. Past experience provides sufficient evidence that these reforms will not happen voluntarily. Grassroots organizations advocating the interests of the poor have the responsibility to ensure that the corrupt political elite is not allowed to usurp resources that will be released through debt relief.

ENDNOTES

1. An earlier version of this paper was presented in a lecture sponsored by the Center for Ethics and World Societies, Colgate University, Hamilton, New York, March 1, 2001. The author is grateful to Prof. Michael Johnston and participants at the Center presentation for comments. The author is also grateful to the John Molson School of Business for funding this research and to Ms. M. Roquebrun for valuable research assistance.

2. See Table 1 in Brooks, Ray, Mariano Cortes, Francesca Fornasari, Benoit Ketchekmen, Ydahlia Metzgen, Robert Powell, Saqib Rizavi and Kevin Ross. 1998. *External Debt Histories of Ten Low-Income Developing Countries: Lessons from Their Experience.* Working Paper of the International Monetary Fund, WP/98/72 (May). The annual average ratio of debt-to-exports ranged from 296 percent (Kenya) to 2512 percent (Nicaragua) during 1991-95. The average ratio for ten countries was 751 percent. Brooks et al attribute increases in debt burdens to exogenous (external as well as internal) shocks as well as to lack of internal management and reforms.

3. See, for example, the website of Jubilee 2000 http://www.j2000USA.org/debt/edpack/effects.html (viewed 25 March 2004).

4. Nominal oil prices increased from $2.11/barrel in 1960s to more than $36/barrel in 1980, increasing the oil import bill for oil importing countries seventeen fold. Due to the nature of the product, the price elasticity in the short-term tends to be close to zero—making it difficult to reduce the quantity of imports in response to price increases.

5. Developing countries depended too heavily on exports of commodities, and terms of trade for commodities have generally tended to worsen, especially if time value of price movements is taken into account. See Jain, Arvind K. 1987. "Time Preference for Price Deviations and Terms of Trade," *Economics Letters* 22:2-3, pp. 303-307.

6. See Jain, Arvind K. 1986. "International Lending Patterns of U.S. Commercial Banks." *Journal of International Business Studies* 17:3, pp. 73-88, and Jain, Arvind K. 1986. "Bank Size and International Lending Patterns." *Economics Letters* 22:1, pp. 55-59, on the patterns of distribution of loans by the commercial banks. The situation was not helped by the fact that competitive forces in the banking industry allowed banks to find comfort in herding behavior.

7. See Daseking, Christina, and Robert Powell. 1999. *From Toronto Terms to the HIPC Initiative: A Brief History of Debt Relief for Low-Income Countries.* Working Paper of the International Monetary Fund, WP/99/142, for a discussion of the links among export credits, foreign aid and deficit financing.

8. For a brief discussion of the lack of analysis preceding the loans, see Jain, Arvind K. 2000. "Governance of Global Financial Markets: Risk of Hubris." In Frenkel, M. and M. Rudolf. *Risk Management: Challenge and Opportunity.* Berlin: Springer, Berlin, pp. 238-240, and Jain, Arvind K. 1993. "Dictatorships, Democracies, and the Debt Crisis." In Riley, Stephen P. (ed.). *The Politics of Global Debt.* New York: St. Martin's Press, pp. 69-82.

9. Records of the hearings by a US Congress Committee show no evidence that any attempt was made to recognize the role of corruption in Mexico's debt crisis that commenced in 1982. Almost the entire discussion was devoted to the external causes of the crisis and the need for "macroeconomic" adjustments. United States. House of Representatives, Committee on Foreign Affairs. 1984. "The Mexican Economic Crisis: Policy Implications for the United States." Washington, D.C.: U.S. Government Printing Office.

10. This summary of the HIPC initiative draws upon Boote, Anthony R., and Kamau Thugge. 1997. *Debt Relief for Low-Income Countries and HIPC Initiative.* Working Paper of the International Monetary Fund, WP/97/24 (March); and the details of the list of countries included in this section and in Table 1 are from International Monetary Fund International Monetary Fund. 2003. "Heavily Indebted Poor Country (HIPC) Initiative: Status of Implementation." Washington D.C.: IMF, unpublished paper.

11. Levels of debt were measured by calculating a net present value (NPV) of all debt owed. Loans given by international banks were calculated at their face value but the loans given at concessional terms (usually loans given by export financing banks in the industrialized countries) were converted into values that would be equivalent to the values of loans that would have been given by commercial banks. The objective of this discounting of concessional loans at market interest rates was to make the loans given by banks and those given by public agencies comparable in terms of discussion of funds required for the HIPC initiative. Since the interest rate on a concessional loan is not the market interest rate, a debt forgiveness of, say, $1 million will cancel a bank loan of $1 million but a concessional loan of *more than* $1 million.

12. Paris Club is an informal forum where debtor countries negotiate with creditors. The club does not have a fixed membership. From 1976 to December 1996, this club had organized 169 reschedulings involving US$52.3 billion of debt. See Daseking, Christina, and Robert Powell. 1999. *From Toronto Terms to the HIPC Initiative: A Brief History of Debt Relief for Low-Income Countries.* Working Paper of the International Monetary Fund, WP/99/142, Table 1.

13. International Monetary Fund, 2003, "Heavily Indebted Poor Country (HIPC) Initiative: Status of Implementation." Washington D.C.: IMF, unpublished paper.

14. Daseking, Christina, and Robert Powell, 1999, *From Toronto Terms to the HIPC Initiative: A Brief History of Debt Relief for Low-Income Countries.* Working Paper of the International Monetary Fund, WP/99/142, Table 3.

15. This account is summarized from Beattie, Alan. 2001. "Zambia's Deadly Virus." *Financial Times Weekend*, July 21-22, p. I.

16. Charlotte Denny, Charlotte. 2001. "Corruption Busters." *Guardian Weekly*, July 12-18, p. 11.

17. Jain, Arvind K., 2001. "Corruption: A Survey." *Journal of Economic Surveys* 15:1, pp. 92-3.

18. Kaufmann, Daniel. 1998. "Research on Corruption: Critical Empirical Issues." In Jain, Arvind K. (ed.). *Economics of Corruption.* Boston: Kluwer Academic Press, p 133.

19. Wade, Robert. 1985. "The Market for Public Office: Why the Indian State is Not Better at Development." *World Development* 13:4, pp. 467-97.

20. Gupta, Sanjeev, Hamid Davoodi, and Erwin Tiongson. 2001. "Corruption and the Provision of Health Care and Education Services." In Jain, Arvind K. (ed.). *The Political Economy of Corruption.* London: Routledge, pp. 111-141.

21. Mauro, Paolo. 1995. "Corruption and Growth." *Quarterly Journal of Economics* 110:3, pp. 681-712.

22. Tanzi, Vito, and Hamid Davoodi. 2001. "Corruption, Growth, and Public Finances." In Jain, Arvind K. (ed.). *The Political Economy of Corruption.* London: Routledge, pp. 89-110.

23. Direct taxes refer to those levied on income and wealth and indirect taxes to those that are based on consumption. Direct taxes place greater burden of tax revenues on

higher income earners—who—in corrupt environments—have more control over what kind of taxes are paid.

24. Gupta, Sanjeev, Hamid Davoodi, and Erwin Tiongson. 2001. "Corruption and the Provision of Health Care and Education Services." In Jain, Arvind K. (ed.). *The Political Economy of Corruption.* London: Routledge, pp. 111-141.

25. Shleifer, Andrei, and Robert Vishny. 1993. "Corruption." *Quarterly Journal of Economics* 108:3, pp. 599-617.

26. See the website http://www.dbonline.concordia.ca/jain/mainglobalization.htm for extensive literature on effects of globalization.

27. For a brief survey of importance of governance for development, see Grindle, Merilee S. 2000. "Ready or Not: The Developing World and Globalization." In Nye, Joseph S., and John D. Donahue (eds.). *Governance in a Globalizing World.* Washington, D.C.: Brookings Institution, pp. 178-207.

28. See Bartram, Sohnke M., and Gunter Dufey. 2001. "International Portfolio Investment: Theory, Evidence, and Institutional Framework," *Financial Markets, Institutions and Instruments* 10:3, pp. 85-155, for evidence and the importance of this assertion.

29. An imperfect example would be the asymmetry in the way large firms like Monsanto have been able to protect their inventions of genetically modified seeds while at the same time other firms have expropriated and patented knowhow—for example, in the area of traditional medicines—technology that can be said to belong to society at large.

30. For a brief description of the negotiation process see Beamish, Paul W., Allen J. Morrison, Philip M. Rosenzweig, and Andrew C. Inkpen. 2000. *International Management.* Boston: Irwin McGraw, pp. 204-210.

31. Hart, Jeffery A., and Aseem Prakash. 1999. "Globalization, Governance, and Strategic Trade and Investment Policies." In Prakash, Aseem, and Jeffrey A. Hart (eds.). *Globalization and Governance.* London: Routledge, pp. 252-253.

32. Rajan, Raghuram G., and Luigi Zingales. 1998. "Which Capitalism? Lesson from the East Asian Crisis." *Journal of Applied Corporate Finance* 11:3, pp. 40-48.

8

Seventy-one Years of PRI Come to an End?
Electoral Reform in Mexico

Andrea S. Falken

If there is one consistent theme in the debate over reform, it is that free, honest, and competitive elections are essential. Electoral reform promises no anti-corruption miracles, but without it citizens face far bigger challenges. Mexico's presidential election of 2000 was a landmark in electoral reform; for the first time a challenger defeated the candidate of the long-entrenched ruling PRI party, and did so in a country where electoral abuses had become deeply rooted traditions. Andrea Falken examines electoral reform in this chapter, focusing not only upon the problems that were tackled but also upon the social and political context. Corruption and electoral fraud were only part of the PRI story, and the victory of Vicente Fox in 2000 was only one step toward continuing reform; indeed, as his term enters its final stages he is struggling politically on several fronts while some elements of PRI are actively rebuilding. Nevertheless Mexico is an encouraging example for all democracies—the US included—as they search for ways to improve the quality of electoral democracy.

> *"The PRI never loses, and when it loses, it cheats."*
> - *El Universal* columnist Rafael Álvarez Corderno

> *"It's not that we have Fox; it's that we have a choice."*
> - Adolfo Aguilar Zinzer, journalist turned Fox advisor

I. Introduction

On July 2, 2000, in what was arguably the most transparent election ever to take place in Mexico, the Institutional Revolutionary Party (PRI)—the ruling political party for the previous seventy-one years—lost the presidency to the National Alliance Party (PAN). This historic event captured the attention of Mexicans and foreigners alike well before the actual day of the election. Ever since President Ernesto Zedillo made a promise not to elect his successor through the traditional party mechanism–the institutionalized *dedazo* (pointing of "the big finger") and instead proposed to hold a presidential primary election, the presidential campaign of 2000 had taken a different tone. Intellectuals raced to predict the outcome of the election and heatedly debated the possibilities among each other since for the first time there was more than one. Major daily papers worldwide carefully covered the series of events culminating in the opposition's win. On election day, the world's attention was focused on the events in Mexico, with much of the international community hoping to view, and some even directly helping to ensure, the results of numerous electoral reforms and political changes. The common hope was that this would be a more transparent election. Increased transparency would, in turn, allow for more competition between political parties in the future, and competition, it is widely hoped, will provide a natural check on any future governing party.

The scope of the change thus envisioned should not be underestimated. Indeed, until the early 1990s, Mexico's electoral system had fostered corruption, rather than restraining or creating alternatives to it. Although Mexico was nominally a constitutional democracy, in practice it lay much closer to authoritarian rule. To maintain its dominance, the PRI either bought votes with material goods or coerced them by means of intimidation tactics. Presidential elections were not free, fair and competitive, but rather democratic facades that lent legitimacy to leaders handpicked by the regime and preordained to win, by electoral fraud if necessary. As a result, Mexican citizens had lived under a virtual monopoly of party power since the 1920s, with the PRI winning all thirteen presidential elections between 1929 and 1994.

Despite a shady history that created doubts as to the feasibility of a fair election and reports of irregularities only days before polling day, as officials tallied the votes on election night Vicente Fox Quesada, the PAN candidate, pulled ahead. As the results accumulated, it became clear that 2000 would be the year when a presidential candidate from an opposition party would win in Mexico. While this historic change was made possible by many factors of both domestic and foreign origin, this article focuses specifically on the anti-corruption reforms that shaped the 2000 election, and on the question of whether the increased electoral competition these reforms helped bring about will help check corruption in the future.

Party structure

An understanding of corruption in Mexico begins with a look at the scope
and structure of the PRI. Political parties are vehicles by which the electorate
and government organize themselves in a democracy. Parties conduct campaigns, raise and spend money and, both during and between election campaigns, help structure elite competition. By these criteria, PRI was both less and
more than a political party as we normally use the term. Certainly it was a for-
midable electoral force and formed the backbone of the Mexican political elite
but lacking were the more democratic party functions – those allowing citizens
to voice their interests, organize themselves, and make meaningful political
choices. As Schultz and Williams explain it, "In democracies, parties are established to obtain political power. In Mexico, in contrast, *the* party was established
to retain (not acquire) political power." They conclude that the structure of the
PRI suggests that it did not truly qualify as a political party.[1]

The pervasiveness of the PRI and its close association with governmental
institutions has also made it much *more* than the typical political party. So
closely linked were the party and the government that the PRI was often referred
to simply as 'the party of the state'; accordingly, citizens long had a difficult
time distinguishing between the two, as is demonstrated by their interchangeable
use of the terms 'government' and 'PRI'. PRI was not merely a component of
political life in Mexico, and it certainly was not an outgrowth of public interest
but was, rather, a tool of elites who dominated political life and the state. It com-
prised the whole of the Mexican political system—a one party system. "Mexico
could be accurately described until 1988 as a one-party, one-branch system
dominated by an omnipotent president."[2] In this "interpenetration of party and
state" the PRI resembled what Mair calls a "cartel party".[3] Mair's model is particularly interesting in that it acknowledges a role for various "opposition" parties in the functioning of a cartel, and suggests ways in which codependent party
organizations can hold political hegemony. Sartori also emphasized such relationships in his often-cited definition of the pragmatic hegemonic party:

> The hegemonic party neither allows for a formal nor a *de facto* competi-
> tion for power. Other parties are permitted to exist, but as second class,
> licensed parties; for they are not permitted to compete with the hege-
> monic party in terms and on an equal basis.[4]

In PRI's Mexico there were no truly competitive political forces outside of
the party. Smaller "opposition" parties such as the Popular Socialist Party (PSP)
and the Authentic Party of the Mexican Revolution (PARM) were easily bought
off, coming to endorse the PRI in exchange for patronage and local offices. Such
collusion, however, was limited, suggesting either that the PRI was unable to
incorporate other parties by bargaining or did not need to do so. I would liken
the PRI to another type of oligopoly—the price-leadership (also known as
Stackelberg) model.[5] This model allows for one large and several small firms—

or, in this case, political parties—and describes action-taking in two distinct steps: first the larger, stronger firm makes a decision, and then the weaker firms react to that move. There is no need to demonstrate active collusion in the price leadership model, and yet the dominance of the super-firm remains unquestionable. PRI might be likened to a dominant firm with supreme power. By this model, smaller opposition parties such as the PAN and PRD merely reacted, doing what they could to minimize the effects of the party of the state, leading to a political party system that is anything but competitive.

A Word about corruption

Mexico and the PRI are frequently referred to as corrupt. But that is scarcely the whole story with regard to the decline of the PRI and the consolidation of democracy. Indeed, few who condemn corruption in Mexico fully understand the complexity of the situation. What does "corruption" really mean? According to Johnston, corruption is the "abuse of a public role or trust for the sake of some private benefit".[6] If we regard the PRI's elites and its clients as beneficiaries, it neatly fits this definition of corruption. Indeed, the party took advantage of the country's electoral processes to benefit the party itself and members of the elite, engaging in clearly nefarious practices to retain control of and to exploit the state. Under the PRI, *la mordida* (the bribe) became institutionalized and the party was a tool by which individuals and interests could plunder the state for private benefit.

But "corruption" by itself is insufficient to describe what seems to be a much broader-reaching phenomenon. Perhaps we do not even possess the vocabulary to accurately and objectively discuss the situation. Since corruption has often, if not always, been seen as a property of particular government organizations or of limited groups of individuals, the term connotes a system that at least claims to uphold norms and values that transcend self-interest. However, in other cases, including that of Mexico, "corruption" takes the form of a web of complicity embracing most of government and political life. Under the PRI, there was no recourse or appeal to another branch, sector or organization, for all were involved in corrupt deeds, directly or indirectly. The PRI has thus been described as having a "corporatist structure":[7] party members no longer retained individual responsibility for their actions. Culpability was dispersed throughout the party as an institution, making actions less risky for members of the PRI as individuals. Further, PRI tactics made it difficult for opposition parties to mount any viable competition and nearly impossible for citizens to hold the Mexican government accountable for its acts. The PRI's breadth contributed not only to its ability to commit corrupt acts, but also to the overall weakness of political competition in Mexico, and to the continuing problems in Mexico's development as a democracy.

II. Politics—and More—PRI Style

The PRI established and maintained its hegemony through a variety of techniques. The following discussion is limited to a few examples of the creative electoral practices that helped sustain the PRI, although its shadier dealings were by no means reserved for election time.

Vote buying

Particularly in the rural states and the slums outlying Mexico City, the PRI was known to make deliveries of essential supplies such as tortillas, clothing and other badly needed items with the expectation that recipients would vote PRI. In other cases, the party made promises prior to election day of what was to come after individuals voted in its favor. The PRI delivered paved roads, electricity and other modern conveniences, winning the loyal support of a large segment of poor rural Mexicans. An aspect of this vote buying especially striking to foreigners is that, as with many other corrupt electoral practices, the PRI made no attempt to conceal it. The distribution of gifts to constituents prior to elections is still not considered a crime according to Mexican law—nor is it in many places in the U. S.—and was very much accepted in the political climate of the country. The real problem with the party's handouts lay in the fact that many recipients were not aware that while they could accept these gifts they had no obligation to vote PRI. During the late 1980s, vote buying became increasingly institutionalized with the advent of President Salinas de Gortari's social spending programs PRONASOL and PROCAMPO. Not surprisingly, because local PRI officeholders distributed these resources, they were soon converted into patronage by which the PRI could obtain votes.

Electoral fraud

As a May 27, 2000 *Washington Post* article entitled "How to Vote Twice in Mexico" somewhat humorously illustrated, it was exceptionally easy for many years to commit voter fraud in Mexico.[8] Like those of its northern neighbor, Mexico's voter registry has long been incomplete. It also contained many repeat names useful to the ruling party in vote stealing. These were a reflection, among other factors, of frequently used names and a system known as *domicillo conocido* (known residence). In small towns and makeshift slums lacking house numbering, voters simply wrote *domicillo conocido* on their registration forms, indicating to a visitor looking for the individual that he must simply ask around, for that person's residence would be commonly known within the village. It is a system that has existed since ancient times but one that made it nearly impossible to distinguish among individuals with common Mexican names. Because of this and other sorts of confusion, PRI officials were able to manipulate the use of voter identification cards. The cards were made, bought and sold just like any other coveted form of identification.

Aside from voter identification problems, blatant vote stealing was commonplace. Dan La Botz has chronicled some of the corrupt election day techniques used within polling places to steal the vote, noting their sometimes-amusing English translations. For example, the PRI professional vote stealers were known as *mapaches* (raccoons). These individuals rode the *carrusel* (carousel) to different polling stations, carrying with them *urnas embarazadas* (pregnant ballot boxes)—ones that had been pre-stuffed with votes—and making *tacos* at the polling places: by folding their ballots in half, PRI vote stealing brigades could wrap several additional marked ballots within a single one. PRI controlled voting stations would also change the location of the polls at the last minute, creating the phenomenon of *ratones locos* (crazy mice), as voters scurried to find their polling station.[9]

Intimidation

Because of its broad scope, the PRI could control citizens' everyday lives and intimidate them with the threat of using official powers to their detriment. Even more serious than the possibility of withdrawing a family's government-paid benefits or denying it future ones was the very real threat of violence against opponents. Patrick Oster gives the account of several *campesino* men who "disappeared" during an anti-PRI demonstration: police pushed Abelardo Velasco and three others into a truck well after the violence of the demonstration had cleared. They were never seen again. The PRI was only infrequently and minimally held accountable for its crimes, and this was even less likely when an incident involved mistreatment of indigenous or poor Mexicans. Rural peasants were a dime a dozen to the party; those responsible for even the most heinous crimes were rarely prosecuted. Independencia, the place of the disappearance mentioned in Oster's book, is not coincidentally located in the poorest, most southern, illiterate and indigenous state in the country—Chiapas. "People die or are tortured in such places with little notice from the rest of the country."[10]

Intimidation was particularly a problem in rural states experiencing resistance movements. The Zapatista National Liberation Army (EZLN) in Chiapas, and the Popular Revolution Army (EPR) and People's Revolutionary Army (ERPI) in Guerrero, have organized multiple armed uprisings. Ostensibly to keep the peace, government forces remained stationed throughout these states, creating a situation of low-intensity warfare. Under the PRI, citizens endured military training and armed military checkpoints along main roads that detained and searched all who passed, thereby intimidating both natives and outside observers. Other events, such as the December 22, 1997, Massacre at Acteal in Chiapas, gave indigenous peasants further reason to be wary of government forces. On that date, between 50 and 150 government-supported troops, dressed in a variety of local uniforms—local police, army and, just to confuse the responsibility of the attack, the Zapatista's own characteristic ski masks—descended upon the small autonomous village of Acteal with the intent of wiping out its population. The armed troops killed forty-five and injured twenty-six, 80 percent of whom were women and children. Among them were five pregnant women, whose bellies the soldiers slashed with machetes and babies pulled from the womb. Years after the attack, the survivors remaining in Acteal continued to live in fear of the government troops stationed only 100 meters up the road; many soldiers stationed at this checkpoint were the very same ones who had executed the massacre, but who remained unpunished. In addition to regular police and army attacks, the PRI also sponsored violent paramilitaries in the region who damaged the *campesinos'* crops and homes and participated in similar massacres and their respective cover-ups.[11]

The political opposition was also a major target of PRI violence. The Revolutionary Democratic Party (PRD), a growing opposition party formed in September, 1988,[12] lost many party officials and supporters to politically motivated assassinations. From 1988 to 2000, 645 members and activists of the PRD were killed. One PRD congressional candidate, forty-one-year-old Mario Valdéz of Guerrero, endured detainment and torture by local police and took five bullets, one of which left him blind in the left eye, in politically motivated attacks during previous campaigns. The entire family of a member of the opposition would often be put in jeopardy by one individual's activity, as was the case in the kidnapping of the daughter of the national president of the PAN.[13] Because of the hazards inherent in their work, it is no wonder that opposition parties had trouble developing and maintaining strong party cadres.

Media bias

The PRI also had the advantage of unquestioned supremacy in the media. Patrick Oster gives an account of one *periodista's* struggles with autonomy: Julio Scherer García became editor of the Mexico City paper *Excélsior* in 1968, the year of the great civilian protest in Mexico City and a time of oppressive action by the regime against the opposition. Scherer gave critical coverage to events at the time and was soon under fire, both from the government and from a government-supported faction of his own staff. In 1976, when he called an emergency staff meeting, armed rebels took over *Excélsior* for good, converting it to a journalistic appendage of the government.[14]

Obstacles to a free and fair press were hardly limited to this incident. On a daily basis, Mexican reporters had to resist the temptation to supplement their meager salaries with government bribes and with articles paid for by the government though not marked as advertisements. When Scherer began his own paper, he had to buy surplus newsprint from his competition because of the government's monopoly control of newsprint. Like other sectors of the population, including opposition party members and *campesinos*, journalists, too, faced life-threatening job hazards. According to the human rights organization, Freedom House, more journalists were murdered in 1987 in Mexico than in any other country.[15]

In addition, the PRI maintained control of television and radio production, the two more popular modes of obtaining news in Mexico, so that all three media were effectively dominated by the PRI. Citizens heard only superficial radio coverage, watched reporters deliver news from PRI-inspected scripts and viewed delayed transmissions of government censored foreign programs. If a program presented opposition to the government there was no hesitation in shutting it down. Not surprisingly, during election campaigns, the PRI received both more extensive, and more favorable, coverage.

The decline of the PRI

Based on the above description, the Mexican political situation might have seemed hopeless only five years ago—and, indeed, many thought it was. Yet this powerful and pervasive political machine was brought down as a result of a decline in the party's legitimacy and by electoral reforms that created opportunities for greater media and citizen scrutiny.

An extended chain of events helped undermine the PRI's legitimacy and support. Elections in Mexico have always been flawed but beginning in 1988, when it first appeared possible that another party might win the presidency, PRI electoral abuses became even more egregious. In that year, a breakaway faction of the PRI won significant popular support for its candidate, Cuauhtémoc Cárdenas Solórzano. On election day a new computer system, which was supposed to rapidly tally the votes, "shut down," providing the PRI with the cover it needed for vote tampering. In many cases, numbers were so obviously fraudulent that the PRI's totals in a given municipality exceeded the total number of voters registered in that area. "This not only damaged its legitimacy, it created the idea that an opposition force might actually be able to win a Mexican election."[16] In some state elections in subsequent years, public support for opposition candidates for governor was so extensive that violence and protest ensued when apparent winners were denied the official victory. In an effort to calm enraged opposition supporters, the newly elected President Salinas forced the resignation of the several "winning" PRI candidates, putting temporary governors in power until new elections could be held. Salinas's moves were meant to head off worse trouble, such as the ascendance of opposition parties. In a way, it was also an early manifestation of one of the forces that helped to produce the 2000 election result: electoral reform. However, at the same time, the recognition of a handful of opposition wins gave those parties the incentive to cry wolf, contesting the outcome of elections even in some cases when they had not won the election. Furthermore, Salinas's decision to begin overturning election results was a poor move on his part, one that undermined the credibility of the electoral process and the role of popular opinion. By overturning the results of elections run by his government he virtually admitted that those processes, and many of his own party's wins, were fraudulent.[17]

III. Reforming Elections

The 2000 presidential election, by contrast, was predicted to be the fairest of all time in Mexico. This expectation, along with extensive voter education campaigns organized by the Federal Election Institute (IFE) and the Mexican NGO Alianza Cívica, generated excitement and a feeling of voter efficacy. Mexicans understood that political alternation could help check corruption and other abuses. A new sense of nationalism and appreciation for personal liberties was building, and many Mexicans looked forward to election day.

Increased voter awareness

The strong supporter base Fox enjoyed may also have had something to do with a more fundamental change in the Mexican political climate. Mexicans were becoming fed up with the PRI. "They humiliate us and treat us like beggars with their bags of blankets and old clothes," explained one woman, a resident of a slum on the outskirts of Mexico City called Valle de Chalco. The lower classes, whose votes could normally be bought by the PRI, were no longer so easily convinced. Another neighbor echoed that exasperation: "They think they can buy our dignity; they are wrong".[18] This increasing frustration and rage was vital to the alternation of power. Residents of Mexico City's slums had endured one too many indignities. Domínguez and McCann link such a shift in public values to the emergence and later consolidation of democracy.[19]

Increasing media coverage drew attention to the widespread abuses of power. The speed at which information could travel with the use of modern technology facilitated international understanding of Mexican events. Both governmental and non-governmental groups harnessed the power of the Internet to publicize their causes and gain support. One particularly good example of the effective use of the internet for grassroots mobilization was by the Zapatistas own leader, the so-called *Subcomandante* Marcos. Marcos was determined to make the world aware of the PRI's crimes against the indigenous peoples of Mexico. Through the use of the internet, Marcos sent his stirring manifestos from the depths of the Lacandon jungle to international NGOs and media, thereby garnering a large following abroad.

Debate format

Another novelty in the 2000 election was the fairer, U.S.-style presidential debate, agreed to—after some controversy—by all three candidates. Debates in the past hadn't really been debates at all, but were designed to allow the PRI to dominate opposition candidates. For example, in previous televised election debates, viewers could see and hear PRI candidates clearly, but whenever an opposition candidate began to speak, the television set suddenly displayed blue or red interference and merely static in place of audio reception. It was no secret that this "interference" was orchestrated by the PRI. In the 2000 debate, a time-keeper was charged with ensuring the candidates were given equal amounts of time. Each was allowed an introductory statement, opening statements for the three subcategories of debate and opportunities to voice open-ended opinions on those themes and during the concluding period. This debate format seemed most beneficial to Fox; a naturally commanding speaker, he possessed a familiarity with American-style debates that enabled him to come out on top, while Cárdenas (the PRD candidate) and Labastida (PRI) became mired in party muck time and time again. The two opponents unwisely addressed the issues of past corruption, enabling Fox to address broader issues.

The Main Elements of Electoral Reform

Legal Changes – during the administrations of Salinas and Zedillo
<u>1990</u>
Electoral violations made a criminal offense.

<u>1994</u>
Provision for foreign observers added to the electoral code.
Special Federal Prosecutor for Electoral Crimes (FEPADE) created.

<u>1996</u>
Federal Election Institute (IFE) changed from an executive to autonomous status. José Woldenberg becomes the independent leader.
Established new electoral registry systems to prevent the exclusion of voters and result tampering.
Created new system for selecting local election officials.
Clarifies the provisions for observation by NGOs and by representatives of parties.
Monitored allocation of paid advertising time.
Campaign finance laws revised.

Civil Society
Alianza Cívica, an independent observer group is formed in 1988 as a result of the blatantly fraudulent election. It becomes one of the nation's leading watchdog organizations, studying media coverage, conducting exit polls, and cosponsoring two observer delegations with Global Exchange.

Global Exchange, another NGO, based in San Francisco plays a key role in bringing two international observer delegations, the first two months prior to election day and the second on election day. These delegations resulted in two critical reports that are widely used in international reporting and research.

Media
Grupo Reforma newspapers
Posts an 800 number tip-line for citizens to report irregularities.
Sends reporters with mobile phones to remote voting stations.
Discourages reporters from accepting bribes by paying a reasonable salary.

Electoral procedures

The most striking aspect of the 2000 presidential election, however, was the thoroughness of electoral reform. Beginning in 1986, official electoral reforms had begun to break down the hegemonic structure of the PRI. In that year, new legislation introduced public financial support to campaigns, created a tribunal to investigate complaints over electoral irregularities and made it possible for opposition parties to supervise polling stations alongside their PRI counterparts.[20] At first, PRI officials agreed to reforms for the sake of appearances and, in fact, the early measures did little to eliminate disparities between parties. Later, when President Salinas took office after the highly contested 1988 election, electoral reform became a more serious issue; even Salinas recognized the importance of reforming, at least to some extent, as a way to regain some of the legitimacy his party had lost.

While at its creation merely another appendage of the PRI, the IFE has since been transformed. Its role in Mexican electoral politics changed dramatically, particularly over the *sexenio* (six year term) between the 1994 and 2000 presidential elections. From 1988 to 1998, five major electoral reforms—all of which were the subject of much debate among parties—took place, affecting two presidential elections.[21] Now a genuinely autonomous body, IFE has worked to standardize electoral processes and eliminate opportunities for fraud. The IFE has also been instrumental in bringing in foreign observers to analyze elections.

The result has been a significant decline in what have become known as "electoral irregularities". IFE, working with a variety of Mexican and international NGOs, cracked down on voter fraud in 2000, spending billions of pesos to issue 60 million photographic voting credentials, and to redesign *casillas* (ballot boxes) and voting booths.[22] Officials even claimed to have eliminated the PRI's secret funds, often used in past years to buy support and elections. All of this proved that the effects of dismantling the informal structures of authoritarian rule can prove profoundly destabilizing to the party in power.[23] This destabilization, in turn, allows opposition parties a chance to attain power and, in the case of an opposition win, sets a precedent for future electoral competition.

IV. Continuing Challenges

While the pace of reform quickened prior to the 2000 election, evidence from both election day and the campaign period suggests that further electoral reform is still required.

Media coverage

During the 2000 election, the unequal treatment of the different parties and their candidates in the media, while significantly diminished from earlier years, continued. Though certain enlightened newspapers such as the *Grupo Reforma* chain did everything they could to curb corruption, including posting front-page notices with an free telephone tip-line for voters to call in and report irregularities, papers such as Mexico City's *Excélsior* remained firmly in the PRI camp.

Josh Tuynman, national editor of *The News*, the country's only English language paper, resigned when his publisher ordered him not to run stories or pictures on Fox. Reporters at many papers continued to accept government bribes and to run articles paid for by candidates but not labeled as advertisements.[24] Television and radio programs also continued to be slanted. In Chiapas, a pre-election survey showed that the PRI received 57 percent of the airtime while the PAN was left with 11 percent and the PRD with 18 percent.[25] Another continuing problem was reporters' inability to obtain accurate data. The government's reluctance to permit the free flow of information was as much a barrier to the free press in the 2000 election as more obvious censorship and intimidation had been a few years earlier.

Rural targets

Despite IFE efforts and the honest desire of most citizens to see free and fair elections, some irregularities remained. Both the pre-election delegation sent by the San Francisco-based NGO Global Exchange and its election day delegation noted deficiencies in the electoral process, particularly in rural and indigenous regions. Among other problems, there were still no electoral materials in indigenous languages. Delegates also reported that IFE had trouble recruiting and training qualified volunteers to run polling stations in those areas, and that high levels of militarization in certain states continued to affect how and whether individuals voted.[26] Most noticeable was the way the federal government distributed particularly large numbers of public works projects such as clinics, roads and bridges in the months preceding the election.[27] The PRI's increased reliance on this tactic was probably to compensate for the loss of other now-defunct vote-stealing techniques. Increased social spending immediately before the election had the effect of making voters look more favorably upon the PRI. Although programs were actually funded by federal agencies, rather than by PRI itself, as in years past most rural recipients of such benefits did not distinguish between the two. In fact, not long before the election one driving through the small towns of Mexico could still see the influence of the PRI. Electricity poles were painted with the party's acronym to remind residents who brought utilities to the people. While increased public spending and the distribution of policy benefits before election time remains common today in many other countries, including the United States and the United Kingdom, in this case these handouts were directed to PRI supporters and villages, and withheld from opponents. Furthermore, they came after years of neglect and abuse—problems that would surely return following another PRI victory on election day.

Why did voters not see through such tactics? Perhaps they did not have the luxury of paying attention to the PRI's political agenda. They were poor farmers who desperately needed handouts and who were not accustomed to the idea of real electoral alternatives. In an environment of institutionalized corruption, a "take what you can get" attitude might have even been necessary to the survival of some of the poorest communities. In any event, both the PRI and other parties as well had long viewed elections in those terms. Opposition parties did, never-theless, remain on the lookout for vote buying during and before the election. In Chilapa de Alvarez, Guerrero, PRD officials exposed PRI's distribution of beans and cornmeal before the election. They also obtained a letter from a local PRI leader requesting more government-subsidized supplies to hand out because, in his own words, "we have a lot of competition from the PRD". As Rogelio Go-mez, director of the Mexican NGO Civic Alliance, noted, "the form of coercion has gotten more sophisticated". The PRI's manipulative tactics had not disap-peared; they had simply become subtler—in part because of increased national and international scrutiny.[28]

Post-electoral obstacles

Will Mexico's partially-reformed electoral system strengthen democracy and help control corruption? Clearly, there is still much to change. Interestingly, a great deal of this change must begin in the minds of the Mexican people. Citizen confidence in the democratic system is essential in its success. According to Roderic Ai Camp little confidence existed in any facet of the Mexican political system largely because of the high degree of perceived corruption: "76 percent of Mexicans believe that many or all members of the government are corrupt." There is also a general lack of confidence in political parties and in the electoral process.[29] The long-standing cynicism in these institutions has not vanished just because of the new strength of opposition parties. Critics such as linguist Noam Chomsky contend that regardless of who won the election, it represented "a minimal or null change since it does not modify the true structure of power".[30] To some degree this skepticism is understandable: the mere election of a new party does not guarantee systemic change. Still, major segments of Mexican society, and of the international community, hope and expect that Fox will fulfill at least some of his campaign promises. This is a necessary condition for long-term democratic change within the country, and for the emergence of a degree of faith in the government. There must be a limit to Mexican skepticism and a be-ginning point to trust. And even if a fairly elected president is willing to under-take dramatic change, sometimes his efforts to bring about reform are not enough. International events also limit his power to bring about change on a national level. That has become made evident during the years following the September 11th, 2001 terrorist attacks upon Mexico's closest and most influen-tial neighbor, the United States. Unfortunately, Fox's ability to fulfill at least some of his campaign promises—a task that does not rest solely in his hands—could prove an important condition for long-term democratic change within the country, and for the emergence of a degree of faith in the government.

V. Conclusions

Mexico's 2000 presidential election was an important lesson about both the value, and the limits, of electoral competition—both in itself and as a strategy for reform. While a change in the ruling party may be a step toward democratic consolidation in that it indicates increased electoral competition, citizens must recognize that it is not a change dramatic enough to rapidly renovate the entire Mexican political system—nor should it be. While Fox's election has undoubtedly been good for electoral competition and political life in Mexico, whether he is effective as President, particularly given the tense international climate during his *sexenio*, is another question entirely. This election merely indicates that citizens now have one important way to hold their elected officials accountable—if they choose to employ it.

In the 2000 election, many of the PRI's manipulative tactics could not survive within the context of a newly reformed electoral procedure. Others, as we have seen, became more intense and sophisticated. Still, Mexicans attitudes were turning a corner and adopting new democratic ideals. Most importantly, the PRI's cover of stability—for generations, its bedrock appeal—had been blown; its legitimacy had eroded to the point where it was virtually nonexistent. Meanwhile, citizens were taking greater notice of these injustices and beginning to assert themselves. The opposition was also getting smarter and tougher. Fox was able to overcome the archaic and faltering PRI electoral machine because of these combined forces. His own determination, character and strategy aided him to some extent, but much of his victory must be attributed to external circumstances, which luckily fell into place simultaneously. He was fortunate to have two poorly suited presidential candidates opposing him and to run at a time when the PRI's legitimacy had declined so extensively. He also reaped the benefits of a vastly reformed electoral system, and of a strong international presence and far-reaching educational campaign.

As the 2000 election approached, *The Economist* predicted, "until political power starts alternating, Mexico will not get some of the changes it most urgently needs".[31] So is Mexico now on the road to democracy and reduced corruption? Political competition and alternation are certainly a start, but only a start. As Mainwaring describes the process, Mexico has just completed the first step in the transition. The first stage in the transition to democratic consolidation begins with doubts about the regime and ends with the "competitive" election of a new government.[32] Democratic consolidation does not end there; much more must happen. In short, competition and political alternation are a necessary but not sufficient condition for the consolidation of democracy. Alternation and competition may prove to be an impetus for further corruption control in the long term, but in the short run may be disruptive: post-election headlines such as "Defeat Ruptures Mexican Party" suggest that the election will profoundly affect the structure of the PRI in coming years.[33] This may lead to further reform, but could also produce a political climate in which governance itself is difficult. The task now is not to sustain the PAN and turn it into a reincarnation of the PRI, but to support democratic change that will bring a variety of parties into office. The distinction between fundamental and sustainable change and a "shallow electoral façade" is an important factor in the consolidation of democracy.[34] While Fox may not be as sinister as Boullosa and others maintain, his election is only one step toward democratization. The real change will result from what Fox's successes or failures in office. The 2000 election was indeed historical and dramatic, but an increase in political competition is only one of several important steps on the road to democracy. It was tempting for Mexicans and foreign scholars alike to hail this election as a major democratic change but, in fact, the change has yet to begin. If Fox can avert mass disillusionment, democracy has a chance; but as the 2006 election approaches perceptions of his presidency are mixed at best. It is up to his administration to convince Mexicans that a democratic transition can and must continue. This latter stage is, if anything, likely to prove even more challenging than what has been accomplished already.[35] But at the very least, parties will be more careful in future; even the PRI, should it make a comeback, may have to earn popular support rather than buy or steal it. In this way, increased electoral competition may help check corruption in Mexico.

ENDNOTES

1. Schultz, Donald E., and Edward J. Williams. 1995. *Mexico Faces the 21st Century.* Westport, CT:
Greenwood Press, p. 30.
2. Ai Camp, Roderic. 1999. "Democracy through Mexican Lenses." *The Washington Quarterly* 22:3 (Summer), pp. 229-242.
3. Mair, Peter. 1997. *Party System Change: Approaches and Interpretations.* Oxford: Clarendon Press, p. 108.
4. Sartori, Giovanni. 1976. *Parties and Party Systems: A Framework for Analysis (Vol. 1).* Cambridge: Cambridge University Press, 1976, cited in Prud'home, Jean-Francois. 1998. "The *Instituto Federal Electoral* (IFE): Building an Impartial Electoral Authority." In Serrano, Mónica. *Governing México: Political Parties and Elections.* London: Institute of Latin American Studies, p. 140.
5. Hogendorn, Jan S. 1995. *Modern Economics.* Englewood Cliffs, N. J.: Prentice-Hall, p. 204.
6. Johnston, Michael. 1982. *Political Corruption and Public Policy in America.* Monterey, CA: Brooks-Cole, p. 4.
7. Moreno, Alejandro. 1998. "Part Competition and the Issue of Democracy: Ideological Space in Mexican Elections." In Serrano, Mónica. *Governing México: Political Parties and Elections.* London: Institute of Latin American Studies, p 72.
8. Anderson, John Ward, and Molly Moore. 2000. "How to Vote Twice in Mexico." *Washington Post* 27 May, p. A18.
9. La Botz, Dan. 1995. *Democracy in México: Peasant Rebellion and Political Reform.* Boston, MA: South End Press, p. 193.
10. Oster, Patrick. 1990. *The Mexicans: A Personal Portrait of the People.* New York: Harper and Row, p. 156.
11. Global Exchange/*Alianza Cívica* International Delegation. 2000. "The Pre-Electoral Conditions in Mexico 2000." (June). San Francisco: Global Exchange.
12. La Botz, Dan. 1995. *Democracy in México: Peasant Rebellion and Political Reform.* Boston, MA: South End Press, p. 123.
13. Moore, Molly. 2000. "In Mexico, Ballots and Bullets." *Washington Post* 28 June, p. A16.
14. Oster, Patrick. 1990. *The Mexicans: A Personal Portrait of the People.* New York: Harper and Row, p. 188.
15. *Ibid.*, p. 193.
16. NACLA (North American Council on Latin America). 1997. "Contesting México" *NACLA Report on the Americas* 33 (Jan./Feb.), p. 13.
17. Domínguez, Jorge I., and James A. McCann. 1996. *Democratizing Mexico: Public Opinion and Electoral Choices.* Baltimore: Johns Hopkins University Press, p. 174.
18. Thompson, Ginger. 2000. "In Mexican Slum, Two Views of The Government's Help." *New York Times* 26 June 2000.
19. Domínguez, Jorge I., and James A. McCann. 1996. *Democratizing Mexico: Public Opinion and Electoral Choices.* Baltimore: Johns Hopkins University Press, p. 24.
20. Prud'home, Jean-Francois. 1998. "The *Instituto Federal Electoral* (IFE): Building an Impartial Electoral Authority." In Serrano, Mónica. *Governing México: Political Parties and Elections.* London: Institute of Latin American Studies, p. 145.

21. *Ibid.*, p. 139.

22. Dillon, Sam. 2000. "Clean Vote Vowed in Mexico, but Fraud Dies Hard." *New York Times* 28 June.

23. Serrano, Mónica. 1998. *Governing México: Political Parties and Elections.* London: Institute of Latin American Studies, p. 11.

24. Anderson, John Ward. 2000. "Mexican Papers Use Impartiality to Influence Change." *Washington Post* 23 June, p. A20.

25. Anderson, John Ward. 2000. "Mexico's Dinosaurs Resurgent." *Washington Post* 23 May, p. A23.

26. Global Exchange/*Alianza Cívica* International Delegation. 2000. "The Pre-Electoral Conditions in Mexico 2000." (June). San Francisco: Global Exchange, p. 33)

27. De la Garza, Paul. 2000. "In México, A Blurry Line between Aid, Vote Buying." *Chicago Tribune* 6 June.

28. Anderson, John Ward. 2000. "Mexican Party Puts Campaign into Overdrive." *Washington Post*, 24 June, p. A17.

29. Ai Camp, Roderic. 1999. "Democracy through Mexican Lenses." *The Washington Quarterly* 22:3 (Summer), pp. 229-242.

30. Cason, Jim, and David Brooks. 2000. "La Alternancia es Más Ilusión que Paso Democrático Real: Chomsky." *La Jornada* 27 June 2000.

31. *The Economist.* 1999. "The End of an Affair." 2 October, pp. 38-9.

32. Mainwaring, Scott, Guillermo O'Donnell, and J. Samuel Valenzuela. (eds.). 1992. *Issues in Democratic Consolidation: The New South American Democracies in Comparative Perspective.* Notre Dame, IN: University of Notre Dame Press, p. 2.

33. Sullivan, Kevin. 2000. "Defeat Ruptures Mexican Party." *Washington Post.* 12 July, p. A33.

34. Ai Camp, Roderic. 1999. "Democracy through Mexican Lenses." *The Washington Quarterly* 22:3 (Summer), pp. 229-242.

35. Mainwaring, Scott, Guillermo O'Donnell, and J. Samuel Valenzuela. (eds.). 1992. *Issues in Democratic Consolidation: The New South American Democracies in Comparative Perspective.* Notre Dame, IN: University of Notre Dame Press, p. 2.

9

Building Social Action Coalitions for Reform[1]

Michael Johnston
Sahr J. Kpundeh

Getting citizens involved in reform on a sustained basis is not just a matter of identifying corruption as a problem, and will not work if we simply urge them to attack corruption in support of the public good. That sort of reform encounters classic collective-action problems; most citizens will wait for others to assume the costs and risks of working for reform, secure in the knowledge that better government—should it be attained—will benefit all. Michael Johnston and Sahr Kpundeh argue that building citizen action coalitions to fight corruption requires careful thought about the sorts of incentives that are needed, and that can be found, to motivate and reward citizen participation. They conclude that even where money and other material incentives are scarce, there are ways to encourage people to join together to back reform. The key lies in understanding what draws people into cooperative action in the first place.

I. Sustaining Reform

Societies rarely bring corruption under control through penalties, deterrence, or morality campaigns alone. Anti-corruption *coups* and the "one-man show" strategy usually do more harm than good—even if actually intended as reforms, which usually they are not—weakening civil society and the press and substituting intimidation for transparency and accountability. Reform is a long-term process bearing real costs and risks, and thus requires a system of incentives that can sustain it.

Historically, people have often reduced corruption in the course of doing other things—usually, while defending themselves against official abuse or the unfair advantages of others.[2] The process was sustained not so much by a vision of good government, but by the self-interests of people who saw a less corrupt system as both necessary and possible. Today's high-corruption societies cannot afford to wait and see whether such outcomes eventually occur. Modern corruption can be deeply entrenched domestically[3] and integrated into powerful international economic and political networks. The pace of change in the world economy and the harm corruption does to growth[4] mean that a society not making progress against corruption is vulnerable to forces beyond its control, and is missing opportunities that will not last forever. The challenge is to build an anti-corruption force rooted in society, possessing real influence, and sustained by credible incentives, and to build it quickly.

We suggest that *social action coalitions*, building broad-based cooperation among private parties and, as far as possible, working with government, can institutionalize opposition to corruption and reward good government. Such coalitions are a way to create a visible, legitimate reform movement quickly, and allow groups to "borrow" size and resources from each other as they work together. Even more important in the long run, the internal incentive systems of coalitions can *sustain* reform, counteract some of its costs, and protect members from reprisals after the initial enthusiasm has faded. This is particularly critical, for anti-reform forces are likely to mobilize in response to coalition activities. In a way, we propose to build a "clean machine": like urban political machines, a broad-based, effectively-led organization that rewards diverse constituencies for active support. Unlike corrupt machines, however, the coalitions we have in mind are open, honestly managed and aimed at reform.

Many groups are working to build anti-corruption coalitions.[5] The best-known effort is Transparency International, but others such as The Asia Foundation and USAID have also been involved. These drives often begin with much fanfare, and in some places they thrive. Too often, however, strong coalitions prove difficult to sustain, particularly where they are needed most. Even ardent advocates are likely to agree that we do not know enough about making the transition from launch to long-term viability. We believe the problems lie not in the strategy itself, but at the level of incentives—that is, how to offer benefits to supporters that others do not receive, and how those incentives compare to the costs and risks of reform. Analysis at that level does not lead us to a neat all-purpose coalition blueprint; it does, however, identify some of the things coalitions can offer and some of the basic problems to be overcome.

"Political Will" and civil society

Two of the most frequent responses to corruption are to call for "political will" on the part of officials and to urge the strengthening of civil society. Both ideas have obvious merit. "Political will"—credible and demonstrated commitment to reform—is essential to overcoming apathy and outright opposition, to setting clear priorities, and to mobilizing people and resources.[6] Committed anti-corruption leadership can have important demonstration effects: officials who witness real changes in their institutions and see corrupt colleagues losing jobs and going to jail are more likely to mend their ways than those whose leaders wink at misconduct (or, worse, actively participate in it). Without demonstrated political will, anti-corruption programs become empty gestures, or camouflage for continued abuses.

A strong civil society—self-organizing cooperative activity at the level between the state and the household—is critical as well.[7] As elusive as "strengthening civil society" may be in practice, it can provide anti-corruption agencies with critical information and feedback, uphold a framework of values,[8] build the organizational base and skills citizens need to take act on shared problems, and help open alternatives to mistreatment by corrupt officials. Where civil society is comparatively strong, corruption attracts what Weber called "social sanctions": popular condemnation that reinforces, and in many societies, carries more weight, than official standards of conduct. Where civil society is weak, on the other hand, moral frameworks may be weak and confronting corruption may be futile or downright risky; everyday dealings among citizens, and with officials, may be a game of *sauve qui peut*.

Political will at the top, and a strong civil society, can reinforce each other—a pattern seen in many low-corruption countries. Particularly where electoral democracy is viable, civil society can reward leaders and parties demonstrating effective leadership and penalize those who fail, thus making leadership roles more secure.[9] Even where democracy is only partially functional, the support of civil society can be valuable. For their part, leaders with the will to carry out reforms can also provide citizens a measure of security—both for reform and civil liberties generally—and open up political and economic alternatives to corrupt exploitation. Again, this does not require fully-functional democracy.

But political will and a strong civil society seldom emerge simply because they are needed. They are *outcomes,* not inputs, of broad-based political and social changes, and thus cannot be invoked as a *deus ex machina*. Where they exist, they grew out of long processes of change. Political will is not just a matter of elites' deciding to be good: they must have reason to think that it is in their interests to do so. So too with a strong civil society: we cannot just urge citizens to act. They need leadership, protection, and an organizational base. They need to know about each other—literally, that they are not alone. These are high thresholds, particularly for those who are vulnerable to corruption because of poverty, powerlessness, and isolation. Where can they, and we, begin?

II. Coalitions as a better strategy

We suggest that *coalition building* is a promising way to strengthen and link political will and civil society. By "coalitions" we mean *self-conscious, freely-organized, active, and lasting alliances of elites, organizations, and citizens sharing partially overlapping political goals—in this instance, including but not restricted to the control of corruption—and a basic commitment to peaceful reform.*[10] The *social action coalitions* we have in mind unite elites and civil society in a multi-faceted program of reform.[11] They are distinct from formal party coalitions,[12] but are more concrete than mere coordination or consultation groups.[13] They must be able to resolve internal conflicts, redirect members' actions in limited ways, and back up a strategy of action with meaningful incentives not available to outsiders.

Such coalitions—particularly those involving significant numbers of formal organizations—are not easy to build and even more difficult to sustain. At their best, they offer a little something to almost everyone; but that is also one of their main problems, for they must trade in a diverse range of incentives that may conflict with each other. And circumstances matter: if the regime is repressive and openly exploitative, or skilled at using its resources to undermine the coalition, the most determined efforts may come to naught.

Minimal conditions

Social action coalitions will not thrive everywhere, nor will they always be the best anti-corruption strategy. To succeed, they require *a functioning state* rather than the misrule of dictators, private armies or *mafiyas*. A reasonable level of *order* is also essential; pervasive violence (as in Colombia), famine or disease (as with the African AIDS crisis), or social disintegration (as in Zaire or parts of Russia) can render coalition-building impossible and corruption a secondary problem. *Meaningful boundaries between state and society* are essential too; in practice this means working limits on both official power and private influence, and the "space" required for a viable civil society and private economy. Where *basic civil liberties*—freedom to organize, assemble, and voice criticism of the regime—and *freedom from routine coercion* are a reality, people and groups will feel more secure about opposing corruption.[14] Equally important is a *reasonably free press*; not only can it become a "watchdog", it is also essential to publicize coalition's activities and to enable key incentives, as we shall see.

Also useful at the outset, if not essential, is a *crisis or opportunity* making clear why action against corruption is imperative.[15] Hong Kong's famous ICAC—whose anti-corruption strategy included extensive public involvement from the beginning—originated after a corrupt police official's escape touched off mass demands for reform. Its first step toward winning public confidence was to bring him back to Hong Kong for trial and imprisonment. *Outside support* from NGOs, aid partners and international organizations, including law-enforcement, pro-democracy and anti-corruption groups, will provide essential resources, expertise, and encouragement. Ultimately, however, reform must become the norm, not a crisis issue, and coalitions must be self-sustaining. Early opportunities will give way to different, but no less difficult, challenges as the coalition matures.

Strategic questions

Coalition building, in practice, poses many difficult questions. Who are the basic constituencies, and what do we ask of them? Virtually everyone suffers where corruption is serious, so in one way anyone is a potential member. But most costs of corruption, even if clearly understood, are long-term and widely-shared; some of the most important costs—lost political opportunities, reduced accountability of government—are intangible or difficult to document. The costs are often most compelling for those who have the least. Beneficiaries, on the other hand, have resources, connections, and a tangible stake in corruption. Thus many citizens may not feel a compelling reason to act against corruption at any one time, nor perceive a meaningful chance of success if they did.

What sort of relationship should a coalition have with the regime—fighting from the opposition corner, or cooperating? To some extent the answer depends upon the political options generally available. In a multi-party democracy a coalition must be nonpartisan, for reasons of credibility and adaptability, and can take a critical stance regarding specific corruption problems without directly antagonizing the powerful. But elsewhere competition is more apparent than real,[16] or democracy is nonexistent. In those cases people may respond to corruption evasively or illicitly, rather than confronting it directly,[17] even if they sympathize with reform and stand to gain from it in the long run. An adversarial stance will be counterproductive or dangerous, but too little independence will make credibility difficult to win.

Without doubt, reform coalitions must be forthright about opposing corruption. But in general they should seek cooperative relationships with the regime, *offering officials reasons and incentives to oppose corruption, and helping them develop the means with which to do so.* Such a stance will reduce the likelihood of official reprisals, thus helping coalition leaders control strain within the coalition[18] by keeping risks moderate and evenly shared among members. For those reasons, it should not become an investigative body, a whistleblower, or a force of anti-corruption vigilantes. Non-corrupt political leaders will not welcome such disruptions, and at the very least may withdraw their support and curtail access to information. Corrupt leaders, or those "on the fence" about reform, may become much more hostile. Instead, the emphasis should be on locating, uniting, and supporting those both within and without government who oppose corruption, providing the information and incentives they need to act effective against it. Providing technical information and expertise will do more to institutionalize reform than any additional fear of exposure or punishment that may flow from the coalition's own activities. Efforts to publicize—and to give regime leaders and coalition backers *the opportunity to take credit* for—anti-corruption successes can create positive incentives to reform now lacking in many high-corruption societies.

Overly close cooperation, of course, bears risks too. A coalition too closely linked to the regime will have little credibility. It may be used and co-opted by leaders who using the symbols of reform to conceal their stake in the *status quo* but will suffer equally when such wrongdoing is revealed. In particular, the coalition should resist any temptation to become a certification body. From the coalition's standpoint, giving anti-corruption "seals of approval" involves large risks and few rewards. They may entail complicated analysis beyond the capacity of coalition members; once given, such approval will be difficult to withdraw. Credit for successes will flow to those being "certified", while the coalition will be seriously damaged should recipients turn out to be corrupt.

III. Building and Sustaining Social Action Coalitions

Social action coalitions offer many advantages, but they are not easy to build. A good idea and the prospective benefits of controlling corruption are not enough. In the medium term, they must compete—and, in some respects, can conflict—with members' existing interests and agendas. Not only does opposing corruption often involve real costs and risks; some coalition members may have to forego corrupt benefits and relationships from which they benefit now, as well as the superficial sense of security to which they have grown accustomed.

Backers will include organizations as well as individuals, and lasting coalitions among organizations are rare.[19] For organization leaders there are many reasons not to join a coalition, or to support it in more than perfunctory ways, while the payoffs are small and uncertain. Joining a coalition may be a drain upon scarce resources, and can muddle an organization's identity. Adding a new mission, even as a partner in a broader front, may induce or worsen internal strains (members of a business group, for example, may want honest administration but oppose restrictions on political contributions). Anti-corruption activity may threaten carefully-nurtured relationships with government or opposition officials. *Autonomy* is of particular importance to organizational elites,[20] and may appear threatened by a substantial commitment to a coalition—the more so as the coalition grows in size and strength. Leaders of formal organizations will likely calculate costs and benefits more ruthlessly than individuals; after all, the decision will have usually more serious implications for the group. Coalition-builders will need to persuade elites that their groups' resources, unity and autonomy will not be threatened, that they may even increase in a less corrupt public arena, or that they are at significant risk should corruption go unchecked. An understanding of organization leaders' calculations, and of how they differ from those of individuals, will be important: while an individual's decision to support or leave a coalition will ordinarily not make a major difference, an organization's choice may be very important indeed.[21]

This is not to suggest that organizations will never join a coalition; more likely they will give symbolic support but withhold the sorts of hard resources, and public backing in time of controversy, needed for sustained effort. For mass-membership organizations, the problems may be less pronounced, particularly if there arises a clear-cut threat or some attention-getting event.[22] A mass membership, perhaps possessing less of a stake in connections to politically powerful figures, may press the leadership to support anti-corruption efforts, and it may be tempting for leaders to do so as visible evidence they have taken action. But such a process will be easier where civil society is comparatively strong and free to criticize the regime—conditions that may not apply where corruption is worst—and organizations without a significant mass base will remain difficult to enlist in the movement.

For both individual and potential organizational allies, reform has real risks and costs. Opposing corruption means taking on powerful interests, often in a framework where institutions and the rule of law are weak. Many people and groups will have been compromised by corruption. Others may have a stake in the status quo, such as a useful friendship with a patron. Active support of reform will mean foregoing those benefits in exchange for the uncertain prospect of something better—indeed, most likely something widely-shared—at some uncertain point in the future. Particularly for the "first movers" who come out early for reform it will be tempting to be a free rider.[23] A different, but equally problematical, logic applies to "blocking coalitions":[24] those who benefit from the early stages of reform but then seek to prevent further progress. We might imagine a group of businesspeople who, by resisting corruption among government inspectors in their industry, manage to lower their own costs, but then oppose the higher taxes necessary to pursue similar reforms might benefit others.

This does not mean coalition-building is futile. Skillful leadership can make the current costs of corruption, and the future benefits of reform, credible and compelling. And we should not underestimate the demonstration effects of finding a few prominent "champions" both inside and outside government—people who are willing to lead the fight, and to show possible opponents of corruption that they are not alone. The goal, rather, is to foster broad-based anti-corruption activity at many levels of society, *based upon self-interest and a sense of security,* rather than crusades doomed to become noble failures. Reform can take on a life independent of particular leaders' agendas, and of the efforts of any one anti-corruption group. A successful anti-corruption coalition may, in the long run, fade into the background of the vibrant civil society it helped create (though there will always be need for a group to keep the corruption issue alive). Getting to that point is, of course, a long and challenging process. How can we build this sort of coalition, and what can hold it together over the long run?

What's in it for me? Thinking about incentives

James Q. Wilson's classic work *Political Organizations*[25] offers an enduring typology of the incentives that motivate and reward organizational participation. Wilson challenges the economism of Olson[26] and others who argued that organizations seeking broadly shared goals would fall prey to "free rider" problems. Wilson, noting that such groups *do* form and persist for long periods, and that people act out of diverse motives, reasoned that successful organizations must offer members more than just a chance to achieve a goal. These incentives, he argued, were of four major types:[27]

Material incentives: rewards of tangible value, such as money or goods.

Purposive incentives: the accomplishment of a significant goal—often, the formal purpose of the organization. Members of a group that succeeds in cleaning up a city's parks do create a benefit available to all residents, but still derive a special satisfaction flowing from their membership and contribution toward that goal.

Specific solidary incentives: ". . . intangible rewards arising out of the act of associating that can be given to, or withheld from, specific individuals. Indeed, their value usually depends on the fact that some persons are excluded from their enjoyment." Such incentives include offices, honors, and other recognition; the prestige accruing to a donor who provides a "naming gift" to a university ethics center, for example, would be a large specific solidary incentive.

Collective solidary incentives: ". . . intangible rewards created by the act of associating that must be enjoyed by a group if they are to be enjoyed by anyone." These include the prestige of affiliation; sociability and fellowship; and perhaps a degree of exclusivity.

Wilson also identified sub-categories important to our discussion. *Material* incentives may be *exclusive* or *individual*. The former are available to all members, but only to members (the mutual insurance schemes created by immigrant organizations in nineteenth-century American cities, or by village associations in African cities today, are examples; so are the discounts on goods or insurance offered by fraternal and professional groups). The latter are given to some members and withheld from others (and are never offered to outsiders); patronage jobs distributed by a political machine are a classic example, but so are salaries paid to staff. Among *purposive* organizations Wilson identifies *goal-oriented*, *ideological*, and *redemptive* organizations. The first try to bring about specific changes in their surroundings (e.g., cleaner parks), while the second mount a comprehensive critique of society or of human nature and envision sweeping change (*e.g.* a new system of property ownership). The third, which Wilson acknowledges as difficult to define, not only seeks to change society at large but also ". . . to change its members by requiring them to exemplify in their own lives the new order". Religious sects or roving bands of militant vegans might fit this category. It is tempting to think of anti-corruption groups as redemptive, but in most instances they are not; in fact, for Wilson such groups face special problems.

Putting incentives to work

The most obvious incentives for an anti-corruption coalition are purposive: it exists, after all, to pursue reform. But a coalition model both allows and requires the use of diverse, overlapping incentives aimed at multiple constituencies. The broader-based the coalition we envision, the more true this is. At the same time, different sorts of incentives serve different purposes, and to some extent become critical at different phases in the coalition's life cycle. Thus, while a social action coalition aimed at controlling corruption will be many things to many people and groups, it cannot survive or be effective simply by proclaiming a noble purpose, or by bombarding the problem with good ideas.

Where corruption problems are deeply entrenched, two interrelated problems will arise immediately. First, reformers will have few material resources to sustain themselves, much less to offer to others. Second, their agenda, and thus its purposive incentives, may seem risky and unlikely to succeed.

The first problem will be familiar to anyone who has ever belonged to an organization—particularly so, to those who have watched a group become so consumed with fund-raising that it loses sight of its original purposes. But it has other ramifications as well: one reason reformers will be short of material resources is because of the power of corrupt interests, who monopolize many opportunities within an economy that is unlikely to be robust to begin with. Many businesses and individuals will deal with corrupt officials and their clients—responding to corruption illicitly, in Alam's[28] terms—or tolerate and avoid them (responding evasively), because they perceive few alternatives. Joining an anti-corruption coalition (in effect, responding directly) thus means taking on risks and costs, if only in the form of new uncertainties, for which the coalition may offer little compensation.

Thus arises the second problem: while reduced corruption would bring substantial benefits, material and otherwise, that is a long-term and uncertain prospect. Purposive incentives will always be central to the coalition, but there are important choices, particularly with respect to sustaining support and effectiveness over the long run. An incentive system based mostly on purposive appeals is "fragile": it is open to multiple interpretations and vulnerable to outside events. An anti-corruption agenda in particular may seem goal-oriented to some and redemptive to others, with conflict over targets and tactics the likely result. Changes in the coalition's environment—an election result, new economic circumstances, or the rise of some hotter new issue, for example—can weaken the appeal of purposive incentives quickly and decisively.

It is tempting to think of an anti-corruption crusade in redemptive terms, or to make a comprehensive ideology out of reform. But Wilson notes that purposive incentives must be relatively non-controversial if they are to sustain an organization.[29] Causes rather than issues, and cooperation rather than conflict, will be essential if the coalition is to avoid threatening the interests of its own members (and particularly, the autonomy of its organizational members) and antagonizing the regime. Efforts are thus likely to take the form, not of the sorts of crusades and condemnations likely to keep a mass constituency aroused, but rather of specific and discrete tasks: raising auditing standards, cutting down the number of steps in routine bureaucratic functions, or building information networks are examples. These, in turn, will require staff and leadership with considerable sophistication and staying power—and such a staff will need to be paid.

Purposive incentives thus must be supplemented by others that will attract the sustained backing of people and groups able to contribute funds and other scarce resources. *Specific solidary* incentives[30] and *exclusive* material incentives rather than the *individual* varieties that are likely to be in such short supply— and that might prove corrupting, or conducive to disruptive internal competition, if they were available—are critical in this regard. *Specific solidary* incentives can be targeted to particular members and benefactors: offices, honors and citations, and exclusive access to information can motivate individuals, civic groups and journalists to back the coalition. The staff salaries and resources noted above also fall into this category; purposive appeals might launch the coalition, but solidary resources are critical in sustaining it.

Collective solidary resources are of real value, even if not targeted to specific recipients: sociability, prestige and a sense of mutual support may be of value especially where civil society is weak. Wilson points out that many such appeals—notably, prestige—require an audience in order to be effective:[31] leaders may hand out all manner of "Corruption-Fighter" awards, for example, but if no one hears of them they will be of little value. A relatively free press can thus be an essential supplement to an incentive system.

Social action coalitions are unlikely to have extensive *individual material* incentives, as noted; if they are available they are likely to be controlled by corrupt officials. But a coalition can provide *exclusive material* incentives: things of real value, perhaps created by the coalition's own efforts, that can be restricted to members only. Access can be controlled, and converted into support, by insisting upon contributions or labor from members. In New York City, for example, teams in a youth soccer organization were given preferential access to a city-owned playing field after they worked to renew its facilities. The immigrant savings groups noted above were founded by very poor people but accumulated significant resources through small individual contributions and provided valuable aid to members. Even where public dealings are deeply corrupt, the members and officials of such groups handle resources honestly. An anti-corruption coalition could emulate this model by setting up a kind of "corruption insurance" in which members pool information and resources, and make binding pacts not to compete corruptly. That could reduce the risks and costs both of corruption itself, and of coalition membership.

What might the overall incentive system of an anti-corruption coalition look like, and which incentives would appeal to what constituents? Tables 9.1 and 9.2 offer some ideas:

Table 9.1: Anti-Corruption Coalition-Building Incentives by Type

| MATERIAL | | SPECIFIC SOLIDARY | COLLECTIVE SOLIDARY | PURPOSIVE |
Exclusive	Individual			Goal-Oriented*
"Corruption Insurance"	Econ benefits of improved economy	Data/information banks •on corrupt agencies, officials •on best practices	Prestige, improved image •domestically, internationally Enhanced autonomy for organizations, press, opposition, civil society groups	Reform as public good Better governance
Technical services: •vulnerability assessments •prevention within orgs •legal advice	Security from better governance	Research products Rewards, recognition	Sociability, fellowship, mutual encouragement	Fair political, economic processes Stronger civil society Enhanced Rule of Law

* Ideological and Redemptive sub-types not recommended

Table 9.2: Anti-Corruption Coalition-Building Incentives by Target Constituency

| MATERIAL | | SPECIFIC SOLIDARY | COLLECTIVE SOLIDARY | PURPOSIVE |
Exclusive	Individual			Goal-Oriented*
Small firms, domestic entrepreneurs and investors	Citizens generally Civil society,	Professional coalition staff, researchers Benefactors, financial supporters	Mass membership Journalists NGO leaders Government elites	Mass membership Aid/lending partners NGOs
	NGOs	Anti-corruption "champions"		Democracy groups and supporters

* Ideological and Redemptive sub-types not recommended

IV. The "Clean Machine": Incentives at Work

The tables above suggest many ways to supplement purposive appeals. Even though it may lack the individual material incentives available to corrupt politicians and bureaucrats, a coalition can offer many other things to a variety of constituencies. Of these, *exclusive material* and *specific solidary* incentives may be the least familiar. They will, however, be the most effective at attracting sustained support from small to medium business firms, domestic entrepreneurs, and investors—precisely those to whom a coalition must turn for material resources. *Information* can be of real value. It may take the form of technical assistance: vulnerability assessments focusing upon corruption risks within or from outside a firm could be performed for active coalition backers. Training programs, advice on auditing requirements and internal control systems, and an information bank on best practices or risk assessments elsewhere can be of real value. Whether these services be provided on a fee basis, or made available to regular subscribers (the preferred option), they are reasons to join and support a coalition, and ways to demonstrate the effectiveness of paid staff. *Recognition* is a similar incentive: coalition leaders should spare no efforts in giving awards, citations, and favorable publicity to key backers as well as to anti-corruption "champions" in government.

Other benefits consist of offsetting the costs of corruption itself. Coalitions could offer a kind of "corruption insurance", which might take several forms: technical assistance (as noted), pooling funds for legal assistance or even for compensation of those hurt most by corrupt demands, and active support for whistleblowers are just a few examples. At another level, the coalition could broker integrity pacts among firms in a sector of industry, or among bidders for large contracts, as exemplified by Transparency International's "Islands of Integrity" initiatives. These can create confidence that one is not just handing advantages to competitors by refusing to pay bribes. Similar services could be offered to government officials: the coalition could monitor and report publicly on privatization schemes, civil service reforms, and campaigns for improved administrative controls, although as noted above its role should be restricted to providing public information, *not* demonstrating the absence of corruption. That remains the responsibility of public officials. The coalition's role is to help them take credit for successes while ensuring that failures will not go unnoticed. It could thus reward political will while strengthening the role of civil society, as suggested earlier.

Collective solidary incentives, such as sociability and prestige, may seem an afterthought or even a luxury. But in fact they will be essential to maintaining mass support and with it, the coalition's visibility and legitimacy. It is no accident that the Hong Kong ICAC's highly-regarded public education campaigns have long included a component of fun and social activity, particularly for young people. For journalists and the leaders of participating organizations, a kind of security can flow from membership of a strong coalition: those who conceal corruption or practice intimidation may think twice if they know their critics are backed by a larger group. Conversely, coalition members tempted by offers of money for silence, for example, have something important to lose if they are found out: membership of a prestigious and visible group. Such incentives may be difficult to quantify, but they show how a solid coalition can, through aggressive use of multiple sorts of incentives, alter the calculus of corruption and reform.

At the outset we suggested that social action coalitions can reinforce political will and help enhance the vitality of civil society by bringing a broad range of constituencies together to oppose corruption. What does this mean in practice?

Strengthening political will

While political, administrative and judicial officials bear much of the burden of reform, a strong coalition can reinforce, and reward, their will to see it through. Simply put, the coalition's support can persuade elites that they have an interest in reform, *via* popularity, enhanced development, a better international image, or simply their own political survival. This entails supporting elites politically and socially when they do pursue reform—no easy task where corruption has become entrenched—while where possible, showing that those leaders do not own the coalition or the corruption issue in the long term. A coalition with a strong grassroots base can also identify the sorts of reform targets that will be seen as most important—advice that committed reform leaders are likely to value greatly. And as outlined above, it can aid them in taking credit for reform successes while making sure that failure is difficult to conceal. It can also provide valuable information on the ways other societies counterparts have dealt with the problem and have benefited from doing so. Such information may not always be fresh news to all leaders, but hearing it from a coalition with a broad base of support can be a powerful encouragement to act in credible and visible ways. Relationships with opposition leaders are a touchy issue here: if they are too weak, reformers will not be credible in society, but if they are too close there may be little access to important figures in government. The key is to cooperate with the regime while remaining open to input and participation from opposition groups (unless circumstances make that too risky), making it clear that the coalition can make room for all in society who oppose corruption.

A coalition in a position to mobilize popular disapproval can also convey pointed political messages. Careful judgment is in order, once again: cooperative ties with the regime are ordinarily one of the coalition's most valuable assets. Moreover, if coalition leaders too frequently condemn failures without also being able to point to successes, followers decide that reform is futile. And as a practical matter, in some of the most corrupt societies popular opinion is of little significance; those who express disapproval may take significant risks only to be drowned out by cheerleaders for the regime. Still, targeted expressions of disapproval (*e.g.* the Sierra Club's "Dirty Dozen" lists of US Congress members) may both demonstrate that disregarding anti-corruption views has real costs while underlining the movement's independence.

Building a stronger civil society

A strong civil society can develop, protect, and express important social values, and can give its members the "space" and organizational capabilities they need to act against corruption. Likewise, it can encourage and protect direct responses to corruption and open up political and economic alternatives to abuse by corrupt officials and their clients. In this way, a strong civil society can reduce the costs of corruption and the risks of opposing it directly. Where those sorts of protections are in place, the short-term rewards of corruption become less tempting, the longer-term and shared costs become clearer, and the incentives to control it become more compelling.

Over the long run, a viable civil society becomes a force for accountability in all but the most repressive societies. It does so through the broad mobilization of many pro-reform interests, becoming the vehicle through which support for political will is most strongly conveyed. Political leaders, in turn, will have reasons to move credibly against corruption, even in undemocratic systems, because doing so can build legitimacy for the regime.

Public education

An effective social action coalition can change the ways people think about corruption. Immediate costs are known to all; but less well understood are the long-term, shared, and intangible costs, such as delayed and distorted development, the loss of political choices and accountability, and the mutual suspicion that can corrode business, political, and personal relationships in societies where corruption is the rule, rather than the exception. The task is to show people how corruption is involved in many of their own problems, both day to day and over the long term. Some of these ideas will be less than obvious, for they are measured in terms of values, security, and opportunities they have never possessed, and which they may believe they will never enjoy.

For that latter reason it is important to break the sense that there is nothing that can be done. Many citizens might resist paying up or concealing illicit deals, and many officials might "blow the whistle" and support reform, if they did not think they would be alone in doing so. They will also know the risks: reporting corruption or resisting corrupt demands often means an uneven fight with powerful officials and their cronies. Those who have paid or taken corrupt payments in the past may fear (with good reason) that those dealings will be used as evidence against them. The answer, in part, is to lengthen the time horizon—to encourage people to look beyond the short-term giving and getting toward the long-term consequences of corruption for themselves and for society. The Hong Kong example suggests that sustained commitment to this sort of public education can succeed in changing attitudes at a basic level (for details on this and other aspects of the ICAC's work in Hong Kong, see Jenny C. Y. Chan's Chapter 6 in this volume).

Finally, an honest public education strategy will include the lesson that reform is costly, and requires sustained support and vigilance. Reform efforts may, in the short term, give the impression that corruption is on the increase, as cases become public knowledge and critics of corruption become more aggressive. Coalition leaders must do all they can to give the public a realistic picture of the likely consequences of reform, lest disillusionment set it. American campaign-finance reform advocates in the 1970s, for example, largely failed to do this, with the result that disclosure requirements created an erroneous perception that the political process was suddenly up for sale while the promised new age of clean politics never quite materialized. As a result, advocates of new reforms now find the public's response is heavily tinged by cynicism.

Alternatives to corruption

The coalition's appeals to civil society will make little sense, however, unless they help open alternatives to exploitation by corrupt figures. One obvious way to perform this function is to gather, share, and disseminate information on the scope of corruption problems, and on effective, workable reforms. Transparency International chapters have had considerable success in performing this function, as has the parent organization in Berlin. The more widely such information is shared, the less vulnerable people may become to pressures from corrupt figures. Gathering and broadly sharing such information is also a way to protect "institutional memory".

At the same time, information sharing has its pitfalls. The process may become an echo chamber in which "knowledge" that "everyone knows" acquires a spurious authority through repetition. Reform is reduced to slogans, as has already happened, to a distressing degree, with terms like "political will" and "civil society". A one-size-fits-all understanding of what corruption is, and of what remedies must be pursued, can result: already, we too often see "corruption" treated as a synonym for "bribery", and essentially as a problem in the liberalization of international trade.[32] When this happens, local knowledge and experience are devalued and reforms reflecting local realities are less likely to emerge.

For this reason, *a social action coalition should develop research and analysis capabilities* if at all possible. These need not be elaborate to be valuable; they can, however, enable a coalition not only to work hard against corruption, but to be smart about that task—providing convincing advice and feedback to elites about corruption problems, and about the progress and perceptions of reform efforts. Perhaps most important, a social action coalition with a least a basic research capability will be much less dependent upon official accounts of corruption and reform. It will also serve as a clear focus for those, within and without a given society, who want to know more about the corruption problems there. The ability to provide credible information on an independent basis can be critical to any effort to identify and open alternatives to current corrupt practices.

V. Conclusion

Coalition building to fight corruption is more of a metaphor than a blueprint: effective social action coalitions will differ considerably in organization, tactics, and agendas from one society to the next. They will also change over time, both as they become institutionalized and "deepen" their incentive systems, and as they respond to events and changes beyond their control. Ironically, early success may bring problems of its own if supporters conclude that the problem has essentially been solved and that their backing and vigilance are no longer needed.

The key to the strategy is a mix of continuity and adaptation. The former depends upon a solid internal economy of incentives, while the latter requires leadership aware of the need for political will and a strong civil society, and of the role a social action coalition can play in linking and supporting them. Even with all of those factors in place, success is far from a certainty, and there will be many setbacks along the way. Still, we have tried to show that even where corruption is entrenched and reformers lack critical resources it is possible to build a base for sustained and effective action. Perhaps the most important thing to remember is that coalitions are merely means toward broader ends—not, in themselves, the solution to the problem, but rather a framework allowing and encouraging people to oppose corruption because it is in their best interests to do so. To the extent that they succeed at this, they will be following the path taken by other societies that have, through contention and over time, brought corruption under control.

ENDNOTES

1. A revised and expanded version of this discussion appears as an introductory section of Johnston, Michael, and Sahr J. Kpundeh. 2002. *Building a Clean Machine: Anti-Corruption Coalitions and Sustainable Reforms.* World Bank Institute Working Paper SN37208 (December).

2. Johnston, Michael. 1993. "Political Corruption: Historical Conflict and the Rise of Standards." In Larry Diamond and Marc F. Plattner (eds.). *The Global Resurgence of Democracy.* Baltimore: Johns Hopkins University Press; Roberts, Clayton. 1980. *The Growth of Responsible Government in Stuart England.* Cambridge: Cambridge University Press.

3. Johnston, Michael. 1998. "What Can Be Done About Entrenched Corruption?", pp. 149-180 in Boris Pleskovic and Joseph E. Stiglitz (eds.). *Annual World Bank Conference on Development Economics 1997.* Washington, DC: The World Bank.

4. Mauro, Paolo. 1997. "The Effects of Corruption on Growth, Investment, and Government Expenditure: A Cross-Country Analysis." In Kimberly A. Elliott (ed.). *Corruption and the Global Economy.* Washington, D.C.: Institute for International Economics.

5. For recent studies of grassroots activism focused at least partly on corruption issues, see Benner, Thorsten, Wolfgang H. Reinicke, and Jan Martin Witte. 2004. "Multisectoral Networks in Global Governance: Towards a Pluralistic System of Accountability." *Government and Opposition* 39: 2 (Spring), pp. 191-210; Ruteere, Mutuma, and Marie-Emmanuelle Pommerolle. 2003. "Democratizing Security or Decentralizing Repression? The Ambiguities of Community Policing In Kenya." *African Affairs* 102: 409 (October), pp. 587-604; Moser, Annalise. 2003. "Acts of Resistance: The Performance of Women's Grassroots Protest in Peru." *Social Movement Studies* 2:2 (October), pp.177-190; and Sater, James. 2002. "Civil Society, Political Change and the Private Sector in Morocco: The Case of the Employers' Federation *Confédération Générale des Enterprises du Maroc* (CGEM)." *Mediterranean Politics* 7:2 (Summer), pp.13-29.

6. See, for Uganda, Ruzindana, Augustine. 1997. "The Importance of Leadership in Fighting Corruption in Uganda." In Kimberly A. Elliott, ed., *Corruption and the Global Economy.* Washington, D.C.: Institute for International Economics.

7. A variety of studies of civil society and "social capital" appear in Pharr, Susan J., Robert D. Putnam, *et. al.* 2000. *Disaffected Democracies.* Princeton, NJ: Princeton University Press; and in Putnam, Robert D. 2000. *Bowling Alone: The Collapse and Revival of American Community.* New York: Simon and Schuster.

8. Cooter, Robert D. 1997. "The Rule of State Law Versus the Rule-of-Law State: Economic Analysis of the Legal Foundations of Development." In Proceedings of the *Annual World Bank Conference on Development Economics 1996.* Washington, D.C.: The World Bank.

9. On corruption among insecure elites see Knack, Stephen, and Philip Keefer. 1995. "Institutions and Economic Performance: Cross-Country Tests Using Alternative Institutional Measures." *Economics and Politics* 7:3, pp. 207–227.

10. On the theory and analysis of coalitions, see Gamson, William A. 1964. "Experimental Studies of Coalition Formation." In Berkowitz, Leonard (ed.). *Advances in Experimental Social Psychology.* New York: Academic Press, Vol. I; Olson, Mancur, and Rich-

ard Zeckhauser. 1966. "An Economic Theory of Alliances." *Review of Economics and Statistics* XLVIII (August), pp. 266-279; Burgess, Philip M., and James A. Robinson. 1969. "Alliances and the Theory of Collective Action: A Simulation of Coalition Processes." *Midwest Journal of Political Science* XIII (May), pp. 194-218; Groennings, Sven, E. W. Kelley, and Michael Leiserson (eds.). 1970. *The Study of Coalition Behavior.* New York: Holt, Rinehart and Winston; Rounds, David. 1970. *Coalitions.* New York: Dutton; Mahon, John F., and Barbara Bigelow. 1990. "Coalitions: The Strategic Bridge within and across Organizations." Boston University School of Management, working paper no. 90-68.

11. For studies of coalitions and public participation in reform, see Tendler, Judith. 1979. "Rural Works Programs in Bangladesh: Community, Technology and Graft." Transportation Department, The World Bank, Washington, D.C; Hede, Andrew, Scott Prasser, and Mark Neylan. 1992. *Keeping Them Honest: Democratic Reform in Queensland.* St. Lucia, Queensland, Australia: University of Queensland Press; Nickson, R. Andrew. 1996. "Democratization and Institutional Corruption in Paraguay". In Walter Little and Eduardo Posada-Carbó, eds., *Political Corruption in Europe and Latin America.* New York: St. Martin's Press, pp. 237-266; Clay, Karen. 1997. "Trade without Law: Private-Order Institutions in Mexican California." *Journal of Law, Economics, and Organization* 13, pp. 202-231; Klitgaard, Robert, and Heather Baser. 1997. "Working Together to Fight Corruption: State, Society, and the Private Sector in Partnership". In S. Taschereau and J. E. L. Campos (eds.). *Governance Innovations: Lessons from Experience, Building Government-Citizen-Business Partnerships.* Washington, D.C.: Institute on Governance, pp. 59-81; Stapenhurst, Frederick, and Sahr J. Kpundeh. 1998. "Public Participation in the Fight against Corruption." *Canadian Journal of Development Studies* XIX:3, pp. 491-508.

12. Geddes, Barbara. 1994. *Politician's Dilemma: Building State Capacity in Latin America.* Berkeley: University of California Press. Rose-Ackerman, Susan. 1999. *Corruption and Government: Causes, Consequences, and Reform.* Cambridge: Cambridge University Press, esp. Ch. 11.

13. Wilson, James Q. 1973. *Political Organizations.* New York: Basic Books, pp. 267-68)

14. (Isham, Jonathan, Daniel Kaufmann, and Lant Pritchett. 1996. "Civil Liberties, Democracy, and the Performance of Government Projects." Washington, D.C.: The World Bank, Policy Research Department, Poverty and Human Resources Division.

15. Wilson, James Q. 1973. *Political Organizations.* New York: Basic Books, p. 275.

16. Mair, Peter (with Richard S. Katz). 1997. "Party Organization, Party Democracy, and the Emergence of the Cartel Party". In Mair, Peter. *Party System Change: Approaches and Interpretations.* Oxford: Clarendon Press, pp. 93-119; Johnston, Michael. 2002. "Party Systems, Competition, and Political Checks against Corruption." In Heidenheimer, Arnold J., and Michael Johnston (eds.). *Political Corruption: Concepts and Contexts. Third Edition.* New Brunswick, N.J.: Transaction Publishers, pp. 777-794.

17. Alam, M. S. 1995. "A Theory of Limits on Corruption and Some Applications." *Kyklos* 48:3, pp. 419–35.

18. Wilson, James Q. 1973. *Political Organizations.* New York: Basic Books, pp. 30-31.

19. *Ibid.,* p. 267.

20. *Ibid.,* pp. 272-75.

21. *Ibid.,* pp. 20.

22. *Ibid.,* pp. 203-4.

23. Olson, Mancur. 1965. *The Logic of Collective Action.* Cambridge, MA: Harvard University Press.

24. Rose-Ackerman, Susan. 1999. *Corruption and Government: Causes, Consequences, and Reform.* Cambridge: Cambridge University Press; De Janvry, Alain, and Elizabeth Sadoulet. 1989. "A Study in Resistance to Institutional Change: The Lost Game of Latin American Land Reform". *World Development* 17. pp. 1397-1407.

25. Wilson, James Q. 1973. *Political Organizations.* New York: Basic Books.

26. Olson, Mancur. 1965. *The Logic of Collective Action.* Cambridge, MA: Harvard University Press.

27. The following discussion draws upon Wilson, James Q. 1973. *Political Organizations.* New York: Basic Books. pp. 33-51.

28. Alam, M. S. 1995. "A Theory of Limits on Corruption and Some Applications." *Kyklos* 48:3, pp. 419–35.

29. Wilson, James Q. 1973. *Political Organizations.* New York: Basic Books, p. 43.

30. *Ibid.,* pp. 208-210.

31. *Ibid.,* p. 40.

32. Johnston, Michael. 2002. "Measuring The New Corruption Rankings: Implications for Analysis and Reform." In Heidenheimer, Arnold J., and Michael Johnston (eds.). *Political Corruption: Concepts and Contexts. Third Edition.* New Brunswick, N.J.: Transaction Publishers, pp. 865-884.

Part III

Data and Research Resources

10

Guide to Locating the Literature on Corruption

Mary Jane Walsh

The renewed emphasis, over the past fifteen years, upon corruption as a social and political problem has produced information, evidence, case studies and quantitative date at an unprecedented pace. Gaining access to that information and finding ways to organize it are critical elements of analysis and reform. In this concluding chapter, Mary Jane Walsh provides a field guide to the world of information on corruption, in the process providing solid pointers on how to search for materials on a range of topics. This chapter is not itself a bibliography or master list of sources. Moreover, electronic databases, search engines, web-sites and other information sources change so rapidly than any list will rapidly become dated. Still, this compilation will help anyone be aware of the scale of information that is becoming available and is a useful introduction to ways of using a variety of sources most efficiently.

I. Introduction

During the 2000-2001 academic year, when Colgate University's Center for Ethics and World Societies (CEWS) theme was "Corruption: wealth, power and democracy", I volunteered to act as "official bibliographer" for the center. My task was to create a list of all the writings of each speaker, and lists for further reading for those inspired by a particular presentation. Little did I know what I had gotten myself into. It became obvious that while concern about corruption has been with us for some time, the literature and research resources on the issue have skyrocketed only in recent years. Take, as an example, books about political corruption (not including campaign finance) published in the English language. Publishing output remained well below fifty books per year until the mid 1970's. In 1990, a dramatic rise in output began that peaked in 2000, when 287 books in English were published. Although out put has declined in recent years, it is still twice that of the pre-90's era.[1]

At the same time, use of the Internet as a research tool was increasing, adding to the literature. On the Internet, authors may act as editor, peer reviewer, and publisher, and readers must scrutinize results of an Internet search even more carefully than the results of a search in a reputable database, index, or bibliography. Further complicating tracking the literature of corruption is its interdisciplinary nature. While much of the writing about corruption in government appears in the political science literature, there are also significant contributions from economics, sociology, law, anthropology, history, and philosophy, and, of course, from a variety of news sources.

This chapter, an outgrowth of the year's work for CEWS[2], is a guide to locating information about corruption. It is not a list of recommended books and articles, but rather sources to use and strategies to employ to find the most appropriate information for your needs from a universe of resources that can only continue to grow over the coming years. With apologies to the Chinese philosopher: "Give a man a fish and you feed him for a day. Teach a man to fish, and you ruin his weekends for a lifetime."

The emphasis of this guide is on locating information about political corruption in the social science literature, particularly those in political science:

- published from 1980 to the present
- written in English
- written for the scholar and for the "informed public"
- covering political/administrative corruption and fraud; not corruption in fields such as business, sports, art, or science; not specialized topics such as campaign finance.

Finding articles in popular magazines and newspapers, dissertations, or non-print (television, radio, video) materials will not be discussed. Nor is finding United States government documents—a major research discussion in its own right.

II. Background Information

Have no idea what civil society is? How about rent-seeking? (No, it's not what your landlord does monthly.) Want to gather quickly some information about a particular country or region? These are the sources to use to gather background information, define a term, or clarify an issue. Entries in most sources include a brief bibliography for further reading.

Introductory texts

Rose-Ackerman, Susan. *Corruption and Government: Causes, Consequences, and Reform.* Cambridge: Cambridge University Press, 1999.

Divided into four parts: Corruption as an Economic Problem, Corruption as a Cultural Problem, Corruption as a Political Problem, and Achieving Reform.

Politics of Corruption series, edited by Robert Williams *et al.* and published by Edward Elgar Publishing in 2000.

A four volume series, each volume is a collection of previously published writings grouped around a theme: *Explaining Corruption, Corruption in the Developing World, Corruption in the Developed World,* and *Controlling Corruption.* In most libraries, you will find each volume cataloged separately.

Heidenheimer, Arnold J. and Michael Johnston, eds. *Political Corruption: Concepts and Contexts.* 3rd ed. New Brunswick, NJ: Transaction Publishers, 2002.

A compilation (the third volume in a series dating from Heidenheimer's original volume in 1970) of writings, some classic studies of the nature and development of corruption, others newly penned. Arranged in fourteen parts, covering historical and modern studies, development, economics, methodology, and different geographic areas.

Dictionaries/Encyclopedias - topical

Roberts, Robert North. *Ethics in U.S. Government: An Encyclopedia of Investigations, Scandals, Reforms, and Legislation.* Westport, CT: Greenwood Press, 2001.

The title says it all: brief entries about people, events, concepts, and legislative reforms; each with suggested readings. Includes an eight page timeline of important invents

Political Science.

Lipset, Seymour Martin, ed. *The Encyclopedia of Democracy.* Four vols. Washington, D.C.: Congressional Quarterly, 1995. See Donatella della Porta. "Corruption". pp. 310-312.

Krieger, Joel, ed. *The Oxford Companion to Politics of the World.* 2nd ed. New York: Oxford University Press, 2001.
See Michael Johnston. "Corruption". pp. 177-178.

Bogdanor, Vernon, ed. *The Blackwell Encyclopaedia of Political Institutions.* Oxford: Blackwell Reference, 1987.
See Alan Doig. "Political Corruption". pp. 445-446.

Social Sciences.
Smelser, Neil J. and Paul B. Baltes, eds. *International Encyclopedia of the Social & Behavioral Sciences*. Twenty-six vols. Amsterdam: Elsevier, 2001. See Y. Mény and L. de Sousa. "Corruption: Political and Public Aspects". pp. 2824-2830.

Sociology.
Borgatta, Edgar F., ed. *Encyclopedia of Sociology*. Five vols. Detroit: Macmillan Reference USA, 2000. See Richard McGrath Skinner. "Political and Governmental Corruption". pp. 2123-2138.

Philosophy.
Becker, Lawrence C. and Charlotte B. Becker eds. *The Encyclopedia of Ethics*. 2nd ed. Three vols. New York: Garland Pub, 2001. See Lewis Anthony Dexter & David Braybrooke. "Corruption". pp. 344-346.

Craig, Edward, ed. *Routledge Encyclopedia of Philosophy*. London and New York: Routledge, 1998. Also available online. See Mark Philp. "Corruption". pp. 674-677.

Economics.
Not useful as introductory starting points, but very useful when looking for information about related topics, such as rent-seeking or bribery, are:

Eatwell, John, Murray Milgate, and Peter Newman, eds. *The New Palgrave : A Dictionary of Economics*. New York: Stockton Press, 1987.

O'Hara, Phillip Anthony, ed. *Encyclopedia of Political Economy*. London and New York: Routledge, 1999.

Dictionaries/Encyclopedias - geographic

Ember, Melvin, and Carol R. Ember, eds. *Countries and their Cultures*. New York: Macmillan Reference USA, 2001.
    Produced with the support of the Human Relations Area File, Inc. at Yale University, emphasis is on "what is and what is not commonly shared culturally by the people who live in a country." Entries cover history and ethnic relations, food and economy, social structures, gender roles, urbanism and architecture. The bibliographies for further reading included for each country are good, but somewhat dated for some countries. Essays about some cultures also available online as part of an *eHRAF Collection of Ethnography* subscription.

Europa yearbooks (Europa Publications Limited, London).

Published annually, all Europa yearbooks follow the same format: introductory essay about the history, politics, geography, and economy of each country, basic statistical data, and a directory of the government, political organizations, publishers and media, finance, trade and industry, transportation, and tourism organizations. The country essays in the regional yearbooks are more extensive than those in the *Europa World Year Book*, and they include current bibliographies. Each regional yearbook begins with a general survey of the region, including important documents, a list of organizations (mostly non-governmental organizations) and their activities in the region, and a bibliography about the region as a whole. The current Europa yearbooks are:

> *The Europa World Year Book*
> *Africa South of the Sahara*
> *Eastern Europe, Russia and Central Asia*
> *The Far East and Australasia*
> *The Middle East and North Africa*
> *South America, Central America, and the Caribbean*
> *The Territories of the Russian Federation*
> *Western Europe*

Economist Intelligence Unit reports. Available with subscription: http://www.eiu.com (March 7, 2004).

> *Country Reports:* analysis and forecast for two hundred countries covering politics, economic policy, foreign trade and payments. Some *Country Reports* are available as part of a subscription to EBSCO's *Business Source Premier* database.
> *Country Risk Service*: EIU ratings of risk over the next two years in one hundred markets. Includes politics, economic policy and structure, currency, debt, and the banking sector.

Library of Congress Country Studies. Library of Congress Federal Research Division and U.S. Dept. of the Army. Available: http://lcweb2.loc.gov/frd/cs/ (March 7, 2004).

Book length studies of each country or region that describe and analyze "the historical setting and the social, economic, political, and national security systems and institutions of countries throughout the world and . . . the interrelationships of those systems and the ways they are shaped by cultural factors. Focuses primarily on lesser known areas of the world or regions in which U.S. forces might be deployed . . . At present, 101 countries and regions are covered. Notable omissions include Canada, France, the United Kingdom, and other Western nations, as well as a number of African nations." The date of information for each country appears on the title page of each country and at the end of each section of text. Also available in print in many libraries.

Country Information. International Monetary Fund.   Available: http://www.imf.org/external/country/index.htm (March 7, 2004).

Arranged by country, this website provides links to basic financial data, and the full text of IMF country reports, press releases, statements and speeches, and country policy documents.

III. Search Tips

The computerization of library catalogs and periodical indexes and abstracting services was a major leap forward in information retrieval. Not only can you construct sophisticated searches combining multiple concepts, you also can cover multiple years of publication in a single search. However, computers are still dumb; they will only search for the exact combination of keystrokes that you enter. It is all too easy to accidentally retrieve information about Venetian blinds when you wanted information about blind people in Venice, to be over-whelmed the sheer number of results from one search, or underwhelmed by re-trieving nothing at all. To get the best results from a computer search, you should be familiar with the concepts, operations, and functions discussed briefly in this section.

Vocabulary

There are four things to remember about vocabulary when searching databases:

1. Any given concept may be described by multiple words. For example, when you are planting your tomatoes, are you digging in soil, dirt, earth, or the ground?
2. It is possible for one word to have multiple meanings. For example, is a slug a slimy creature that gets in the way of planting your tomatoes, a form of ammunition, or a unit of mass?
3. When in Rome (or Paris or London), do as the natives do—use their vocabulary, not yours. You'll be much happier with your search results. And yes, each database uses its own terminology, so you may have to become multi-lingual (see number 1, above).
4. Not only do databases vary in the terminology they use as subject head-ings, they also vary in the way that they enter authors' names. You may have to search LAST NAME FIRST NAME or LAST NAME, FIRST NAME or LAST NAME-FIRST INITIAL. Yes, punctuation may make a difference.

Good databases use a controlled vocabulary—a list of subject headings that they use, consistently, to describe certain concepts. Every item about a particular concept should have the same subject heading assigned, enabling a searcher to retrieve everything in the database about that subject in one search. Better data-bases provide access to a thesaurus of their subject headings, complete with cross-references from alternative terminology, so that you can easily identify what subject heading(s) they use to represent the concepts that make up your topic. If you plan to search multiple databases, or must search a database with poor or no controlled vocabulary, it is helpful to create a list of words that describe each concept you will be searching (think Monty Python's famous "Dead Parrot" sketch).

If a database does not provide you with a thesaurus, begin your search with the terminology that is natural for you and quickly scan the results looking for one or two good titles. When you find them, look at the assigned subject headings, then use those subject headings to refine and focus your search.

In addition to knowing what subject headings are used, you also must know how they are assigned. Indexers and catalogers follow two basic guidelines in assigning subject headings:

1.   they assign the most specific subject headings possible that describe the entire contents of the item in hand, and
2.   they only assign subject headings for topics that make up 20 percent or more of a item's total content.

For example, a book about Nigeria will have the subject heading NIGERIA, not the subject heading AFRICA. A book with one chapter each about every country in Africa will have the subject heading AFRICA, not subject headings for each country, because each chapter would not constitute 20 percent of the total contents.

Design your search to work with these cataloging guidelines: begin with specific subject headings and broaden your search as necessary. Turn to Monty Python again for inspiration, this time to their "Cheese Shop" sketch: begin your search with specific terms (BRIE, CHEDDAR, PORT SALUT, WENSLEYDALE), but be willing to broaden your scope as necessary (CHEESE).

Boolean operators
The Boolean operators AND, OR, NOT are used to combine concepts.

AND. All words connected with AND must be somewhere in the records retrieved. For example, the subject heading search:
CORRUPT PRACTICES AND DEFENSE CONTRACTS
will retrieve records with both the subject heading "corrupt practices" and the subject heading "defense contracts". AND is typically used to connect words that describe different concepts, or with multiple words that, when combined, describe one specific concept. The more terms that are connected with AND, the fewer records will be retrieved. In some databases, AND is assumed if you type a space (*e.g.*, political corruption is the same as political AND corruption). In some databases, a space acts as a proximity operator (see below), not a Boolean operator.

OR. At least one of the words connected with OR must be somewhere in the records retrieved. For example, the keyword search:
CHINA OR CHINESE
will retrieve records that contain either the word "China" or "Chinese" or both words. OR is typically used to connect synonyms or antonyms, or when retrieval of any one of a number of concepts is acceptable. The more terms that are connected with OR, the more records will be retrieved.

NOT. The word following the operator NOT will not appear in any of the records retrieved. For example, the subject heading search:
POLITICAL CORRUPTION NOT CAMPAIGN FINANCE
will retrieve records with the subject heading "political corruption". None of the records retrieved, however, will have the subject heading campaign finance, even if there are records with both subject headings assigned. NOT can be used to winnow a large set of records, or to exclude a word that appears in your results, but is inappropriate to your search. The more terms that are connected with NOT, the fewer records will be retrieved. Using NOT frequently eliminates some useful records.

Proximity operators

Proximity operators indicate how close together, and in which order, you wish words to appear. They vary from database to database, but the most common are <space>, ADJ, NEAR, SAME, WITHIN, and PRECEDES. The operators may indicate adjacency, within a certain number of words (*e.g.*, WITHIN/3), or in the same field, sentence, or paragraph. Adjacency is not the same as word order (*i.e.*, the results may have your words in a different order than you entered them). In fact, adjacency may not always be adjacent. For example, in *GPO Access* databases[3], ADJ means that the word after ADJ must be, within twenty characters, the word before ADJ. Check each database for its rules governing proximity.

Operator order

Each database has a specific order in which it performs the individual components of your search. Typically, proximity operators are performed before Boolean operators. AND is typically performed before OR, and NOT is almost always the last Boolean operator to be performed. However, some databases perform all operations in the exact order in which you enter them. Use parentheses to group together operations to get the intended results. Operations inside parentheses are performed before any other operations. For example, the following searches would retrieve very different results:
AFRICA AND BRIBERY OR RENT ADJ SEEKING
AFRICA AND (BRIBERY OR RENT ADJ SEEKING)

The first search would retrieve records about bribery in Africa, or records about rent-seeking anywhere (not necessarily in Africa). The second search would retrieve records about either bribery in Africa or rent-seeking in Africa.

Truncation/Wildcards

Truncation symbols and wildcards allow you to look for variant spellings or versions of a word. A truncation symbol used at the end of a word-stem will retrieve any record that has words beginning with the combination of letters entered (*e.g.*, administ* will retrieve administer, administrate, administrates, administrator, administrators, administration, *etc.*). Truncation can backfire. For example, if you truncate China as Chin*, searching for China, China's, or Chinese, you will also retrieve records with the words chin, chinchilla, or chintz. If you truncate cult as cult*, searching for the singular or plural, you will also retrieve records with the words culture, cultivate, or cultivator. Unless your database provides a specific truncation symbol for plurals, it can be more effective to enter both the singular and the plural than to truncate. The most common truncation symbols are the asterisk (*) and the question mark (?), although the plus sign (+) and the exclamation point (!) are also used.

Wildcard symbols are typically used for internal spelling variations; *e.g.*, color or colour; women or woman. The most common such symbols are the question mark (?) and the pound sign (#), and some databases allow you to indicate how many letters can be changed.

Limiting

Other advantages to computer searching include the ability to limit by language of publication, year of publication, document type (*e.g.*, book, journal article, website), or occasionally by type of content (*e.g.*, review of the literature, book review, bibliography). You can often limit where in a record your search terms might appear (*e.g.*, only in the subject headings or only in the titles).

In the following sections we turn to the major computer-searchable databases; a working knowledge of the techniques discussed above will make all them considerably more useful as information sources.

IV. Finding Books

Despite many predictions to the contrary, the book is not dead. Book publishing (*i.e.*, materials treated as books by catalogers) about political corruption has increased dramatically in the last decade; the English language output alone almost quadrupled between the 1990 and 2000.

Most academic and research libraries have access to *WorldCat*, the online union catalog of more than forty-five thousand OCLC (Online Computer Library Center) libraries in seventy-six countries.[4] The database is used by member libraries to catalog their own collections and to facilitate interlibrary loan (borrowing among the libraries). Each record is linked to a list of libraries that own the item. *WorldCat* is available as one of the OCLC FirstSearch databases.

All FirstSearch databases offer three different levels of searching: Basic, Advanced, and Expert. I recommend Advanced Searching because it provides the most flexibility without having to know the search syntax. The search tips that follow for FirstSearch databases are designed for Advanced Searching.

WorldCat. OCLC.

Years covered online: 1000 B.C.-

Subjects covered: all.

Materials indexed: all formats, including books, government documents, dissertations, manuscripts, serial titles, scores and sound recordings, websites, and video materials.

Publishing information: updated daily.

Suggested subject headings:

    CORRUPTION

    CORRUPTION INVESTIGATION

    POLITICAL CORRUPTION

    PUBLIC ADMINISTRATION – MORAL AND ETHICAL ASPECTS

    POLITICAL ETHICS

    CIVIL SERVICE ETHICS

    LEGISLATIVE BODIES – ETHICS

    MISCONDUCT IN OFFICE

    BRIBERY

    FRAUD

The subdivision CORRUPT PRACTICES can be used with names of individual corporate bodies (including government agencies) and with activities, types of industries, and types of organizations.

Search tips:

"Keyword" searches Geographic Code, Map Data, Title, Note, and Subject Heading fields, and can be limited to one field (*e.g.*, title). The words may appear in any order unless otherwise indicated by proximity operators.

"Phrase" searches require an exact match (order, punctuation, *etc.*), and are best conducted by using the browse index button to the right of each search box.

Can combine results of multiple searches. Good for complex searches with multiple synonyms for each concept—do one search for each concept and then combine.

Thesaurus available, click on subject icon above the search button.

Boolean:

    AND, OR, NOT

Proximity:

W	adjacent, in order entered
W#	within # of words, in order entered
N	adjacent, in any order

	N#	within # of words, in any order

Truncation:

	+	simple plurals (-s and -es)
	#	single character
	*	multiple characters

Wildcard:

	?	0-9 characters, can specify number

Limits:

Year of publication
Language
Document type
Items on the Internet
Holding libraries

V. Finding Articles in Periodicals

Unless you are looking for articles in current issues of periodicals, scanning individual issues of periodicals is not the fastest, most efficient, or preferred method of finding more than a few articles. For years, indexes and abstracting services have provided simultaneous access to the contents of many periodicals, one year at a time. Now, databases (electronic indexes and abstracting services) provide simultaneous access to the contents of many years of many periodicals. It remains to be seen whether a comprehensive, multi-disciplinary periodical database, the equivalent of WorldCat, will ever emerge. It may not be practical, given the sheer number of articles published each year. What is gaining momentum is movement towards even more electronic access to periodicals in the form of *full text online*. Although significant progress has been made, the era portrayed in Star Trek has not yet arrived (or we wouldn't spend so much time in planes, trains, and automobiles, let alone in libraries). Until then, we must continue to rely on a variety of indexes and abstracting services, print and electronic, to conduct comprehensive searches, and continue to make paper copies of the articles that we find, whether online, on microfilm, or in paper, so that we can read them at our leisure in the setting of our choice.

The following indexes, abstracting services, and databases are recommended for identifying articles about corruption. Not included in the list are indexes that cover newspapers and popular magazines, and indexes that cover primarily pre-1980 material (*e.g.*, the C.R.I.S. indexes). Also not included are a number of indexes whose focus is a geographic area, such as *Bibliography of Asian Studies* or *International African Bibliography*. Emphasis is given to databases, indexes, and abstracting services with substantial coverage of the political science literature. Years covered online are based on the years available from the provider listed; some databases are available from more than one provider.

Political and social sciences

International Political Science Abstracts. Basil Blackwell. Online examined August 2001

Years covered paper: 1951-

Years covered online (SilverPlatter): 1969-

Subjects covered: Political science, international relations, public administration. Materials indexed: Selectively indexes more than six hundred scholarly periodicals and yearbooks. Publishing information: Paper published bi-monthly; cumulated annually. Annual subject and author indexes. Abstracts arranged in six categories: Political science method and theory, Political thinkers and ideas, Governmental and administrative institutions, Political process: public opinion, parties, *etc.*, International relations (international law and foreign policy), and National and area studies.

Suggested subject headings/descriptors:
> For articles not limited to one geographic area, use:
>> ADMINISTRATIVE REFORM
>>
>> CORRUPTION
>>
>> ETHICS
>
> For articles about a geographic area:
>> Names of countries and larger geographic areas, *e.g.*, USA, NORDIC COUNTRIES, AFRICA. States and cities are subdivisions of the country and topical subdivision, *e.g.*: USA – ELECTIONS – NORTH CAROLINA. In paper version, geographic subject headings are cross-referenced from subject headings like corruption, not double-listed.
>>
>> Suggested subdivisions to use with geographic subject headings:
>>> CORRUPTION
>>>
>>> ADMINISTRATIVE REFORM
>>>
>>> DEMOCRACY
>>>
>>> DEMOCRATIZATION
>>>
>>> ETHICS
>>>
>>> HUMAN RIGHTS
>>>
>>> CIVIL SOCIETY AND STATE

Online search tips:

Assignment of descriptors in online database is poor; many citations have no subject headings. Use "Words anywhere" search, which searches Author, Title, Source, Notes, Descriptors, Abstracts, and Accession, ISBN, and ISSN Number fields.

To narrow a search, look for terms in title OR subject. Can limit search terms to subject, but will miss many articles.

You can combine results of multiple searches. Good for complex searches with multiple synonyms for each concept—do one search for each concept and then combine.

The Index function lists all searchable words in the database. The Suggest function is similar to a thesaurus.

Boolean:
> AND, OR, NOT

Proximity:

ADJ	adjacent, in order entered
<space>	adjacent, in any order
NEAR	in same sentence, in any order
NEAR#	within # of words, in any order
WITH	in same field

Truncation:
> *   multiple characters

Wildcard:
> ?   one character or none, anywhere in word except first character

Limits:
> Language of abstracts
> Update year (year entered into database)

Paper search tips:

Subject index in paper version appears to be complete. Most articles are listed under geographic subject headings.

International Bibliography of the Social Sciences. SilverPlatter.
Years covered online (SilverPlatter): 1951-
Subjects covered: Anthropology, economics, political science, sociology, and related fields.
Materials indexed: 2,600 social sciences journals and six thousand books each year.
Publishing information: Online equivalent of the *International Bibliography of...* series published by UNESCO/Tavistock. Source of data is British Library of Political & Economic Science of the London School of Economics & Political Science.

Suggested subject headings/descriptors:
> ADMINISTRATIVE CORRUPTION
> POLITICAL CORRUPTION
> CORRUPTION
> Geographic subject headings of various levels; *e.g.*, ASIA, SUB-SAHARAN-AFRICA, U.S.A., PARIS

Search tips:

An article with a city geographic descriptor will also have descriptors for the country and sometimes the state/province, or region; *e.g.*, records with the geographic descriptor BOSTON will also have the descriptors MASSACHUSETTS and U.S.A..

"Words anywhere" searches Author, Title, Source, Abstracts (when available), Notes, Descriptors, Abstracts, and Accession, ISBN, and ISSN number fields.

Descriptor phrases are hyphenated. Searching ADMINISTRATIVE-CORRUPTION automatically limits search to descriptor field.

Combine descriptor searches with keyword searches not limited to any field. There are few abstracts

You can combine results of multiple searches. Good for complex searches with multiple synonyms for each concept—do one search for each concept and then combine.

The Index function lists all searchable words in the database. The Suggest function as similar to a thesaurus, suggesting terms to search.

Very few abstracts.

Boolean:
     AND, OR, NOT

Proximity:

ADJ	adjacent, in order entered
<space>	adjacent, in any order
NEAR	in same sentence, in any order
NEAR#	within # of words, in any order
WITH	in same field

Truncation:
     *   multiple characters

Wildcard:
     ?   one character or none, anywhere in word except first character

Limits:
     Language
     Year of publication
     Publication type
     Subset of choice: Political Science, Sociology, Economics, or Anthropology

International Bibliography of Political Science. UNESCO/Tavistock.
Years covered paper: 1951-
Years covered online (SilverPlatter): see *International Bibliography of the Social Sciences.*
Subjects covered: Political science and related fields such as political philosophy and law.
Materials indexed: Scholarly books and periodicals, research reports, dissertations, specialized bibliographies.
Publishing information: Annual publication. Arranged by broad subject areas; author and subject indexes. No abstracts.

Suggested subject headings:
>ADMINISTRATIVE CORRUPTION
>
>POLITICAL CORRUPTION
>
>CORRUPTION
>
>Geographic descriptors of various levels, *e.g.*, AFRICA, ITALY, BOSTON.

CSA Worldwide Political Science Abstracts. Cambridge Scientific Abstracts.
Examined August 2001
Years covered online: 1975-
Subjects covered: Political science and related fields, such as international relations, law, and public administration and policy.
Materials indexed: As of August 2001, web resources, books, dissertations, and approximately 920 serial titles; expected to reach at least 1250 serial titles. Serials are classed in three categories: core (all articles indexed), priority (more than 50 percent of articles indexed), and selective (less than 50 percent of content indexed).
Publishing information: A new database from Cambridge Scientific Abstracts, formed by the merger of the back files of *ABC Pol Sci* and *Political Science Abstracts.* Actively under construction, so subject to change.

Suggested subject heading/descriptors (a combination of the two original databases subject headings):
>CORRUPTION
>
>CORRUPTION OF AND ILLEGAL INFLUENCE OVER DECISION-MAKERS
>
>POLITICAL DEVELOPMENT OR POLITICAL DEGENERATION
>
>INFLUENCE
>
>BRIBERY
>
>Geographic terms of various levels, *e.g.*, AFRICA, ITALY, MASSACHUSETTS, MOSCOW

Search tips:

Advanced Search provides most flexibility without needing to know fields and search syntax.

"Keyword" searches Title, Abstracts, Identifiers, and Descriptors fields; identifiers are words and phrases describing the article assigned by indexer, but not in the thesaurus.

Future possibility: combine keyword or descriptor search with classification; *e.g.*, de = (corruption) and cl = (national level politics). At this time, no list of classification terms.

Descriptors from merging of two databases are not harmonized. A new thesaurus, based on the *ABC Pol Sci* subject headings, was implemented in 2000.

Since 2000, many records include list of references cited.

Book reviews have no descriptors.

Boolean:

       AND, OR, NOT

Proximity:

<space>	adjacent, in order entered
WITHIN #	within # of words, in any order
NEAR	within ten words, in any order
BEFORE	in order entered, but not necessarily adjacent
AFTER	not necessarily adjacent

Truncation:

*	multiple characters
?	single character; use as many ? as characters desired

Wildcard:

*	multiple characters
?	single character; use as many ? as characters desired

Limits:

Language

Year of publication

Publication type

ABC Pol Sci: Advance Bibliography of Contents: Political Science. ABC-Clio.
Years covered paper: 1969-2000
Years covered CD-ROM: uncertain <1984-?>
Subjects covered: Political science, as well as related areas such as economics, sociology, law.
Materials indexed: Periodicals.
Publishing information: Lists the table of contents of periodicals. Arranged by periodical title; author and keyword indexes. Published monthly; indexes cumu-

late annually and every five years. CD-ROM publication is uncertain, online publication still available (not examined). Continued in paper as *CSA Political Science & Government: a guide to periodical literature* (not examined) and online as part of *CSA Worldwide Political Abstracts* (see above).

Suggested subject headings/descriptors:
>   CORRUPTION
>
>   BRIBERY
>
>   INFLUENCE
>
>   Geographic areas at all levels, *e.g.*, AFRICA, LATIN AMERICA, UNITED STATES, LOUISIANA, CHICAGO. Very few entries under names of cities or U.S. states.

Print search tips:

Two or more subject terms assigned as a string to each article. Articles appear in the subject index under all subject terms assigned; no cross-references or subdivisions needed.

CD-ROM search tips:

Article Search displays results in reverse chronological order. TOC Search displays results arranged by journal title (Table of Contents).

"Subject" searches Descriptor and Title fields; "Descriptor" searches Descriptor field.

<F2> allows you to browse an alphabetical list of all words used in a field.

Boolean:
>   AND, OR, NOT

Proximity:

ADJ	adjacent, in order entered
ADJ#	within # of words, in order entered
NEAR	adjacent, in any order
NEAR#	within # of words, in any order

Truncation:

*	multiple characters
?	single character

Sage Public Administration Abstracts. Beverly Hills, CA: Sage Publications.
Examined August 2001
Years covered paper: 1974-
Years covered online (FirstSearch ECO): 1998-
Subjects covered: All aspects of public administration, including politics, law, economics, civil and human rights, government, trade, immigration, public health, social services, environmental protection, and banking.
Materials indexed: Books, articles, pamphlets, government publications, significant speeches, legislative research studies.
Publishing information: Paper published quarterly; annual index.

Subject headings/identifiers:
    CORRUPTION
    POLITICAL CORRUPTION
    POLITICAL REFORM
    FRAUD
    ADMINISTRATIVE ETHICS
    PROFESSIONAL ETHICS
    BRIBERY

Search tips online:

Searching a database (*Sage Public Administration Abstracts*) within a FirstSearch database (*Electronic Collections Online*) can be confusing.

In Advanced Searching always enter "Sage public administration abstracts" in one search box as a Source Phrase. Enter identifiers or keywords or authors in other search boxes.

Journal, volume, pages, date information displays in the Source field as Full Text; no full text available online.

"Phrase" searches require an exact match (order, punctuation, *etc.*), and are best conducted by using the browse index button to the right of each search box.

"Keyword" searches the Title, Identifiers, and Abstract fields. The words may appear in any order unless otherwise indicated by proximity operators.

You can combine results of multiple searches. Good for complex searches with multiple synonyms for each concept—do one search for each concept and then combine.

Boolean:
    AND, OR, NOT
Proximity:
W		adjacent, in order entered
W#		within # of words, in order entered
N		adjacent, in any order
N#		within # of words, in any order

Truncation:
     +   simple plurals (-s and -es)
     #   single character
     *   multiple characters
Wildcard:
     ?   0-9 characters, can specify number
Limits none, instead searches can be done for:
     Year of publication, Language

P.A.I.S. International. Public Affairs Information Service.
Years covered online (FirstSearch): 1972-
Years covered paper: 1915-
Subjects covered: Government and politics, public and social policy, population, human rights, international relations, law, industry.
Materials indexed: Periodicals, books, U.S. government documents; about 3,600 sources.
Publishing information: Published monthly; cumulated annually; a paper cumulative index covers 1915-1974. Several preceding titles.

Suggested subject headings:
     CORRUPTION. Can subdivide geographically down to state level: AFRICA, ICELAND, NEW YORK (STATE)
     POLITICAL ETHICS
     PUBLIC OFFICIALS – ETHICS
     BRIBERY

Search tips online:
     "Phrase" searches require an exact match (order, punctuation, *etc.*), and are best conducted by using the browse index button to the right of each search box.
     "Keyword" searches Abstract, Descriptors, Journal Name, and Title fields. The words may appear in any order unless otherwise indicated by proximity operators.
     You can combine results of multiple searches. Good for complex searches with multiple synonyms for each concept—do one search for each concept and then combine.
     Thesaurus is available online, click on subject icon above the search button.

Boolean:
     AND, OR, NOT

Proximity:
     w   adjacent, in order entered
     w#   within # of words, in order entered

N	adjacent, in any order
N#	within # of words, in any order

Truncation:

+	simple plurals (-s and -es)
#	single character
*	multiple characters

Wildcard:

?	0-9 characters, can specify number

Limits:

Year of publication
Language
Document type
Government document
Electronic document
Government level
Holding libraries
Full text available

Social Sciences Index. H.W. Wilson. Examined August 2001
Years covered online (FirstSearch): 1983-
Years covered paper: 1974/75-
Subjects covered: Anthropology, area studies, community health and medical care, criminal justice and criminology, economics, family studies, geography, gerontology, international relations, law, minority studies, planning and public administration, policy sciences, political science, psychiatry, psychology, social work and public welfare, sociology, urban studies, and women's studies.
Materials indexed: About 550 English language journals.
Publishing information: Published monthly, cumulated annually. Preceded by *Social Sciences and Humanities Index* (1965-1974).

Suggested subject headings:
CORRUPTION IN POLITICS
CORRUPT PRACTICES
POLITICAL ETHICS
POLITICAL TRUST (IN GOVERNMENT)
BRIBERY

Online search tips:
"Phrase" searches require an exact match (order, punctuation, *etc.*), and are best conducted by using the browse index button to the right of each search box.

"Keyword" searches the Abstract, Source Phrase, Subject, and Title fields. The words may appear in any order unless otherwise indicated by proximity operators.

You can combine results of multiple searches. Good for complex searches with multiple synonyms for each concept—do one search for each concept and then combine.

Boolean:
> AND, OR, NOT

Proximity:

W	adjacent, in order entered
W#	within # of words, in order entered
N	adjacent, in any order
N#	within # of words, in any order

Truncation:

+	simple plurals (-s and -es)
#	single character
*	multiple characters

Wildcard:

?	0-9 characters, can specify number

Limits:
> Year of publication
> Document type
> Holding libraries
> Full text available

Social Science Citation Index. Institute for Scientific Information.
Years covered online: 1956-
Years covered paper: 1956-
Subjects covered: Anthropology, archaeology, area studies, business & finance, communications, community health, criminology, demography, economics, educational research, environmental studies, ergonomics, ethnic group studies, family studies, geography, geriatrics & gerontology, health policy, history, international relations, law, linguistics, management, marketing, nursing, personal management, philosophy, political science, psychiatry, psychology, sociology, statistics, substance abuse, urban planning & development, women's studies.
Materials indexed: About 1,725 journals completely and 3,300 journals selectively; some books.
Publishing information: Paper published in three parts: Source Index (access by author), Subject Index (access by words in article titles), and Citation Index (access by cited author). Online version (*Web of Science*) can be searched in combination with *Science Citation Index*, if desired.

Search tips:
No "subject headings" as defined in other databases. "Topic" searches the Title, Abstract (where available), and Keyword fields. Keywords are either sub-

mitted by authors (beginning with 1991), or are added by the publisher when the word or phrase appears frequently in the titles of cited references. Use as many synonyms as reasonable.

Unique feature is the ability to search existing items for the articles that have cited them (cited reference/cited author search). Useful if you know of a seminal work or author in the field.

Very difficult to search in paper version; online recommended. If using paper index, begin subject searches in the Permuterm Subject Index, author searches in the Source Index, and cited author searches in the Citation Index.

Boolean:
          AND, OR, NOT (space is the same as AND)
Proximity:
          SAME   same sentence or keyword phrase
Truncation/Wildcard:
          *   multiple characters
          ?   single character

VI. Databases/Indexes/Abstracting Services in Related Disciplines
Multi-disciplinary

ArticleFirst. OCLC.
Years covered online: 1990-
Materials indexed: fifteen thousand journals, good for current literature.

Ingenta Library Gateway. Ingenta.
Years covered: varies with title.
Materials indexed: about 28,425 journals, good for current literature.

ProQuest Direct. Bell & Howell Information and Learning. Examined August 2001
Years covered online: varies with title, generally 1985-
Materials indexed: two thousand periodicals, including scholarly journals, magazines, business publications, and newspapers, Full text online for about 1,200 periodicals, beginning with 1992.

Academic Search Elite and *Academic Search Premier*. EBSCO. (*Elite* not available for review)
Years covered online: varies with title; one hundred titles back to 1965 or first issue (whichever is more recent).
Materials indexed (*Premier*): periodicals: 7,888; full text online: 4,450; peer-reviewed full text online: 3,500.

WilsonSelectPlus. H.W. Wilson. Examined August 2001

Years covered online: 1994-
Materials indexed: one thousand periodicals selected from H.W. Wilson's General Science Abstracts, Humanities Abstracts, Reader's Guide Abstracts, and Wilson Business Abstracts. Text online, but no graphics.

Law

Lexis-Nexis Academic Universe - Legal Research Files.
Years covered online: varies with title
Materials indexed: five hundred law reviews, three hundred legal newspapers, magazines & newsletters; court cases, laws, and patents. Text online, but no graphics.

Index to Legal Periodicals. H.W. Wilson. Examined August 2001
Years covered online: 1981-
Years covered paper: 1929-
Materials indexed: About 925 legal journals, yearbooks, institutes, bar association organs, law reviews, and government publications originating in the U.S., Canada, Great Britain, Ireland, Australia, and New Zealand.

Economics

EconLit. American Economics Association.
Years covered online (EBSCO): 1969-
Years covered online (JSTOR): 1963-latest three years
Years covered paper (various titles): 1963-
Materials indexed: periodicals, working papers, books, dissertations.

International Bibliography of Economics. UNESCO/Tavistock.
Years covered online (SilverPlatter): see *International Bibliography of the Social Sciences*
Years covered paper: 1953-
Materials indexed: scholarly books, essays, scholarly articles in specialized journals, research reports, thesis, dissertations, and government documents.

Sociology

Sociological Abstracts. Sociological Abstracts, Inc.
Years covered paper: (journals) 1952- , (books) 1974-
Years covered online (Cambridge Scientific Abstracts): 1963-
Materials indexed: 1,809 journals, conference papers, dissertations, books.

International Bibliography of Sociology. UNESCO/Tavistock.
Years covered paper: 1952-
Years covered online (SilverPlatter): see *International Bibliography of the Social Sciences*

Materials indexed: scholarly books and journals, research reports, dissertations, government documents, and specialized bibliographies.

Anthropology
Anthropological Index Online. Royal Anthropological Institute. Examined August 2001
Years covered online: 1957-
Materials indexed: journals.

Abstracts in Anthropology. Greenwood Press.
Years covered paper: 1970-
Materials indexed: about one hundred journals.

International Bibliography of Cultural and Social Anthropology.
UNESCO/Tavistock.
Years covered paper: 1955-
Years covered online (SilverPlatter): see *International Bibliography of the Social Sciences*
Materials indexed: scholarly journals, books, and essays.

Philosophy
Philosopher's Index. Philosophy Documentation Center, Bowling Green State University.
Years covered paper: 1940-
Years covered online (SilverPlatter): 1940-
Materials indexed: journals, books.

History
America: History and Life. ABC Clio.
Years covered paper: 1964-
Years covered online (ABC Clio): 1964-
Materials indexed: two thousand journals. Covers U.S. and Canada.

VII. Bibliographies

Bibliographies are a valuable shortcut to locating information. Bibliographers spend a great deal of time finding, culling, and sometimes annotating, lists of information sources (books, journal articles, government documents, dissertations, *etc.*) so that you don't have to. Like the periodical databases discussed previously, this is an arena where the Internet shines. Unlike those periodical databases, the majority of online bibliographies are free. The first entry below represents the only substantial, fairly current, print bibliography available. Bibliographies provide citations, and sometimes abstracts and/or keywords; most of the sources below do not provide full-text.

Johansen, E. R. (1990). *Political Corruption: Scope and Resources, An Annotated Bibliography*. New York: Garland Publishing.

The only substantial print bibliography about political corruption. Lists popular and scholarly books, periodicals, dissertations, government documents, and court cases published between 1970 and the late 1980's. Does not include campaign finance or police corruption. Some items annotated. Chapters: Legal Writings; Theoretical Frameworks; Appellate Cases; Corruption in Elections and in the Public Office in the United States; Business-Government Corruption; Public Opinion and Corruption; Federal Statutes, Hearings, and Government Documents; State and Municipal Corruption and the Political Machines; Historical and Comparative Studies; Detection, Control, and Correction Practices. Index contains subject, author, and case name entries.

AnCorR Web: Anti-corruption Ring Online. Organization for Economic Cooperation and Development Anti-Corruption Division. Available: http://www1.oecd.org/daf/nocorruptionweb/index.htm (March 7, 2004).

". . . one of the world's largest information centres on corruption and bribery. With collections on a variety of corruption-related (predominantly economic, political, business and legal) topics, the ANCORR WEB offers you more than five thousand selected references to books, journals, papers, reports and other documents, as well as a large number of downloadable resources."

CORIS: Corruption On-line Research and Information System. Transparency International. Available: http://www.transparency.org/coris/ (March 7, 2004).

Searchable databases of publications (news clippings, reports, legal texts, books, periodical articles, research studies, conference papers and proceedings and a variety of grey literature), country profiles, project activities, anti-corruption experts, and seminars). More than six thousand references and one thousand full text documents. Can search by TI keywords, title, or author.

Bibliography. World Bank Institute. Governance and Anti-Corruption Resources Center. Available: http://www.worldbank.org/wbi/governance/bib.htm (March 7, 2004).

Divided into several sections: Working papers and articles, Books, Case Studies, and Links to other resources (numerous).

Corruption: A Selected and Annotated Bibliography. Norwegian Agency for Development Cooperation. Available: http://www.norad.no/default.asp?V_DOC_ID=646 (March 7, 2004).

Selective, well annotated list of books, journal articles, working papers and websites. Arranged in three chapters: general literature on corruption, geographically organized materials, and internet resources. No search engine. Best to print the table of contents and use it to browse. Links to various sections are at the top of the page.

Johnston, Michael. *Corruption in Post-Communist Societies: Central Europe and the Former Soviet Union.* Available: http://people.colgate.edu/mjohnston/default.htm (March 7, 2004). Created April, 1999; revised April 20, 2001.

". . . emphasis here is on corruption, and on materials published in English since 1989." Divided into two sections: print resources and internet resources. Keywords provided for each entry; search function available. Internet resources primarily links to organization websites (see **Organizations**, below).

Johnston, Michael. *Corruption, Development, and Democracy: General Bibliography.* Available: http://people.colgate.edu/mjohnston/genbib.htm (March 7, 2004). Created November 12, 1999.

Lists books, journal articles, and working papers ". . . relating to corruption as a factor in democratization and economic development. For the most part, this bibliography does not overlap the more specialized list of sources on *Corruption in Post-Communist Societies*", above.

Van Wyck, J.J. & Mary C. Custy. *Contemporary Democracy: A Bibliography of Periodical Literature, 1974-1994.* Washington, D.C.: Congressional Quarterly, 1997.

Lists articles from more than 1,400 serials from the social sciences. Arranged alphabetically by author, subject index. Limited number of entries about corruption.

VIII. Organizations
The following organizations have web pages with substantial information about corruption.

Lists of websites

World Bank Institute. Governance and Anti-Corruption Resources Center. *Links* Available: http://www.worldbank.org/wbi/governance/links.htm (March 7, 2004).

Partners. Available: http://www.worldbank.org/wbi/governance/donorpartnerships.html (March 7, 2004).

Extensive lists of organization websites with corruption information.

Johnston, Michael. *Corruption in Post-Communist Societies: Web Resources.*
Available: http://people.colgate.edu/mjohnston/websources.htm (March 7,
2004). Created April, 1999; revised April 20, 2001.
    ". . . links to organizations and publications concerned with corruption issues
in formerly-communist nations. Many of these organizations will have concerns
with other issues and regions as well. . . "

Hughes, David. Colgate *University Libraries Subject Research Guide: Think
Tanks and Research Institutes.* Available:
http://exlibris.colgate.edu/gateway/thinktanks.htm (March 7, 2004). Last updated September 24, 2001.
    Links to lists of organizations.

Selected organizations
Transparency International. Available: http://www.transparency.org/ (March 7,
2004). Last updated October 30, 2001.
    TI is a "non-governmental organisation dedicated to increasing government
accountability and curbing both international and national corruption."

World Bank sites:
World Bank Institute. Governance and Anti-Corruption Resources Center.
Available: http://www.worldbank.org/wbi/governance/ (March 7, 2004).
    Links to full-text of publications, datasets, news, conferences, and "learning
programs".
World Bank. Public Sector Governance. *Anticorruption.* Available:
http://www1.worldbank.org/publicsector/anticorrupt/index.cfm (March 7, 2004).
    Links to World Bank resources, publications, events about anticorruption
programs.

OECD Anti-Corruption Division. Available:
http://www.oecd.org/document/34/0,2340,en_2649_37447_2028706_1_1_1_37
447,00.html (March 7, 2004).
    Most useful section is the *AnCorR Web: anti-corruption ring online,* listed in
bibliography section, above.

Accountability, Transparency and Anti-corruption. United Nations Development
Programme. Democratic Governance Group. Available:
http://www.undp.org/governance/account.htm (March 7, 2004).
    Mostly discussion, position, and conference papers.

GRECO: Group of States against Corruption. Council of Europe. Available:
http://www.greco.coe.int/ (March 7, 2004).
    "The GRECO was conceived as a flexible and efficient follow-up mecha-
nism, called to monitor, through a process of mutual evaluation and peer pres-

sure, the observance of the Guiding Principles in the Fight against Corruption and the implementation of international legal instruments adopted in pursuance of the Programme of Action against Corruption. Full membership of the GRECO is reserved to those who participate fully in the mutual evaluation process and accept to be evaluated." Website contains guiding documents, evaluation reports of members, and links to other organizations websites.

Anti-Corruption Gateway for Europe and Eurasia. Transparency International – Russia and American Bar Association – Central European and Eurasian Law Initiative. Available: http://www.nobribes.org/default.htm (March 7, 2004). Last updated October 2, 2001.

"A significant entrance way to information about combating corruption. It offers primary materials and direct links to major information sources for anti-corruption practitioners and analysts engaged in Eastern Europe and the former Soviet Union. The Gateway serves as an easily accessible repository of anti-corruption project documentation, legislation, regional and international agreements, news, survey results, reports, and research."

Anti-Corruption Resources. United States Agency for International Aid. Available: http://www.usaid.gov/democracy/anticorruption/ (March 7, 2004). Last updated May 12, 2003.

". . . information about and links to the growing collection of anti-corruption resources that are available on the internet, and descriptions of the anti-corruption programs currently operated by USAID, other government agencies, and the many USAID partners who are active in the effort to combat corruption."

United States Office of Government Ethics. Available: http://www.usoge.gov/ (March 7, 2004). Last updated October 31, 2001.

News, laws, regulations, and advisory opinions, training materials, forms, and links to other websites. Emphasis is on United States.

United States General Accounting Office. Available: http://www.gao.gov (March 7, 2004).

The GAO is independent, nonpartisan agency that works for the U.S. Congress. It examines federal programs and executive branch agencies, evaluating, auditing funds, and investigating allegations of illegal and improper activities. GAO Reports are updated daily.

Hong Kong Independent Commission on Corruption. Available: http://www.icac.org.hk/eng/main/index.html (March 7, 2004). Last reviewed October 12, 2001. News, reports, statistics, legislation. Limited to Hong Kong.

ENDNOTES

1. Publishing output was determined by searching political corruption as a subject phrase in WorldCat (see "Finding Books", above) and limiting the results to English language books/texts. Numbers are slightly high, as some titles have more than one record in WorldCat.

2. See http://groups.colgate.edu/cews/archives/2000_2001/resources/default.htm

3. A collection of databases produced by the U.S. Government Printing Offices.

4. The Research Library Group (160 university, national, and research libraries) has a similar database named *RLIN*.

About the Contributors

John Brademas, president emeritus of New York University, served as president from 1981 to 1992. During that time, he led the transition of NYU from a regional commuter school to a national and international residential research university. Before coming to New York, he served as U.S. Representative in Congress from Indiana for 22 years (1959-81), the last four as House Majority Whip. In Congress he earned a reputation for his leadership in education and the arts. Former chairman of the President's Committee on the Arts and the Humanities and National Endowment for Democracy, he is president of the King Juan Carlos I of Spain Center of New York University Foundation. He is a Fellow of the American Academy of Arts and Sciences and member of the National Academy of Education (USA), The Academy of Athens, European Academy of Science and Arts and National Academy of Education of Argentina.

A graduate, B.A., <u>magna cum laude</u> of Harvard, he was a Rhodes Scholar at Oxford University where he earned a D.Phil. in Social Studies. He has been awarded honorary degrees by 52 colleges and universities, the most recent of which was the University of Oxford (2003). He is author of *Washington, D.C. to Washington Square*; with Lynne P. Brown, *The Politics of Education: Conflict and Consensus on Capitol Hill*; and *Anarcosindicalismo y revolucion social en España (1930-1937)*. Among other honors he has received is the Hubert H. Humphrey Award of the American Political Science Association for outstanding public service by a political scientist.

Jenny Chi Yuen Chan is a native of Hong Kong. Before relocating to New York City in December 1999, she worked with the Independent Commission Against Corruption (ICAC) of the Hong Kong Government as a translator/interpreter. She was heavily engaged in the translation of documents and interpretation work in the office dealing with liaison on behalf of ICAC with various levels of the People's Procuratorates (Prosecutors Office) in the People's Republic of China before and shortly after the historic Handover of Hong Kong in July 1997.

Ms. Chan received her Bachelor's degree in Chinese from the University of London and Master's degree in Mass Communications from the University of Leicester, and studied Japanese at International Christian University in Tokyo. She has been granted corresponding membership by the American Translators Association and admitted to the National Association of Judiciary Interpreters and Translators (NAJIT). She is also a member of the Institute of Linguists in the UK and the International Association of Forensic Linguists.

Among her publications are research papers entitled "Between Cantonese and English in Court", for the 3rd Biannual Conference of the International Association of Forensic Linguists at Duke University in September, 1997; and "Legal Translation in Hong Kong: Cultural and Linguistic Aspects", for the *21st Century Kunming International*.

Andrea Suarez Falken participated in the 2000-2001 activities of the Center for Ethics and World Societies as a Lancy Fellow. She has traveled throughout the Americas and has conducted field research in Chiapas and other parts of Mexico. Most recently she has been an English- and Spanish-language teacher in Spain and France. Funding from the Lancy Foundation supported the research on which her analysis of Mexico is based.

Arvind K. Jain is Associate Professor of International Finance and Business, Department of Finance, Concordia University, Montreal, Canada. He has been a faculty member at Concordia University in Montreal since 1990. He earned his Ph. D. from The University of Michigan, Ann Arbor. His other degrees are from the Indian Institute of Technology, Bombay; Indian Institute of Science, Bangalore; and Carnegie-Mellon University, Pittsburgh. Before joining Concordia, he taught at Indiana University, McGill University, The University of Michigan and the University of Dar es Salaam. He has held short-term or visiting appointments at Pennsylvania State University; State College, International University of Japan; and University of Otago, New Zealand. In addition, he has taught at Helsinki School of Economics, Finland; Tianjin University, China; the University of Havana, Cuba; Czech Management Center, Celakovic; *Centro de Enseñanza Tecnica y Superior,* (CETYS Universidad), Mexico; and *Universidad Catolica del Norte*, Antofagasta, Chile. Besides teaching, he has worked in industry and in the public sector in India, the United States, Tanzania and Mexico.

Dr. Jain's current research focuses on the impact of corruption on economic development, management of exchange risk, and capital markets. His research papers dealing with corruption, agency theory and the debt crisis, capital flight, international lending decisions of banks, oligopolistic behavior in banking, foreign debt and foreign trade of developing countries, impact of culture on saving behavior, and commodity futures markets have appeared in the *Journal of International Business Studies, Journal of Money, Credit and Banking, Economics*

Letters, Journal of Economic Psychology, Journal of Economic Surveys, and other academic journals. He has written two books, *Commodity Futures Markets and the Law of One Price* (1981), and *International Financial Markets and Institutions* (1994), and has edited two volumes on corruption: *Economics of Corruption* (Kluwer Academics, 1998) and *The Political Economy of Corruption* (Routledge, 2001). He is on the editorial board of two journals, including the *Journal of International Business Studies.*

Michael Johnston is the Charles A. Dana Professor of Political Science and Director, Division of Social Sciences, at Colgate University in Hamilton, New York. During 2002-03 he was an NEH Fellow and Member of the School of Social Science, Institute for Advanced Study, Princeton, NJ. For the 2000-2001 academic year he was Director of the Center for Ethics and World Societies, which presented a year-long interdisciplinary series of programs on the theme, "Corruption: Wealth, Power, and Democracy." He has studied corruption since 1975, and from 1985 through 1996 was a founding Co-Editor of the journal *Corruption and Reform.* He is author of *Political Corruption and Public Policy in America,* Co-editor (with Arnold Heidenheimer and Victor LeVine) of *Political Corruption: A Handbook,* and Co-editor (with J. B. McKinney) of *Fraud, Waste, and Abuse in Government.* A revised edition of the Heidenheimer, Johnston, and LeVine *Handbook* was published by Transaction Press in late 2001. He has been a consultant to The World Bank, OECD, UNDP, The Asia Foundation, the New York State Commission on Governmental Integrity, the US Agency for International Development, and several commercial firms. Prof. Johnston is a member of the Board of Directors of Transparency International-USA.

Sahr John Kpundeh is a Senior Public Sector Specialist in the World Bank with expertise in helping countries implement country-level strategies for reform of public institutions and strengthening state capacity. He has been a consultant to the United States Agency for International Development, the United Nations Development Program, and several other commercial firms on issues relating to anti-corruption and good governance. Dr. Kpundeh is the author of *Politics and Corruption in Africa: A Case Study of Sierra Leone (*University Press of America, 1995*);* Co-author of *USAID Handbook for Fighting Corruption* (USAID Technical Publication Series, 1998); Co-editor of *Corruption and Integrity Improvement Initiatives in Developing Countries* (UNDP/OECD, 1998); Co-editor of *Curbing Corruption: Toward a Model for Building National Integrity (*1999, The World Bank*);* editor, *Democratization in Africa: African Views, African Voices* (National Academy Press, 1992*);* and several published articles on issues of governance and corruption. From 1991 to 1995, Dr. Kpundeh was Program Officer of the Panel on Issues in Democracy and States in Transition at the National Academy of Sciences, Washington, D.C. A Sierra Leone national, Dr.

Kpundeh received his Ph.D. and Masters degrees from Howard University in Washington, D.C., with concentration in African Political Systems, Political Economy, and International Relations.

Susan Pharr is the Edwin O. Reischauer Professor of Japanese Politics, and Director of the U.S.-Japan Relations Program, Harvard University. A member of the Council on Foreign Relations, Susan Pharr has been a visiting scholar or fellow at the University of Tokyo, Keio University, the Woodrow Wilson International Center of Scholars, and at the Brookings Institution. She has served as Senior Social Scientist with the Agency for International Development.

At Harvard, Pharr serves on the steering committee of Harvard's Asia Center and the Executive Committees of the Weatherhead Center for International Affairs and the Reischauer Institute for Japanese Studies.

Pharr's works include *Political Women in Japan* (1981); *Losing Face: Status Politics in Japan* (1990); *Media and Politics in Japan* (with Ellis S. Krauss, 1996), and *What's Troubling Democracies?* (with Robert D. Putnam, 2000), as well as numerous articles. From 1985 to 1987 she held the Japan Chair at the Center for Strategic and International Studies in Washington. Among her many research interests are Japanese domestic politics, international political economy of development, and international relations of Asia. She is currently writing a book on political ethics and public trust in advanced industrial democracies, focusing on Japan with comparisons to Italy and the United States.

Louise Shelley is a Professor in the Department of Justice, Law, and Society and the School of International Service at American University, Washington, D.C. She is founder and Director of the Transnational Crime and Corruption Center (TraCCC). She is a leading United States expert on crime, law, and law enforcement in the former Soviet Union and an internationally-recognized expert on issue of transnational organized crime and corruption.

Dr. Shelley received her undergraduate degree *cum laude* from Cornell University in Penology and Russian Literature. She holds an M.A. in Criminology from the University of Pennsylvania. She studied at the Law Faculty of Moscow State University on IREX and Fulbright Fellowships and holds a Ph.D. in Sociology from the University of Pennsylvania. She is the recipient of Guggenheim, NEH, Kennan Institute and Fulbright fellowships, as well as a MacArthur Grant to establish the Russian Organized Crime Study Centers.

As an advisor to the U.S. government on the problems of post-Soviet organized crime, Dr. Shelley has testified before the House International Relations Committee and other congressional committees on several occasions. She is the author of *Policing Soviet Society* (Routledge 1997), as well as numerous articles and book chapters. Professor Shelley is currently Co-editor of *Demokratizatsiya*, the journal of post-Soviet democratization, and *Trends in Organized Crime*. Since 1995, Dr. Shelley has conducted programs in coordination with specialists in Russia, and more recently in Ukraine, on the problem of organized crime. In this role, she is often called upon by many multi-national organizations and international universities to speak on the subject of organized crime and corruption.

Donald R. Sherk, who most recently was Senior Advisor to the African Development Bank, has combined a career in international trade, investment and developmental policy working in major international development institutions such as the Asian Development Bank, African Development Bank, and OECD. While working for the U.S. Department of Treasury he held appointive positions as the U.S. Executive Director to the African Development Bank, the U.S. Alternate Director to the Asian Development Bank and for a brief period represented the United States on the Board of the Inter-American Development Bank. In addition he has had a multifaceted academic career and has worked in a variety of private sector positions. As a graduate student he wrote a Masters Thesis on foreign investment in Australia while a Fulbright Scholar in Canberra, Australia. After finishing his PhD at the University of Iowa and teaching for a number of years in Boston, he returned to the Pacific as a staff economist for the Asian Development Bank. As a member of the South Pacific Division of the ADB he was involved in formulating economic policy papers and project development for the South Pacific members of the Bank. Dr. Sherk has specialized in development policy strategies, project finance, regional trade and investment patterns in Africa and the Asia/Pacific area, and multilateral economic policy formation. He has served on a number of international advisory bodies dealing with the multilateral development banks and has undertaken extensive training programs in macro-economic fields in several developing countries.

Alice N. Sindzingre is a Senior Research Fellow, *Centre National de la Recherche Scientifique* (CNRS), Paris, as well as research associate and visiting lecturer at the School of Oriental and African Studies (SOAS, Department of Economics, University of London). For many years she has studied development issues with an emphasis upon comparisons between Africa and Asia. Her work on social networks as an aspect of, and influence upon, corruption and development has drawn international recognition. In addition to work on problems of corruption she studies rent-seeking, institutional aspects of development, and the processes and implications of global economic and political liberalization.

Mary Jane Walsh holds a Bachelor of Music degree from the Crane School of Music at SUNY Potsdam and a Master of Library Science from SUNY Albany. She is an Associate Professor in the Colgate University Libraries, where her primary duty is managing the federal depository collection.